The Personalization of Democratic Politics and the Challenge for Political Parties

ECPR Press

ECPR Press is an imprint of the European Consortium for Political Research. It publishes original research from leading political scientists and the best among early career researchers in the discipline. Its scope extends to all fields of political science, international relations and political thought, without restriction in either approach or regional focus. It is also open to interdisciplinary work with a predominant political dimension.

ECPR Press Editors

Editors

Ian O'Flynn is Senior Lecturer in Political Theory at Newcastle University, UK.

Laura Sudulich is Senior Lecturer in Politics and International Relations at the University of Kent, UK. She is also affiliated to Cevipol (Centre d'Étude de la vie Politique) at the Université libre de Bruxelles, Belgium.

Associate Editors

Andrew Glencross is Senior Lecturer in the Department of Politics and International Relations at Aston University, UK.

Liam Weeks is Lecturer in the Department of Government and Politics, University College Cork, Ireland, and Honorary Senior Research Fellow, Department of Politics and International Relations, Macquarie University, Australia.

The Personalization of Democratic Politics and the Challenge for Political Parties

Edited by
William P. Cross, Richard S. Katz and Scott Pruysers

Published by the European Consortium for Political Research, Harbour House, 6-8 Hythe Quay, Colchester, CO2 8JF, United Kingdom

Copyright © William P. Cross, Richard S. Katz and Scott Pruysers, 2018
Copyright in individual chapters is held by the respective chapter authors.

All rights reserved. No part of this book may be reproduced in any form or by any electronic or mechanical means, including information storage and retrieval systems, without written permission from the publisher, except by a reviewer who may quote passages in a review.

British Library Cataloguing in Publication Data
A catalogue record for this book is available from the British Library

ISBN: HB 978-1-78552-295-6

Library of Congress Cataloging-in-Publication Data Available

ISBN 978-1-78552-295-6 (cloth)
ISBN 978-1-5381-5699-5 (pbk)
ISBN 978-1-78552-296-3 (electronic)

ecpr.eu/shop

Contents

List of Figures

List of Tables

Acknowledgements

Our greatest debt is, of course, to the authors of the chapters in this volume. From the outset, this has been a true team project. The contributors first met in beautiful Banff, Alberta for a two-day workshop at which we discussed the emerging themes and research relating to the personalization of politics. At this meeting, we collectively decided that there was a need for this book. A year later, the group reconvened in Toronto for a further workshop at which draft papers were presented and discussed. Throughout this process, it has been a pleasure to deal with all of the authors who consistently were terrific to work with as they met their commitments and, most important, produced high-level scholarship.

We have benefited throughout our careers from our association with the European Consortium for Political Research and thus are delighted to publish with ECPR in partnership with Rowman & Littlefield International. The editors at both organizations have been great to work with.

We thank the Bell Chair for Parliamentary Democracy at Carleton University for the funding that supported this project. Graduate students Ryan Vienneau and Mark Bencze provided logistical and research assistance along the way.

Finally, as always, we are indebted to our partners, Emma, Judy and Julie, for all their support.

William P. Cross
Richard S. Katz
Scott Pruysers

Chapter 1

Personalism, Personalization and Party Politics

Scott Pruysers, William P. Cross
and Richard S. Katz

This book is about the role and place of individuals—primarily leaders, legislators, candidates and other activists—in modern political life and the implications of this for political parties. Election campaigns, especially in parliamentary democracies, have typically been characterized as contests between competing political parties (Wlezien 2009) because it is parties that aggregate interests, set policy agendas and mobilize voters (King 1969; Dalton, Farrell and McAllister 2011). Moreover, even after the election has been waged, parties remain central players as both legislatures and governments are organized along party lines (Weller 1985). The centrality and importance of political parties is captured in Schattschneider's (1942, 1) classic argument that 'political parties created democracy and modern democracy is unthinkable save in terms of the parties.'[1] From a theoretical perspective, the primacy of the party as an organization was particularly evident during the time of the mass party.[2] In the context of deeply rooted historical animosities based on cleavages such as religion, class and region, individual political actors and their personalities were thought to matter very little compared to ideology and party (Mughan 2000).

Despite the centrality of political parties as organizations, however, individual political actors have been, and will always be, crucially important to democratic politics. After all, parties are often considered to be nothing more than collectives of individuals, or 'teams of men' as Downs (1957) defined them. Cadre parties, with their loose organizational structure, for example, were built around individuals, and election campaigns tended to highlight individual local notables rather than broad national policy or collective identities (Norris 2000; Katz and Mair 1995). Even the mass party took opportunities to highlight its leader and did not focus solely on the collective identity.

As Katz notes in the concluding chapter to this volume, membership applications for the French Communist Party in 1950 included the following oath: 'I hereby join the party of Maurice Thorez'. Despite having a clearly defined ideology and sense of collective identity, the party was, in many ways, defined by its leader. Moreover, as the deeply rooted cleavages that defined politics for generations waned, Kirchheimer's (1966) 'catch-all party' emerged as an alternative to traditional mass-based politics. The emergence of the catch-all party has transformed party competition and has placed a renewed emphasis on individual political actors, specifically with its de-emphasis of ideology and the strengthening of those at the top of the party leadership.

As ideology and formal group identifications (such as class, union affiliation and so on) continue to fade as the primary mechanisms for organizing civic life (Bennett 2012), Western democracies have experienced a significant decline of partisanship and party identification (Dalton and Wattenberg 2000), increased electoral volatility (Bartolini and Mair 1990; Caramani 2006) and a decline of collective identities more generally (Inglehart 1990; Putnam 2000). Importantly, transformations in social and political attitudes and significant changes in political party organization have been accompanied by dramatic innovations in communications technology such as the widespread adoption of the television, and more recently, the Internet and social media. In many ways, these technological changes have served to reinforce the importance of individual personalities (Hermans and Vergeer 2012; Vergeer, Hermans and Sams 2011) by allowing leaders, individual legislators and even candidates to have a more direct and unmediated relationship with voters (Kruikemeier et al. 2013).

Since the emergence of the catch-all party, scholars have increasingly written about the growing importance of individual political actors, especially party leaders and prime ministers, both during election campaigns and inside of legislatures and governments. Although there is still much debate regarding the precise degree, many students of parties and elections have identified a trend towards more candidate and leader-centred politics (Cross and Blais 2012a; Karlsen and Skogerbø 2015; McAllister 2015; Pruysers and Cross 2016a; Wattenberg 1991; Zittel 2015), increasingly individualized campaigns (Cross and Young 2015; De Winter and Baudewyns 2015; Eder, Jenny and Müller 2015; Zittel and Gschwend 2008) and the growing authority of party leaders and chief executives (Poguntke and Webb 2005; Savoie 1999). All of these trends are part of a broader phenomenon that has been labelled the *personalization of politics.*

Although there have been sporadic and somewhat piecemeal attempts in the literature to identify the importance of individual actors, what is lacking is a comprehensive assessment of the role of individuals in democratic politics and importantly, the relationship of this with political parties.

The presidentialization literature (i.e., Poguntke and Webb 2005), for example, focuses exclusively on party leaders and chief executives, leaving out candidates, Members of Parliament (MPs) and a variety of other party individuals who might also deserve study in the context of individualized and personalized politics. Conflation of presidentialization with personalization, of which the literature is often guilty (see, for example, Lobo 2017), is therefore problematic because it restricts our focus to the 'top'.

Likewise, the personalization literature (i.e., Karvonen 2010) focuses too heavily on change over time, and in the pursuit of documenting longitudinal changes, we often lose sight of how central and influential individual actors are even in the absence of change. Indeed, a country's politics may be more *personalized* than another (meaning that persons are more important in the first than in the second), but it may nonetheless experience less *personalization* (the importance of persons is increasing more slowly, if at all). In other words, politics can be highly personalized without personalization. This, of course, is a matter of the baseline from which we start measuring and focusing on the '-ization' of personalization means that this distinction typically is lost. Although the debate regarding the personalization of politics is both interesting and important, it is equally important to assess the degree of *personalism* (i.e., the extent to which politics is personalized).

It is therefore important to take a step back. As a result of the importance of party leaders and chief executives, we are necessarily interested in presidentialization (and the more static presidentialism). Leaders and chief executives, however, are not our only interest. We are also interested in candidates, MPs and party members. Here, the multiple levels identified in the personalization literature is a useful starting point (Balmas et al. 2014), although we identify many more possibilities for personalism than a simple leader-candidate dichotomy. Furthermore, although we are interested in personalization broadly, change over time is not our only interest. Ultimately, we are interested in *personalized* politics. That is, politics in which individual political actors are centrally important, prominent and highly visible. One of the arguments of this collection is that contemporary democratic politics includes a significant degree of personalism. In some respects this might result from recent changes (i.e., personalization), whereas in others it may have been the case for decades or longer.

As students of political parties, however, it is the interaction between personalism/personalization and party politics that is our central interest. Both personalized politics and the personalization of politics have important, though largely undocumented, implications for the way democratic politics is practised and the relative role, function and organization of political parties. Accordingly, we are particularly interested in how the various types and degrees of personalism/personalization interact with, and perhaps influence, party behaviour and organization. Simply put, we seek to uncover the implications of personalization on political parties and consider how personalism influences the 'partyness' of both party and government.

As we will see, the very definition of personalization sets it up as something that occurs at the *expense* of the party and therefore is a phenomenon that weakens the party. As Katz argues in his contribution, in some manifestations this is clearly the case when party primacy, cohesion and unity are undermined by the prominence and visibility of individual actors (be they leaders, legislators, candidates, etc.). Although focus on a single, paramount leader may not always challenge the cohesion and coherence of a party, intraparty competition to become or to replace that leader may put cohesion and coherence in jeopardy, as may the prominence of individual personalities in positions below the top. It may also mean that what the party stands for can change, perhaps dramatically, depending on who is steering the ship. All of this suggests that high levels of personalism and processes of personalization may represent an important challenge to political parties as they are conventionally conceived.

Although this may be the case, we are equally interested in how parties react to personalism and how it influences their organization and behaviour. It may not weaken them as much as encourage—or force in some instances—change in organization, practice/strategy and internal power distribution. Thus, on the other hand, personalization may simply represent an opportunity for the party to rebrand itself, the ability to ride the coattails of a star candidate or popular leader or the possibility of local candidates putting a 'human' face on the distant and impersonal party machine. In this sense, personalism can be a strategic decision of the political party and not something that simply happens to it.

In examining personalization through the lens of party politics, the chapters that follow demonstrate that personalism and personalization are not inherently zero-sum games for political parties. Although these processes certainly have the ability to undermine party cohesion (both during campaigns and inside legislatures) and challenge the primacy of parties, personalization also provides parties with opportunities to connect and engage with party members and voters and to highlight the strengths of their unique 'team' (i.e., individual candidates and leaders). Importantly, however, the relationship and dynamics among person, party and personalism are not the same in every case or consistent over time. Some candidates, for instance, may engage in personalized campaigning in such a way as to undermine the coherence of their party's message, and others in the same party may wage a personalized campaign that is nonetheless consistent with the party's overall message and brand. Likewise, the degree of personalism may change both over time and among different parties in the same country. In better understanding how, when and the extent to which personalization, and personalism more generally, occurs we contribute to a more complete picture of party organization and party government.

PERSONALIZATION AND PERSONALIZED POLITICS

The question of 'what is personalization' is both straightforward and multifaceted. At the most basic level, personalization refers to changing electoral, societal and political norms in which the centrality of individual actors has increased. Rahat and Sheafer (2007, 65), for example, define personalization as 'a *process* in which the political weight of the individual actor in the political process increases over time, while the centrality of the political group (i.e., political party) declines'. Karvonen (2010, 4) sums up the basic premise as follows:

> The core of the personalisation hypothesis is the notion that individual political actors have become more prominent at the expense of parties and collective identities. The central concept denotes a process of change over time: at *t* politics was less personalised than at *t*+1.

Personalism is personalization without the longitudinal change. It denotes the current state of personalized politics and refers to the role and prominence of individual political actors, regardless of change over time. Although the personalization literature focuses on change over time (i.e., personalization as a 'process' rather than a 'state'), many authors have noted that personalized politics is not an entirely new phenomenon. Indeed, Weber's classic form of 'charismatic authority', for example, emphasized how individual leaders could derive personal authority from their charisma.[3] More recently, Bennett (2012, 22) has written that 'personalized politics has long existed, of course, in the form of populist uprisings or emotional bonds with charismatic leaders'. Similarly, Holtz-Bacha and colleagues (2014, 154) have argued that 'in many ways, the personalization of politics is as old and ubiquitous as politics itself', and Karvonen (2010, 2) writes that 'while most authors would argue that the personalisation of politics is a typical feature of contemporary democracies, the phenomenon itself is anything but new'.

Persons always have been important in politics because ultimately they are the only ones capable of seeking political office and of governing. One of the attributes of any politician in a modern democracy is his or her party. But, of course, individuals differ within the same party with regard to: (a) their competence; (b) their policy preferences; (c) their moral character; (d) their personability or sex appeal, and so on. Personalization occurs, for instance, when citizens, voters, the media and political actors themselves place greater emphasis on these personal differences. Suffice it to say, forms of personalism have likely existed for as long as politicians have. The important distinction here, however, is the (potentially) increasing importance of individual actors over time or, at very least, the particular importance that these actors have in contemporary democratic politics.

Beyond this basic definition, however, there is little consensus on the issue of personalization, either conceptually or empirically. Take, for example, the degree of personalization that can be found in western democracies. McAllister (2015, 337) has written that 'there is little doubt that national election campaigns in the established democracies have become more personalized. Leaders are much more prominent now than in the past, and considerable popular attention is directed towards the personalities of the leaders'. Elsewhere, McAllister (2007, 571) has written that 'in a trend that is shared by all of the liberal democracies, politics has become increasingly personalized'. Others, however, are less convinced. Kriesi (2012, 825), for example, claims that 'the empirical evidence concerning the "personalization of politics" thesis is, at best, mixed'. Kriesi concludes that rather than finding evidence of increasing personalization, what can be found are 'large country-specific differences in the overall degree of personalization and of the concentration of attention on the top candidates'.

This tension is borne out empirically as well. Wauters et al. (2016, 3), for instance, reviewed forty articles regarding the personalization of politics and found no clear evidence in either direction. In fact, the studies were almost evenly divided between those supporting personalization (eighteen studies) and those finding no or mixed evidence of personalization (twenty-two studies). Likewise, Karvonen's (2010) large-scale analysis of personalization produced mixed results. Although certain dimensions, such as media attention, provide strong evidence of personalization, evidence relating to the importance of party leaders and individual candidates in vote choice, as well as the changing dynamics of parliamentary democracy, are less clear. Indeed, Karvonen (2010, 101) concludes that the analysis 'does not support the notion that there has been a clear and pervasive trend towards personalisation among parliamentary democracies'. We add to this debate by providing new empirical evidence of the personalization of politics (or lack thereof) in a number of parliamentary democracies.

Holtz-Bacha and colleagues (2014, 155) suggest that much of the inconclusive and contradictory findings in the literature are the result of 'a lack of clarity and agreement about the definition of the term'. This is echoed by Van Aelst, Sheafer and Stanyer (2012, 204) who write that 'it is the lack of conceptual clarity and the absence of common operationalizations which are an important cause of the unclear or conflicting conclusions'. Some studies explore personalization in the media, others consider local campaigns and others still examine voters and how they cast their ballots on election day. Additionally, different institutional settings, different temporal periods of study and baselines and different countries/parties may all contribute to the mixed findings. Indeed, it has been suggested that 'it would be a mistake to assume either that personalization has developed linearly, or that all countries would experience the phenomenon identically' (Holtz-Bacha, Langer, and Merkle 2014, 154). It is therefore unsurprising that different, and often contradictory, conclusions are made given the different foci of various studies.

Acknowledging the conceptual and theoretical deficiencies with the literature, recent scholarship has attempted to provide a clearer definition of personalization, categorize its various types/subtypes and provide empirically tested operationalizations (Adam and Maier 2010; Balmas et al. 2014; Van Aelst, Sheafer, and Stanyer 2012). Rahat and Sheafer (2007), for example, make an important contribution by distinguishing among three types of personalization: institutional, media and behavioural.[4] Institutional personalization refers to rules and institutions that place more emphasis on individuals; media personalization refers to a greater centrality and visibility of individual actors in news coverage; and behavioural personalization refers to the actions of both voters and politicians—voters in how much emphasis they place on candidates relative to parties and politicians in how much emphasis they place on their own campaigns and personalities relative to their party. These are important distinctions because comparing different 'types' of personalization may result in inconsistent results. In other words, within a single jurisdiction, there may be variation across the various types of personalization. With that said, each of these three types likely feed into one another to some degree.

In a similar fashion, Balmas et al. (2014) distinguish centralized forms of personalization from decentralized. Although this is not an entirely new contribution (see Zittel and Gschwend 2008), the authors provide clear definitions of the two subtypes of personalization and provide empirical evidence to demonstrate their differences. Broadly speaking, Balmas et al. (2014) suggest that centralized personalization occurs when 'power flows upward from the group' to a single leader, whereas decentralized personalization occurs when 'power flows downward from the group' to individual candidates/legislators rather than party leaders/executives. This is a useful distinction that helps define the locus of political personalization. Importantly, it demonstrates that personalization is not limited to party leaders and that there are implications for other political actors such as general election candidates. The authors also demonstrate how the earlier Rahat and Sheafer (2007) threefold typology fits within the framework of centralized and decentralized personalization.

Personalization, however, does not only refer to the 'who'. Holtz-Bacha, Langer, and Merkle (2014) are correct to point out that it goes beyond the visibility and centrality of individual political actors. Personalization also refers to the increased focus on the character, personal lives and personality of these individuals. Here, Van Aelst, Sheafer, and Stanyer's (2012) recent work is useful insofar as it distinguishes between two distinct faces of personalization: individualization and privatization.[5]

> The first form of personalization concerns a focus on individual politicians as central actors in the political arena, including their ideas, capacities and policies. . . . We therefore label this first form 'individualization' . . . . The second form of personalization implies a shift in media focus from the politician as occupier of a public role to the politician as a private individual, as a person distinct from their public role. We label this shift in focus 'privatization' (204–205).

This second face of personalization, privatization, has been the focus of far less scholarly work. Nonetheless, there is evidence that both the media and voters focus on personality traits and information related to the personal lives of politicians in addition to their professional competence and performance (Adam and Maier 2010, 216; Bittner 2011; Langer 2011). This, however, is difficult to operationalize as it is challenging to define which personality traits are 'professional' or 'politically relevant' and which are in fact 'personal'. The difficulty in operationalization is likely a contributing factor to the underdevelopment of this aspect in the literature.

These conceptual and methodological innovations have helped to address some of the theoretical deficiencies in the personalization literature. Throughout this volume, we make two additional important conceptual contributions to the study of personalism/personalization. First, despite often being conflated with one another, we argue that personalization and presidentialization should not be used synonymously. Presidentialization is a specific form of personalization, a form that focuses its attention at the top (party leaders and chief executives). As we have just discussed, however, the concept of personalization/personalism is much broader and encompasses other actors such as general election candidates and legislators (among others). To use the two concepts synonymously further entrenches the notion that personalization is primarily about party leaders when this is simply not the case. Personalization occurs at a variety of levels and is in no way limited to the top of the party or government. Furthermore, even when specifically examining personalism among party leaders and chief executives, the two terms should not be confused. High levels of personalism can occur in the absence of presidentialization, whereas presidentialization cannot occur without personalism (see Poguntke and Webb this volume).

Second, although the identification of centralized and decentralized personalization is useful, we suggest that the simple leader-candidate dichotomy that dominates the literature does not go far enough in identifying the various possible levels of personalization. Katz and Mair (1993) convincingly argue that political parties are not completely coherent and unified actors. Three important, and often competing 'faces' of parties have been identified: the party in public office, party in central office and party on the ground. The identification of these three competing faces challenges the conventional view of parties as hierarchical and unified organizations. As Carty (2004, 6) explains, the traditional conception of a political party as 'a single identifiable organization that some group can capture and command' may no longer accurately describe how parties actually organize. Although parties were once hierarchical, *stratarchy* is a more apt description of how many modern parties organize. Given the stratarchical nature of modern parties, it should not be surprising to find personalization manifest at multiple levels within the party and among a variety of different party actors. Our broader conceptualization, however, still fits within the Balmas et al. (2014) framework of centralized and decentralized personalization; we simply identify many more possibilities in each. Centralized personalization, for instance, can include individuals such as chief executives, party leaders, cabinet ministers and other high-profile and prominent politicians at or near the 'top'. Decentralized personalization, by contrast, includes actors such as ordinary backbench MPs, candidates and party members. Personalized politics can therefore be found at the supranational level, the subnational level, the local level and so on.

It should now be clear that personalization is a complex and multifaceted phenomenon. Although personalization refers to the increasing importance, relevance, prominence and even authority of individual actors, it is much more than this; the concept includes more than just candidates and leaders and covers not only the 'who' but the 'what'. Despite this complexity, we can point to several key features of personalism and personalized politics, particularly as they relate to political parties:

- Candidate-centred electoral systems emphasize individual politicians over their collective entities (see chapter 2).
- Citizens take their own evaluations of leaders/candidates into account when casting their ballots (see chapter 3).
- Election campaigns centre increasingly on individual leaders and candidates rather than parties or their platforms (see chapter 4).
- Intraparty democracy stresses individual membership over collective identities in the form of one-member-one-vote (i.e., primaries) for the selection of party leaders and candidates (see chapter 5).
- Individual politicians are highly visible online, especially when considering their social-media activities (see chapter 6).

- Party membership has become individualized and atomized, stressing the individual member over the broader group or subgroup (see chapter 7).
- The behaviour of legislators may deviate from the party and be more individualized (see chapter 8).
- Chief executives are increasingly powerful, especially compared to their parliamentary counterparts (see chapters 9 and 10).
- Election campaigns and the media highlight the private and more personal characteristics of candidates and leaders (see chapter 11).

OUR ANIMATING QUESTIONS AND KEY THEMES

The implications of personalized politics are necessarily widespread and can be found across many different aspects of political parties and our democratic politics more generally. Personalism influences the way election campaigns are waged, how voters determine their preferences, how legislators and governments function and the place and operations of political parties in democratic life. However, in an effort to quantify the precise degree of personalization over time and to uncover the various causes or drivers of personalization, the existing literature has paid far less attention to many of the important questions regarding the consequences of personalism.

The research that does exist, like much of the personalization literature in general, is somewhat mixed. For some authors, the increasing personalization of politics represents a significant challenge for the quality of democracy because it has the ability to downplay substantive debate, overshadow ideology, emphasize personal and often trivial aspects of a leader's life, undermine accountability and weaken party unity (Bennett 2012; Zittel and Gschwend 2008). Others, however, offer a more optimistic outlook, emphasizing the positive implications for individual citizens, the potential empowerment of ordinary MPs and even arguments for enhanced accountability (Kruikemeier et al. 2013; McAllister 2015).

Although many of the chapters throughout this volume document the extent of personalization/personalism, they also seek to address some fundamental questions about the nature of personalized politics, how it manifests, and its consequences for governance, representation, and the state of democracy more generally. The question of what personalization means for political parties is the central animating theme of this volume. Although the importance of this question may seem immediately obvious to some, it has not been adequately explored in the literature. This is not entirely surprising because nonparty scholars, specifically political communications experts, have pioneered and written much of the personalization literature. As a result, the news media is often the central focus and not necessarily political parties.

However, as a process that has the ability to draw focus, visibility, influence and authority away from parties towards leaders, candidates and other individuals, personalization necessarily has implications for the party.

This, of course, is not to say that media personalization is unimportant. It is well-established that media coverage of politics influences voters both in establishing their views of political actors and in making their vote choices. In this way, who or what the media decide to focus their coverage on is vitally important. However, of all the possible manifestations of personalization, the media has been the most studied (Holtz-Bacha, Langer, and Merkle 2014; Kriesi 2012; Langer 2007, 2010; Mughan 2000; Rahat and Sheafer 2007; Van Aelst, Sheafer, and Stanyer 2012; Reinemann and Wilke 2007). We focus our attention, by contrast, on the most understudied aspect: political parties themselves. Within our focus on parties, however, many chapters include an analysis, to some degree, of personalism in the media. Pruysers and Cross, for instance, demonstrate differences between party and leader mentions in national and regional media coverage during the 2015 Canadian general election, as well as analyse how parties portray themselves in their media strategy (press releases, television advertisements and e-mail messages). Likewise, Rahat and Zamir examine new media, exploring how politicians and political parties use social media platforms such as Facebook and Twitter to present themselves to voters, and Thomas, as part of her chapter, examines gendered media coverage of candidates/legislators and considers the implications this has for the personalization of politics. Despite our focus on parties, then, mediated personalization is featured prominently throughout the volume.

When considering personalization and party politics, important questions regarding the interaction of centralized and decentralized personalization arise. Although their work reveals diverging trajectories for centralized and decentralized personalization in the Belgian case, Wauters et al. (2016) demonstrate that the two can coexist. The implications of this coexistence for political parties, however, have not yet been fully explored. What happens when both leaders and candidates run personalized campaigns? Are election campaigns disorganized and devoid of unifying themes among parties? And how do these actors behave inside the legislature once elected, having just run personalized and individualized campaigns? As Zittel (2015, 4) explains, the answers are not immediately obvious:

> the concept of personalization does not imply any clear-cut position on the relationship between party and candidate. Personalized campaigns could signal an adversarial relationship culminating in the mode of openly contradicting party positions in a candidates' campaign communication and thus in individualized campaign politics. However, this relationship also can be supplemental with candidates playing to distinct sub-constituencies while at the same time supporting their parties' platform in their campaigns.

In terms of an adversarial relationship, decentralized personalization has the ability to cause tension within parties for at least two reasons. First, an emphasis on individual candidates/legislators may pose a threat to traditional party discipline. From a parliamentary perspective, the empowering of individuals may ultimately weaken political parties and their general primacy inside of legislatures. Second, the party's message and ideological positioning may be undermined by legislative candidates who run personalized and localized campaigns. When candidates have the ability to focus on specific issues that may be at odds with the national campaign, party cohesion is likely to suffer.[6]

Personalization, however, does not only involve the party, leader and candidates. Indeed, ordinary party members are also implicated in this process. Take, for instance, the movement towards primary elections for leadership selection and candidate nomination (Cross et al. 2016; Cross and Pilet 2015; Hazan and Rahat 2010). Collectives such as convention delegates or the parliamentary party group have lost much of their formal influence over leaders and the direction of party politics. In their place are atomized and individualized party members. According to Katz and Mair (1995) this has served to strengthen the top party leadership and ultimately reduce intra-party accountability. Institutional personalization, in this case, the adoption of primaries, therefore, has consequences not just for how leaders are selected but also the resulting intraparty dynamics.

Beyond intraparty dynamics, personalization also influences the strategic decisions that parties make when waging election campaigns. How much emphasis will a party place on their leader in campaign advertisements and messaging? Do parties focus their campaign attacks on competing parties or competing party leaders? When do local candidates decide to run a campaign that is more about themselves than their party? The degree of personalization in a political system will condition all of these decisions and in doing so will make election campaigns look different—both across time and across countries.

A second animating theme of the book concerns the multilevel nature of personalization. Although there have been both conceptual (Balmas et al. 2014) and empirical (Chiru 2013; Cross and Young 2015; De Winter and Baudewyns 2015; Eder, Jenny and Müller 2015; Zittel and Gschwend 2008; Zittel 2015) examinations of decentralized personalization, the personalization literature remains firmly focused on party leaders and chief executives and often conflates it with presidentialization. So much so that personalization almost immediately conjures images of party leaders. We address this asymmetry by exploring personalization not only at the level of party leaders but also local candidates, legislators (and other prominent politicians) and party members, thereby moving the analysis well beyond a simple leader-candidate dichotomy.

In doing so, we consider the dynamics between the multiple levels and explore implications that this might have on party organization, election campaigns, and governance. Are the processes of centralized and decentralized personalization in competition with each other or can the two forms co-exist? If personalization occurs at multiple levels simultaneously, does the combination of personalized central party campaigns around the leader and individualized local campaigns around individual candidates produce tension once these individuals are inside the legislature? How, if at all, does personalization impact the behaviour of MPs or prime ministers? The implications for both election campaigns and governance are numerous.

The third theme that animates this volume relates to what might be the least studied component of personalization: privatization. Rather than focusing almost exclusively on 'who', we pay particular attention to the 'what'. What is it about party leaders that voters consider when casting their ballot? What kinds of information are candidates and party leaders transmitting about themselves in their campaign communication? What kind of content are politicians posting online? We also consider the broader democratic implications of privatization, specifically whether processes of personalization are gender neutral or whether the process is uneven with gendered effects.

Hart (1994) notes that television has hastened the trend of growing intimacy between voters and leaders, a trend that he suggests is damaging substantial political debate. Echoing this argument, Bennett (2012) also notes that personalization entails a weakening of ideological considerations for voters and less emphasis on policy discussions for election campaigns. Replacing ideology and policy are a variety of other considerations directly related to the individual candidate such as competence, appearance, family life, and so on. Indeed, Zittel and Gschwend (2008, 979) conclude that 'the growing saliency of the personal properties as well as the personal background of main candidates is assumed to put the political issues on the backburner of campaign agendas'.

Although some level of information about candidates' personal lives may be informative for voters, there is a real concern that privatization undermines the substantive elements of political debate. What's more, the concern is not only that ideology and substance are undermined, but that they are also replaced by trivial and often sensational aspects of an individual's personal life (i.e., what they look like, their marriage, etc.).[7] Privatization, as one of the faces of personalization, suggests that personality characteristics, personal achievements and an individual's life outside of politics are becoming increasingly important—both to the media who report on it and voters who consider this information when casting their ballot (Langer 2007; Van Aelst, Sheafer and Stanyer 2012; Van Zoonen 1991). This, however, raises important questions regarding whether personalization is an uneven process and whether its effects are gender neutral.[8]

In terms of the media, there is no shortage of evidence demonstrating gendered news coverage. Indeed, female candidates are typically subject to considerably more attention on their appearance, marital status and sex than their male counterparts (Anderson 2011; Bashevkin 2009; Lawless 2009). Examining the 2004 Conservative leadership election in Canada, for example, Trimble (2007) finds that, among the two leading candidates, fully one-in-three news stories mentioned Belinda Stronach's appearance compared to just 2 percent for Stephen Harper. Similarly, Lawless (2009) argues that the overt sexism and bias in the media experienced by Hillary Clinton in the 2008 Democratic primary may result in fewer women wanting to put themselves in similar situations. The privatization of media coverage around women candidates may therefore act as a significant barrier, preventing women from cultivating a sense of political ambition.

Furthermore, although privatization is often associated with media personalization, it has a much wider application. Privatization can manifest in how candidates portray themselves, as well as what information citizens use to make their voting decisions. In terms of candidate portrayals, women may be punished for presenting certain kinds of personal information (Thomas and Bittner 2017). The gendered nature of privatization may therefore shape the campaign strategies and options available to women candidates. It may also be problematic for women that voters are taking personal characteristics into account when voting, especially because negative stereotypes about women in politics are still quite pervasive. Male politicians, for example, are often viewed as more knowledgeable, trustworthy and convincing than their female counterparts (Aalberg and Jenssen 2007). Stereotypes about women remain in terms of candidate traits and issue competency (Huddy and Terkildsen 1993; Sanbonmatsu and Dolan 2009; see also Pruysers and Blais 2017) as well as potential for electoral performance (Sanbonmatsu 2006). Given the widespread nature of these stereotypes, women candidates/leaders may be at a disadvantage. Thus, personalization in this sense may have negative consequences for the overall health of democracy and for the quality of representation in legislatures.

STRUCTURE OF THE BOOK

Although the relationship between party and personalization/personalism is not necessarily zero-sum and political parties may engage in personalization strategically, personalization has important implications for political parties nonetheless. The chapters in this volume demonstrate that the degree of personalism influences how parties conduct their election campaigns, how they organize and distribute power internally, as well as shape their role in governing. While our focus is generally on consequences and outcomes, there is likely a close feedback loop between cause and effect. Take, for example, the question of electoral systems. Some electoral systems fuel personalism/personalization by being candidate, rather than party, centred. In this sense, the electoral system promotes personalization. Nonetheless, demand for more candidate-centred politics may fuel support for particular electoral systems. In this regard, personalization promotes a certain kind of institutional reform and can shape the institutional architecture of the state. Similarly, it is difficult to untangle whether the movement towards primaries for the selection of party leaders and legislative candidates is a cause or effect of personalization. The answer, perhaps unsatisfying, is both.

To explore the relationship between personalism/personalization and party politics, this volume brings together a diverse set of scholars who study political parties, elections and parliamentary institutions. In terms of empirical data, the subsequent chapters marshal a tremendous amount of information, drawing on a number of existing and original data sets regarding electoral system change, voter behaviour, social-media activity, party communications, the parliamentary behaviour of legislators and constituency candidate campaign strategies. Although the geographic scope varies by chapter, this serves to highlight the widespread and pervasive nature of personalized politics among parliamentary democracies. Importantly, it allows us to uncover variation not only within countries but also between them, reaffirming that personalization is far from a linear or even process.

As noted at the outset, parties perform a wide range of functions. To explore the interplay between personalization and party, we have structured the remaining chapters around the most important activities that parties engage in. Here we can identify the 'electoral arena', the 'party arena', and the 'governance arena'. Taking this approach not only demonstrates how potentially pervasive personalization is, but it also highlights that the implications are far-reaching, impacting many aspects of democratic life including election campaigns, party organization and even governance.

In chapter 2, Jean-Benoit Pilet and Alan Renwick examine the role of the electoral system itself, documenting the move towards more personalized electoral systems around the world as well as the implications of this trend on electoral and party politics. In chapter 3, Amanda Bittner considers the importance of leader evaluations during election campaigns, specifically focusing on the calculus of voters in Canada and the United Kingdom. This section is concluded in chapter 4 in which Scott Pruysers and William Cross explore personalization during the 2015 Canadian federal election, highlighting how competing parties adopt different approaches and how the dynamics of personalization can be different for leaders and candidates within the same party and election.

We then move to the party face of personalization with three chapters that focus directly on the internal workings of political parties and questions of intraparty democracy. In chapter 5, David Stewart examines leadership selection and demonstrates how the move towards more inclusive selectorates is tied to the process of the personalization of party leaders. Note that although the emphasis here is on party leaders, similar conclusions can be made about candidate selection because there has been a similar democratization in this area (Cross et al. 2016). In chapter 6, Gideon Rahat and Shahaf Zamir explore how parties and individual politicians present themselves online and consider whether the online space is a mere reflection of the offline world or whether we can find different trends with respect to the personalization of politics. This is followed by a discussion of party members in chapter 7 in which Anika Gauja considers personalization from the bottom up and explores how membership participation in internal party life is increasingly individualized and specialized.

In the third section, the governance face, our authors consider how personalization influences the governing process and power dynamics inside of legislatures. In chapter 8, Mihail Chiru explores the relationship between personalized election campaigns and the subsequent behaviour of representatives both in the legislature and in representing their districts. In chapter 9, Jonathan Malloy explores the behaviour of party leaders once inside the legislature and considers how personalism and 'personal authority' influence how they interact with their parliamentary colleagues and the implications this has for governance. In chapter 10, Thomas Poguntke and Paul Webb revisit the *presidentialization* of politics thesis, specifically focusing on the nuances that were overlooked in their original work and distinguishing personalization from presidentialization.

The volume ends with two concluding chapters. In chapter 11, Melanee Thomas considers personalization through a gendered lens, demonstrating how the entire process is far from gender neutral. Finally, in chapter 12, bringing together the key findings of the previous chapters, Richard Katz explores the relationship between personalization and party government, revealing that personalization is not necessarily the threat to party that it is often made out to be.

NOTES

1. Similarly, Bryce writes that 'parties are inevitable' (quoted in Dalton and Wattenberg 2000, 3).

2. The mass party, of course, was a phenomenon of the Left. Parties on the Right transformed from elite, cadre parties to catch-all parties. In both cases, personality,

especially leaders, were more important than they seemed to be in the ideologically driven mass party.

3. Weber defines charismatic authority as 'resting on devotion to the exceptional sanctity, heroism or exemplary character of an individual person, and of the normative patterns or order revealed or ordained by him' (1968, 215).

4. For similar, although not identical conceptualizations, see Hermans and Vergeer (2012) and Poguntke and Webb (2005).

5. Van Zoonen (1991) writes of 'intimization', whereas Langer (2010) uses the phrase 'politicization of the private persona'. Note that the use of 'privatization' is somewhat counterintuitive in that it refers to making public that which was previously regarded as private, whereas in the normal etymology of English words, it ought to mean exactly the opposite.

6. The personalities and characteristics of individuals have always mattered. Ranney's (1965) observation in *Pathways to Parliament*, for instance, highlights that the selection of candidates has historically been quite personal. Interestingly, one of the most highly valued personal attributes was loyalty to the party and its message. New forms of personalization, however, seem somewhat different as the personal lives and other attributes of individuals gain prominence.

7. This concern, however, is debated. Mughan (2000) demonstrates, at least in the British case, that fear of unsophisticated voters being manipulated by leader effects and trivial aspects of personalization is unfounded. Indeed, Mughan (2000, 145) concludes that 'the voters most susceptible to leader effects are not in fact the least politically interested and involved, but are the most qualified, as reflected in the possession of characteristics like being politically knowledgeable, caring which party won the election and reading election literature. . . . Moreover, the aspects of the leaders' characters that influence the vote are related to ability to perform well in the job rather than politically irrelevant considerations, like whether they are likeable'.

8. The fact that personalization is a process, however, is important in this regard. Although the treatment of women may differ from men, there may be a convergence over time. We address this possibility in a later chapter.

Chapter 2

Personalization, Personalism and Electoral Systems

Jean-Benoit Pilet and Alan Renwick

Electoral systems are among the most studied elements of democratic politics. Armies of scholars have delineated their types, assessed their effects and at least in more recent years, probed their origins. The overwhelming bulk of this research has focused on how electoral systems relate to interparty competition, particularly the degree to which they encourage a spread of power across a range of parties or its concentration in the hands of just a few. As Shugart (2001, 25) points out, however, electoral rules vary along two crucial dimensions. The interparty dimension—the spread of power across parties—is one. But the intraparty dimension—the distribution of power within parties—is the other. This second dimension has received very little attention; as the title of Colomer's book (2011) says, it is 'the neglected dimension of electoral systems'.

The goal of this chapter is to look at the intraparty dimension of electoral systems and to examine it with the broader topic of the personalization of politics that is the theme of this book. More precisely, in this chapter, we concentrate on the relationship between electoral systems and 'decentralized' personalization (Pruysers, Cross and Katz, this volume; see also Balmas et al. 2014). The literature on the personalization of electoral systems has mostly examined the balance between parties as collective bodies and all individual candidates in electoral systems. The question of the leaders—of 'centralized' personalization—has been addressed much less. The reason for this is that electoral systems attributing a specific role to party leaders are rare in parliamentary systems; for exceptions, we must look to the brief period of the direct election of the prime minister in Israel between 1996 and 2001 (Rahat 2008) or the protection offered to list leaders in Greece and Cyprus. However, the dominant concern in the literature has been with the situation of all candidates in the election dynamics. As a consequence, this chapter focuses on the link between electoral systems and decentralized personalization.

The chapter is divided into four sections. The first discusses how electoral systems affect (decentralized) personalization. Based on this discussion, the second section demonstrates that there has been a trend towards the (decentralized) personalization of electoral systems in Europe, especially since the 1990s. Then, in the third section, we explore the causes of the personalization of electoral systems. We end with a discussion of the consequences of this trend.

ELECTORAL SYSTEMS AND (DECENTRALIZED) PERSONALIZATION

Electoral systems come in many forms. The most basic distinction is often taken to be that between majoritarian systems and proportional systems. This distinction relates to the interparty dimension of electoral systems because it determines the allocations of seats to parties. In this chapter, we look at the other main dimension of electoral systems: the intraparty dimension, meaning how electoral systems allocate seats to individual politicians within parties.

Although this aspect of electoral systems is much less studied than the interparty dimension, scholars have begun to explore it in more depth over the last twenty years (Carey and Shugart 1995; Colomer 2011). The central question in this literature is whether electoral systems make individual politicians or political parties more central in electoral politics. By candidate-centred systems, we do not mean systems that allow voting directly for a candidate. We rather refer to electoral systems that allow voters to make an intraparty choice. It means (1) that voters are offered several candidates per party (unlike most of the time in single member districts [SMDs]), (2) that they are allowed to express preferences among these copartisan candidates, and (3) that these votes for candidates weigh in the allocation of seats to candidates. Candidate-centred electoral systems must also be distinguished from another concept, that of the 'personal vote'. The personal vote refers to 'the part of a candidate's vote share that is unique to him or her' (Coates 1995, 277; see also Cain, Ferejohn and Fiorina 1987; van Holsteyn and Andeweg 2010), rather than to the features of the electoral system as such.

Because the degree of candidate-centredness of the electoral system affects the importance of candidates in voters' choices, politicians adapt their behaviour accordingly. The more candidate-centred the system, the stronger the incentive that politicians face to build up their personal reputations to demonstrate to voters that they are the right people to vote for. This idea is found in the early work of Carey and Shugart (1995) on candidate-centredness. These authors examine how election rules shape candidates' incentives to build up personal reputations. In candidate-centred systems, politicians are more likely to emphasize their own personal attributes during election campaigns; during legislative terms, they will act to make their individual contributions to policy-making visible. By contrast, in party-centred electoral systems, individual politicians tend to be of secondary importance. Political parties—their policy platforms and collective actions—are what drive voters' attention. Campaigns are structured around parties as collective organizations. Individual politicians act as agents of their parties both during election campaigns and once elected.

These conceptual approaches of the intraparty dimension that separate candidate-centred from party-centred electoral systems directly echo the broader literature on the personalization of politics. Going back to Karvonen's definition of the personalization of politics as 'the notion that individual political actors have become more prominent at the expense of parties and collective identities' (2010, 4), the personalization of electoral systems is about whether individual political actors are more central in electoral systems at the expense of parties.

The first challenge to exploring this link between electoral systems and decentralized personalization in greater depth is to capture the degree of candidate-centeredness of electoral systems. A first model was proposed by Carey and Shugart (1995). They classified electoral systems on four dimensions, which they label as ballot, pool, votes and district magnitude. *Ballot* refers to the extent of party control over who is elected. Carey and Shugart allow for three types of ballot: those in which parties present a fixed set of candidates that voters cannot disturb; those where parties determine who their candidates are but voters can change the order of these; and those in which parties control neither access to candidacy nor the order of those candidates (Carey and Shugart 1995, 421). *Pool* distinguishes between systems where a vote cast for one candidate benefits that candidate only or also her or his copartisans. The most party-centric systems are those, including all forms of list-based proportional representation (PR), where a vote for a candidate 'is counted first as a vote for the purpose of determining how many seats are to be allocated to the list' (Carey and Shugart 1995, 421). By contrast, in plurality systems a vote for one candidate does not benefit other candidates at all, be they copartisans or not. *Votes* focuses on the nature of the vote that voters can cast. Carey and Shugart distinguish here between systems in which voters can cast only a vote for a party, those in which they can vote for multiple candidates and those in which they can vote only for a single candidate or subparty list. They argue that candidates face the strongest incentive to cultivate a personal reputation where voters can cast only a single candidate or subparty vote; it is here that the candidate most needs to be the voter's first preference. Finally, *district magnitude* (M) refers to the number of seats per electoral district. Carey and Shugart point out that the effect of changes in M on the importance of candidates' personal reputations depends on the other features of the electoral system. Specifically, they argue that personal reputations become less important as M increases in closed-list systems (where ballot takes the lowest value), but that it rises with increasing M in all other systems.

In a recent book, we have slightly adapted Carey and Shugart's model, shifting from the perspective of politicians to the perspective of voters (Renwick and Pilet 2016). We are thus close to Farrell and Gallagher, who analyse the 'openness' of the electoral system, by which they mean 'how much choice is given to voters' (1998, 56; see also Farrell and McAllister 2006, 11). One consequence of this shift in perspective lies in how we characterize systems allowing voters to cast votes for multiple candidates. For Carey and Shugart, the incentive to cultivate a personal vote is greatest where voters can express just one preference among candidates; it is here that the premium on securing voters' first preference is greatest. In our approach, however, voters have more opportunity to express their preferences among individual candidates where they can express preferences for more than one candidate, particularly where those preferences can be ranked.

Another addition of our approach is that we call for more fine-grained characterization of electoral systems on the intraparty dimension. We believe that there is a need to go beyond the three core dimensions—ballot, vote and pooling—of Carey and Shugart (1995), and beyond the alternative categorization offered by Karvonen, who simply distinguished among closed, semi-open and open-list systems.

Starting from these premises, we have therefore developed the following framework to characterize the degree of personalization of electoral systems. This framework is based on two broad aspects of electoral system personalization: the degree to which voters can express their preferences among candidates and the degree to which those preferences determine who gets elected.

We focus first on the degree to which the electoral system allows voters to express preferences among individual candidates rather than (just) among parties. We propose that the following elements of preference expression should be taken into account:

1. *How many preferences among candidates voters can express*: At one extreme, voters may be able to express no candidate preference at all, where all they can do is vote for a (closed) party list. Or they may be able to express a single candidate preference, as under the single-member plurality (SMP) system and some versions of open- and flexible-list PR. Or they may be able to express multiple candidate preferences: two-round systems with single-member districts allow voters, in effect, to express two preferences; some PR systems give voters three or four preference votes; in Switzerland and in Belgium, voters may cast as many preference votes as there are seats

in the district; under alternative vote (AV) and single transferable vote (STV), voters can cast as many preference votes as there are candidates.

2. *How far voters can differentiate their support for candidates*: Electoral systems also allow voters, in varying degrees, to express order among their preferences. The core distinction is between categorical and ordinal systems. Categorical systems are those in which voters can order two categories of preference: supported and not supported. It is the case in most systems that simply allow voters to express what candidate(s) they support and what candidates they do not support. Ordinal systems are those asking voters to order more than two levels of preference. This is the case when voters are asked to rank candidates (as in STV or AV). It also applies to systems such as the Latvian system of list PR that allow voters to express support, neutrality or opposition to a candidate or to the cumulative vote systems in Switzerland and Luxemburg that allow voters to give candidates no votes, one vote or two votes.
3. *Whether voters can distribute multiple preferences across parties or only within a party*: The third element to take into account concerns whether voters can distribute multiple preferences across parties or only within a party. Some systems—including AV, STV, block vote systems and list systems with *panachage*—allow voters to back candidates across party boundaries. Other systems—in particular, non-panachage list systems (which means, in practice, the vast majority of list systems)—allow voters to support candidates from only one party. The first of these categories clearly allows a greater range of candidate voting than the second; voters in such systems are allowed, if they wish, to think entirely in terms of candidates and not at all in terms of parties.
4. *How far voters have effective intraparty choice*: All of the electoral system features that we have looked at so far relate to voters' ability to express preferences among the candidates. Also important, however, is the degree to which voters actually have a range of candidates to choose from. Most crucially, do voters have an intraparty choice of candidates? On the criteria that we have outlined so far, voters in single member plurality (SMP) systems have exactly the same ability to express candidate preferences as do voters in open-list proportional systems with one preference vote. Yet that is misleading; in the latter case, but not the former, voters can choose among candidates from their preferred party, so thinking about candidates makes sense for party loyalists as well as for voters with weaker partisan ties.[1] To capture these very real differences, we include a dimension focusing on the degree to which even a strong party loyalist is able to express a real choice among candidates. We measure the degree of intraparty choice in terms of the ratio between the number of candidates a party puts up and the number of candidates a voter must vote for to give that party the greatest possible support. The higher this ratio, the greater the degree of intraparty choice.

5. *How great the distance is between voters and individual candidates*: The four dimensions outlined so far concern the degree of candidate preference that voters are formally able to express. In addition, however, we should allow for the impact of the formal rules on the likelihood that voters' choices will, in practice, focus on candidates rather than parties. The most important is the size of the district; by size we mean the district magnitude (the number of seats allocated within the district). As Katz (1980, 30–31) argues, the size of a district makes a difference to the degree to which voters are able to connect with individual candidates; the larger the district, the harder it will be to make such a connection.

The second dimension to incorporate for capturing the degree of candidate-centredness or the degree of personalism of an electoral system is the impact of the votes cast on who gets elected. In respect to this second dimension, we differentiate two main aspects.

1. *The degree to which candidate votes determine the order in which candidates get elected*: Here we capture how far preference votes determine the order in which candidates get elected. We may distinguish three main systems: systems in which intraparty candidate ordering is entirely determined by voters (fully open list); those in which it is determined partly by voters and partly by parties (semi-open/flexible lists); and those in which it is entirely determined by parties (closed lists). One should note that the middle category—flexible lists—is the most common but also the most complex. Flexible-list systems vary a great deal, not just in the degree of list flexibility, but also in both the nature of that flexibility in the nature of the mechanisms that are used to determine the postelection ordering of candidates. For example, countries like Austria, the Czech Republic, the Netherlands and Sweden apply a threshold logic. Candidates are elected in order of the party's preelection list, except that candidates who pass a certain threshold of votes move to the top of the list (and are ordered by the votes they have received). In countries like Belgium, the logic is of transferring list votes (without any preference expression by voters) to candidates first placed on the list by their parties to secure their election. Candidates are elected in the order of the preference votes they have received, but votes cast for the list without expression of preference are ascribed to the top candidate on the party's preelection list and surplus votes are cascaded down that list until all are used. These models (threshold and transfer) are just two examples among several of the variety of flexible list systems.
2. *The degree of vote pooling*: The second and final aspect of the effect that a vote has concerns whether votes pool, whether, that is, a vote cast for

an individual candidate counts in favour only of that candidate or also for that candidate's copartisans.

A final element to clarify is how we treat mixed systems (such as the one used in Germany). In such systems, we treat the parts of the system separately and count changes in either component as significant if they affect at least 20 percent of the seats. In case a reform affects the two components of the mixed system, we then evaluate the effect of the change on the personalization of the electoral system overall.

A TREND TOWARDS MORE PERSONALIZED ELECTORAL SYSTEMS IN EUROPE

The overarching question of this volume is whether and to what extent we can confirm that politics is personalized in contemporary established democracies. To test for this in relation to electoral systems, we have gathered data on electoral systems and electoral system changes in thirty-one European countries (the EU28, Norway, Iceland and Switzerland) between 1945 and 2010 (or since the first democratic elections). Table 2.1 identifies all reforms that we have identified and that have affected one of the dimensions affecting the personalization of electoral systems. Those reforms that reduced personalism are marked 'Down'; those that have increased it are marked 'Up'; those that had mutually cancelling effects on different dimensions of personalism are categorized as 'Neutral'.

As table 2.1 begins to make clear, a clear trend towards the adoption of a greater number of personalizing reforms has emerged over the last three decades. There were small moves towards greater personalization in the 1940s and 1950s. The 1960s saw a complete absence of reforms with any significant effect on personalization, whereas the 1970s saw only one significant move—in Austria in 1970. There was an increase in activity in the 1980s, with five reforms towards more personalized electoral systems.

Yet, the real shift in that direction started in the 1990s. The 1990s and 2000s saw a wave of reforms that increased electoral system personalization, whereas reforms moving in the opposite direction remained rare. Personalizing reforms were passed in Austria, Belgium, the Czech Republic, Greece, Italy, Lithuania, the Netherlands, Romania and Sweden in the 1990s. In the 2000s, such reforms were adopted in Belgium, Bulgaria, the Czech Republic, Estonia, Iceland, Latvia, Lithuania, Poland, Romania, Slovakia and Slovenia.

Table 2.2 breaks down this overall trend into the seven-component dimensions of electoral system personalization. It is apparent that the overall pattern

Table 2.1 Electoral Reforms and Their Effects on Personalization, 1945–2010

	Down	*Neutral*	*Up*	*Total*
1940s			Austria 1949 France 1946 Italy 1948	
	0	0	3	3
1950s	Iceland 1959 Norway 1952	Denmark 1953 France 1951	Germany 1953 Finland 1954 France 1958	
	2	2	3	7
1960s				
	0	0	0	0
1970s	Austria 1970	Cyprus 1979 Denmark 1970		
	1	2	0	3
1980s	France 1985 Greece 1985 Malta 1987		Cyprus 1985 France 1986 Greece 1981 Greece 1989 Netherlands 1989	
	3	0	5	8
1990s	Bulgaria 1991 Italy 1991 Slovakia 1998	Poland 1993 Italy 1993	Austria 1992 Belgium 1995 Czechoslovakia 1992 Czech Republic 1995 Greece 1990 Lithuania 1996 Netherlands 1997 Romania 1992 Sweden 1997	
	3	2	9	14
2000s	Czech Republic 2000 Italy 2005 Malta 2007	Denmark 2006	Belgium 2003 Bulgaria 2009 Czech Republic 2002 Czech Republic 2006 Estonia 2002 Iceland 2000 Latvia 2009 Lithuania 2000 Lithuania 2004 Lithuania 2008 Poland 2001 Romania 2008 Slovakia 2004 Slovenia 2000	
	3	1	14	18
Total	12	7	34	53

Table 2.2 Electoral Personalization in Democratic Europe, 1945–2009, by Dimensions of Personalization

	Number of Preferences		*Differentiation of Preferences*		*Distribution of Preferences*		*Intraparty Choice*		*Voter–candidate Distance*		*Weight of Preferences*		*Pooling*	
	+	–	+	–	+	–	+	–	+	–	+	–	+	–
1940s	3	0	2	0	0	0	2	0	0	0	3	0	0	0
1950s	1	1	1	1	2	0	3	1	1	3	2	1	2	0
1960s	0	0	0	0	0	0	0	0	0	0	0	0	0	0
1970s	0	2	0	1	0	1	3	0	0	2	0	1	0	1
1980s	3	2	1	1	1	1	3	1	1	2	3	2	1	3
1990s	4	3	1	2	1	1	1	3	4	1	8	2	1	1
2000s	4	3	1	1	1	1	2	0	2	3	13	2	1	2
Total	15	11	6	6	5	4	14	5	8	11	29	8	5	7

Note: All positives are increases in personalization; all negatives are reductions in personalization. This means that the reforms shown as positive *reduce* voter–candidate distance and pooling, whereas cases shown as negative *increase* them.

is attributable, in significant part, to just one of those dimensions: namely, the weight attached to voters' candidate preferences in determining who fills a party's seats. Twenty-one reforms increased that weight between 1990 and 2009, whereas just four reduced it. These include changes in a wide range of old democracies—Austria, Belgium, the Netherlands, Iceland and Sweden—as well as newer democracies, including most of the post-1989 democracies in our sample.

By contrast, the remaining dimensions of personalism show little movement in either direction. The other dimension with many reforms is the degree to which voters are able to express preferences, with twenty-six reforms in total over the period. However, there are almost as many reforms decreasing as increasing personalism. The absence of any trend in the degree to which voters can express their preferences is striking.

Overall, these elements clearly confirm that there is indeed a trend across European democracies towards more personalization of electoral systems. The same trend is not observable in other Western democracies (such as Canada, the United States, Australia or New Zealand), but these countries already have very personalized electoral systems. It was in Europe that elections were more party-centred. PR list systems are the most frequent electoral systems, and most often they function with either closed or flexible lists. It is therefore logical that it was in Europe, and especially in those countries that were using rather party-centred systems that the broader trend towards the personalization of politics has translated into a personalization of electoral systems.

This finding is important and goes against what has been reported in previous studies. Karvonen (2010), in particular, concluded there was no clear evidence of any personalization; there were cases of personalization but also of stability or of depersonalization. Karvonen was right; this diversity of configurations is real. But once we take into account more cases—here, thirty-one European democracies—and look at personalizing reforms beyond mere shifts among closed, flexible and open lists, the overall pattern towards greater personalization cannot be denied. We thus already have a strong conclusion to make. Personalization of electoral institutions is indeed happening in Europe, and this trend has emerged in the most recent decades.

THE ORIGINS OF ELECTORAL SYSTEMS PERSONALIZATION

In this third section, we examine the causes of the trend towards more personalized electoral systems in Europe that we described previously. We look at the elements that could account for this trend over the last three decades across European democracies.

Disentangling the causes of electoral system changes is a complex task. As very well phrased by Pippa Norris more than twenty years ago, 'electoral systems are rarely designed, they are born kicking and screaming into the world, out of a messy, incremental compromise between contending factions battling for survival, determined by power politics' (Norris 1995, 3). The literature trying to isolate the main drivers of electoral reforms points towards a wide variety of factors (Renwick 2010; Rahat 2011). Nevertheless, what we are examining in this chapter is not a variety of episodes of electoral reform, but a cross-national trend pointing in the same direction, towards the personalization of electoral systems. It is therefore important to discuss what could be the common grounds on which these reforms are rooted.

We underline four elements. First, as well detailed in the introduction to this volume, the personalization of electoral systems is just one facet of the broader personalization of politics. It is a structural characteristic of contemporary party politics, of how the media are covering politics, of elections as well as of the functioning of the core institutions of representative democracy like government and parliament.

Second, there is an overall decline in satisfaction with the way politics is working in established democracies. We should not portray this pattern in unduly stark terms. Satisfaction with politics and government varies across countries and over time (Norris 2011). Moreover, within countries, citizens are not all equally dissatisfied with democracy, and the reasons for their dissatisfaction vary. Yet, as argued by Dalton (2004, 181), these sentiments are generating support for reforms designed to improve the system of representative democracy (Dalton and Gray 2003), creating 'fertile ground for elites and other political actors to suggest institutional reforms and experimentation'. Similarly, Gallagher (2005) suggests that public dissatisfaction may strongly erode the foundations of electoral systems, and Katz concludes that the major electoral reforms of the 1990s all shared an association with strong regime crisis (Katz 2005). Norris (2011) finds on the basis of a large-scale analysis of 190 independent states around the world from 1993 to 2004 that there is a strong association between negative sentiments among the public towards democratic institutions and the occurrence of electoral reform. To summarize, the growing disengagement of citizens from traditional politics has become more salient, and political elites have concluded that they should do something to demonstrate to citizens that they have received the message. Introducing a more personalized electoral system has often been that 'something'.

The reason for the choice of personalizing reforms as the response to discontentment among citizens is not purely trivial and is the third element that we highlight. This is that voters' dissatisfaction with the state of democracy is directed particularly in the direction of political parties. Research has shown that publics increasingly expect to be able to engage with politics without intermediation by parties. The decline of political parties across most democracies has been well documented. They have lost members (van Biezen, Mair and Poguntke 2012; Webb 2002, 439). Their voters have become less loyal (Dalton 2000; 2004, 33; Webb 2002, 439). Most importantly for our analysis, citizens tend to trust them less (Dalton and Weldon 2005; Webb 2002). Changes in the electoral system that reduce the weight of political parties to the benefit of individual candidates constitute a logical response to this. Politicians assume that voters would prefer systems that limit the role of parties. This does not mean that voters have clear and precise preferences for the personalization of the electoral systems. Most voters are not familiar with the technicalities of election laws. But politicians can hope that they will welcome reforms that can be framed as contributing to limiting the weight of political parties in selecting Members of Parliament (MPs) and as giving more weight to voters in deciding who is to sit in parliament.

The fourth and final element to take into consideration is the observation that public sentiment matters increasingly in shaping electoral rules. Early comparative work on electoral system choice often focused heavily on politicians; politicians were assumed to control the electoral system, and electoral reform would occur only if sufficiently many politicians found change to be in their power-seeking interests (e.g., Benoit 2004; Colomer 2004, 2005). From this perspective, public disengagement from political parties would not be expected to have much impact on the politics of electoral reform; public attitudes, on this account, are just not relevant to outcomes. As research into electoral reform has developed, however, the role of other actors has increasingly been recognized (e.g., Katz 2005; Norris 2011; Rahat 2008; Renwick 2010). Quintal (1970) recognized long ago that potential electoral reformers must attend to 'the costs of voter affect', that enacting reforms that voters dislike or failing to pursue reforms that voters demand could cost politicians support and hence power. This idea, long largely ignored, was revived in Reed and Thies's (2001) distinction between 'outcome-contingent' and 'act-contingent' aspects of decision making. It implies that, even if politicians do largely maintain control over the electoral system, they must attend to public opinion when thinking about reform. Further than that, the public has also been directly involved in various recent processes of electoral reform, be it through referendums, for example, in the United Kingdom, New Zealand, Romania, Slovenia and the Canadian provinces of Ontario, British Columbia and Prince Edward Island or through citizens' assemblies as in Ontario, British Columbia, the Netherlands, and Ireland (see Fournier et al. 2011; Renwick 2010).

These elements—personalization of politics, public dissatisfaction with representative democracy, demands for more citizen participation and a reduced role for political parties and the growing role of citizens in electoral reform processes—combine, we argue, to explain the trend we are witnessing towards more personalized electoral systems. A last important element to underline is that, with these reforms, we can observe that political parties are not passive actors in the process of the personalization of politics. Personalization is not just something that happens to political parties. They are also active partners of this evolution.

EXPLORING THE CONSEQUENCES OF PERSONALIZED ELECTORAL SYSTEMS

The other side of the coin is now to discuss how the shift towards more candidate-centred electoral systems may transform politics. In particular, we explore how it affects voters, on the one hand, and parties and politicians on the other.

Regarding voters, the question is whether they embrace reforms that personalize the electoral system. Such reforms expand voters' capacity to determine which candidates are elected. But the change would only be theoretical if voters do not actually use these new opportunities.

Bowler and Donovan (2013) argue that electoral reforms rarely have the effects expected of them, and a number of authors—notably, Curtice and Shively (2009), Holmberg (2009) and Karvonen (2004)—have questioned whether the impact of variation between countries in the degree of electoral system personalization is as great as is often supposed. On these accounts, changes to the personalization of electoral systems should not have had any noteworthy further effects on electoral and party politics.

To explore these questions, we examine how voters use the new opportunities they are offered to support specific candidates. This variable—voters' usage of their enhanced capacity to decide which candidates are elected—is not easy to capture because voters can express their preferences among candidates through a wide variety of different mechanisms within different systems (list systems with preference votes, ordinal systems such as STV or AV, panachage, and so on). We therefore concentrate on those cases of reform where the impact of a change towards personalization is not too complicated to assess. We focus on five countries: Austria, Belgium, Sweden and the Netherlands, plus Norway for local elections. These five countries use list PR systems, allowing voters to cast preference votes. All have increased the weight of these preference votes in determining who is elected in the recent period (post-1989), giving us easier access to data on preference votes.

Figure 2.1. shows levels of preference voting in the seven elections preceding personalizing electoral reform (specifically, the first of the two such reforms in Belgium, the Netherlands and Sweden) and in all the elections

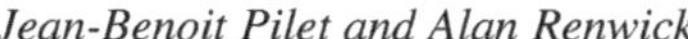

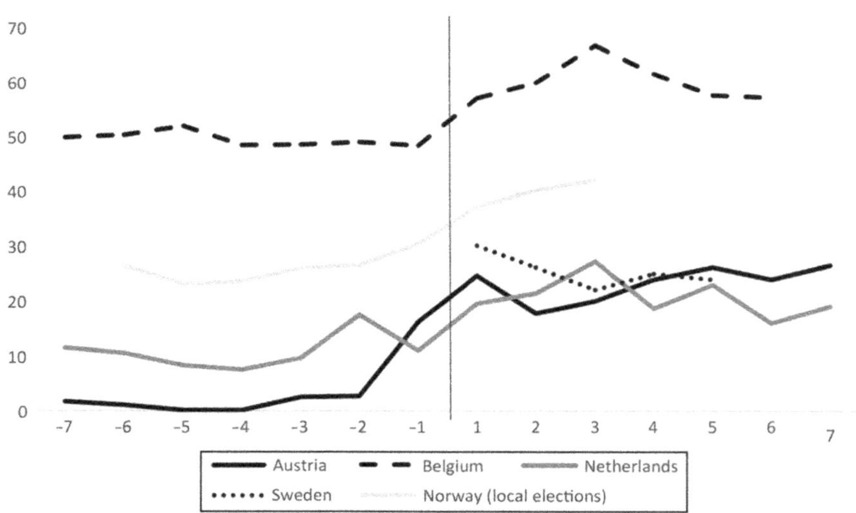

Figure 2.1 The Timing of Electoral Reforms and Changes in Preference Voting (%). *Source: Faces on the Ballot: The Personalization of Electoral Systems in Europe* by Alan Renwick and Jean-Benoit Pilet (2016). By permission of Oxford University Press.

after those reforms in the five countries. The moment of (the first) reform is shown by the vertical line. In Austria, Belgium, Norway and Sweden, the vertical axis denotes the share of voters who decided to cast a preference vote rather than a list vote without any specific preference marked for any candidate. The Dutch system allows voters to cast a valid ballot only by voting for an individual candidate; there is no option to cast a straight party ballot. The proportion of voters who choose to cast a preference vote is therefore not available as a way of measuring preference voting. This system is, however, a flexible rather than fully open-list system; each party determines the order of its candidates on the ballot paper and a vote for the first candidate is, in effect, a vote for that established order. It is therefore standard practice to use the proportion of voters casting their ballot for a candidate other than the top candidate on each list as an indicator of preference voting (see, e.g., Andeweg and Holsteyn 2011). This is what we show on the vertical axis in figure 2.1.

It can be seen that preference voting rose in the first postreform election in every case (hard data are not available for Sweden because preference votes were not even counted before the reform, but it is universally assumed that the rate increased). It also rose following the second reforms in Belgium (between elections two and three in figure 2.1) and the Netherlands (between elections one and two). The only exception is the second reform in Sweden, implemented in 2014 (between elections four and five), when preference voting slightly dipped. Furthermore, preference voting has been higher in all elections since reform than in all elections preceding reform with only one exception; the rate in the Netherlands in 2010 dipped below the level reached before reform in the election of 1986.

These five countries seem to indicate that, indeed, voters are happy to be granted more opportunities to decide which candidates are to be elected. When the electoral system is personalized, voters make use of the new mechanisms of candidate voting.

However, one should be cautious before drawing such a conclusion. What figure 2.1 also makes apparent is that in three of the cases—Austria, the Netherlands and Norway—the rise in preference voting had already begun before reform took place. In Sweden, because of the lack of data, we cannot know whether that occurred. The only clear exception is Belgium; here, preference voting rose almost continuously from 1954 to 1974 (which happens to be the first election on the figure) but then stagnated, not rising significantly again until the first postreform election in 1995. At least in some cases, therefore, causation may flow from voting behaviour to electoral reform.

The next question is what implications personalized electoral systems have for political parties and for politicians. A first element is that it could be expected to diminish the control political parties can exert over which of their candidates enter parliament. In party-centred electoral systems, such as closed list systems or SMP, political parties control this process. They select the candidate(s) who appear on the ballot paper under their name, and voters can simply vote for the party without any opportunity to alter those candidates. In ordinal systems (STV, AV) or in flexible and open list systems, voters may alter the parties' ordering of candidates, potentially changing the allocation of seats to candidates within parties.

The simplest measure of the impact of personalizing electoral reforms on political parties' control over who is elected is to look at the number of candidates who are elected because of the preference votes they received and not because of their position on the list. In systems where parties present ordered lists, as is the case in all flexible-list systems and most open-list systems, we can compare the identity of elected candidates with what would have happened had the final list orderings been the same as those originally submitted by the parties.

Figure 2.2 shows, for the five West European countries that have experienced reforms since 1989 (Austria, Belgium, Iceland, the Netherlands and Sweden), the proportion of deputies who would not have been elected under this closed-list scenario. Of course, the numbers in figure 2.2 take no account of possible changes, induced by list flexibility, in how the parties order their preelectoral lists.

In none of these cases could the change be said to be dramatic. Indeed, in Iceland, by this measure, there has been no change at all; no deputy has been elected solely as the result of preference votes since the first post-war election in 1946. If we lower the bar for change, we can say that the Icelandic reform

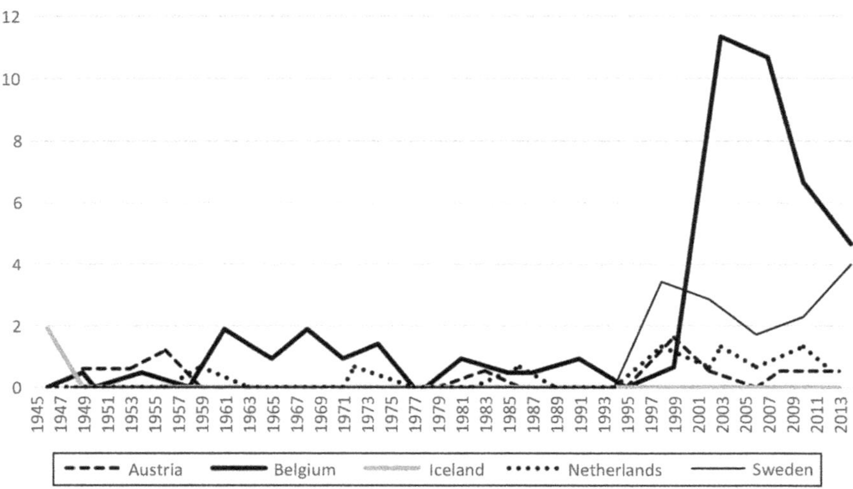

Figure 2.2 Proportion (%) of Deputies Elected as a Result of Preference Votes in Western Europe since 1945. *Source*: *Faces on the Ballot: The Personalization of Electoral Systems in Europe* by Alan Renwick and Jean-Benoit Pilet (2016). By permission of Oxford University Press.

of 2000 has had some slight impact; although there were no cases even of a change in list ordering under either the 1959 or the 1987 rules, there have been four such changes since 2000—two in 2007 and two more in 2009. But none of these changes affected who was elected; in every case, a candidate was demoted by one place, but his (always his) party had secured enough votes to ensure he was elected anyway.

The effects have been only slightly greater in Austria and the Netherlands. In Austria, just one candidate was elected because of preference votes in the ten elections between 1959 and 1990. Since then, there have been six cases where a candidate was elected by this route. Two of these, however, were cases where Jörg Haider—leader of the Freedom Party and later of the Alliance for the Future of Austria—opted for a low list position, was pushed up the list by voters but chose not to take his seat. In the Netherlands, three candidates were elected by preference votes between 1946 and 1989. The reform of 1989, applied only in 1994, had no discernible impact; no candidate was elected by preference votes in that election. The 1997 reform has had some effect and preference votes have affected outcomes in every election since. But the number of candidates elected by preference votes has oscillated between one and two without ever rising higher.

Only in Belgium and Sweden could any significant degree of list flexibility be said, at least by this measure, to have been introduced. In Sweden, whereas no changes in list ordering occurred before the 1997 reform, a number of deputies have been elected because of preference votes at every election since then. Twelve deputies (out of 349) were thus elected in the first election, in 1998. The numbers subsequently fell back, but fourteen were elected by preference votes in 2014 following the further reduction of the preference threshold, of whom only nine would have been elected had the old threshold still been in place. In Belgium, finally, the efficacy of preference voting was always somewhat higher than in the other countries discussed here: between 1946 and 1991, at least one deputy was elected by personal votes in eleven out of sixteen elections, and twenty-three deputies were elected this way in total. Still, that was twenty-three out of a total of 3382 deputies (Dewachter 2003, 123). The first reform had little effect; in 1995, no deputy was elected by preference votes and in 1999 just one was thus elected. Following the second reform, in 2003, however, seventeen deputies—11.3 percent of the total—secured their seats because of personal support. Yet, even in Belgium, the strength of the effect can be doubted because the number of deputies elected this way has fallen at each election since 2003, dropping to just seven in 2014.

Overall, it indeed appears that a first consequence of personalized electoral systems for political parties is that they lose some control over the selection of elected representatives. Yet the changes are not radical. There are indeed more candidates elected despite their position lower down their party's list. But such cases remain a minority.

The impact of personalized electoral systems on political parties as well as on politicians goes, however, beyond the allocation of seats to candidates within political parties. First, as already underlined in the seminal article by Carey and Shugart (1995), the degree of candidate-centredness of electoral systems shapes politicians' incentives to cultivate a personal reputation. Indeed, research has observed that the degree of personalization of the electoral system may have some impact on what politicians do and on the importance they attribute to their personal characteristics. Electoral campaigns may be affected by the personalized nature of the electoral system (see the chapters by Chiru and by Pruysers and Cross, this volume). In more personalized electoral systems, candidates tend to run more individualized campaigns, in which they emphasize their personal identity and political positions and where their actions target their own potential voters (most often in their district) rather than addressing more broadly the entire party electorate nationwide (Zittel and Gschwend 2008; Bowler and Farrell 2011; Zittel 2015).

Personalized electoral systems may also affect how politicians behave once elected. Overall, legislators may tend to favour activities in parliament and outside parliament that contribute to building their personal reputation—such as district presence or case work—when the electoral system is more personalized (André, Depauw and Shugart 2014). Even in their legislative activities, such as bill initiations, legislators are influenced by the reward they could expect personally from voters in more personalized systems

(Braüninger, Brunner and Daübler 2012). Previous research has also shown that personalized electoral systems can facilitate factionalization within parties (Katz 1980). Factions within parties may try to signal their existence via coordinated work or via collective campaigning and would hope to be rewarded by voters as a faction. Factionalized voters would cast preference votes only for candidates of such factions or groups (Marien, Wauters and Schouteden 2017).

Finally, as explored in more depth by Bittner and Malloy in their chapters in this volume, the degree of personalization of the electoral system may also affect the position of the party leader. As explained in the introduction to this chapter, the personalization of electoral system mostly refers to decentralized personalization, as it affects the weight of individual candidates in electoral and party politics. Nevertheless, it is not without consequences for centralized personalization for the role and weight of party leaders. A priori, one may expect that more decentralized personalization would increase the weight of all candidates at the expense not only of the central party organization but also of the central party leaders. Yet, recent research seems to show that things are not that straightforward. In a recent study of Belgian elections, Wauters and his colleagues (2016) show that party leaders have not suffered at all from the personalization of electoral systems in Belgium. In fact, more and more voters have concentrated their preference votes on the party leaders, whereas less prominent candidates have faced growing difficulties in attracting such votes. In other words, centralized personalization has, at least in Belgium, been reinforced in a context of a growing decentralized personalization of the electoral system.

All these elements illustrate that the shifts towards more personalized electoral systems that we have described in the first two sections of the chapter are not merely technical changes. They appear to have genuine effects on the functioning of electoral as well as party politics in contemporary democracies.

CONCLUSIONS: ELECTORAL SYSTEMS, PERSONALIZATION AND THE ROLE OF POLITICAL PARTIES

In this chapter, we have explored the link between personalization and electoral systems. We have first mobilized existing studies that distinguish between candidate-centred and party-centred electoral systems (Carey and Shugart 1995; Renwick and Pilet 2016) to show that a trend exists across European democracies towards more candidate-centred electoral systems.

These first findings enrich the growing literature on the personalization of politics. Over the last twenty years, many studies have been written on various facets of this evolution. The personalization of media coverage of politics, of political parties, and of elections has been discussed and analysed (see Karvonen 2010 for a review). We go one step further and show that personalization is affecting not only the functioning of politics, but also the institutional architecture itself. The heart of the representative process—the electoral system—is being reshaped in many European countries, reducing the role of political parties and increasing voters' capacity to select the candidates who enter parliament. Given that institutions are rather stable, these reforms are likely to leave a lasting footprint in European political systems.

In the third section of this chapter, we have analysed both the origins and the consequences of this trend towards more personalized electoral systems. First, as we showed previously, these changes to electoral institutions have been grounded in a context of public dissatisfaction with representative democracy and growing distrust towards political parties. In reaction, political parties have tried to show that they are responsive to this dissatisfaction by promoting reforms that give voters more say in selecting MPs. In that respect, political parties have lost some control over one of their core functions: the recruitment and selection of political elites. However, they have been able to limit the loss of control. They have enacted reforms to look as though they are responding to popular disengagement and discontent, but they have been able to steer this process. Even if voters now have greater influence over who gets elected, political parties still order the lists of candidates in most democracies, the lists they compose still give a strong signal to voters as to which candidates they should prioritize, and in practice, significant changes to list order generally remain exceptional.

The consequences of personalizing reforms for voters and for parties and politicians are the last facet of the issue that we have explored. We have observed that voters have made use of the opportunities offered to them to vote for candidates, especially within flexible list systems, by increasing their use of preference votes when the weight of these votes on the election of candidates had been increased. For political parties and politicians too, the consequences of personalized electoral systems are not trivial. They have lost some control over access to parliament, and politicians tend to put more emphasis on their personal card, both during campaigns and once in power. Party leaders in particular have in many cases tried to use personalization as an asset. In other words, the personalization of electoral institutions is more than a technical issue. It is not a radical revolution for democratic politics, but as observed in the other chapters of the volume, it constitutes a real shift in politics to which all actors (voters, parties and politicians) are adapting. What we observe is a move towards a new equilibrium between individual politicians, political parties as organizations and party leaders, rather than a radical paradigmatic shift.

NOTE

1. In this respect, we argue that SMP systems are more personalized than closed list systems because voters are allowed to cast a vote for one candidate in the former and not the latter. But SMP systems are less candidate-centred than flexible or open list systems because voters actually do not have any intraparty choice: there is one candidate per party, not several.

Chapter 3

The Personalization of Parliamentary Elections?[1]

Amanda Bittner

The role of party leaders in elections has been debated among scholars for quite some time. While the media focuses on leaders by discussing their appearance, personal lives, and reporting standings in the polls, the impact of party leaders at the ballot box has not always been clear within scholarly research. Some (and a growing number) of the studies have found substantial evidence that leaders play an important role in elections (e.g., Bittner 2011; Johnston 2002; Kinder et al. 1980), others have suggested that once we consider other factors like the economy and partisanship, party leaders cease to have a prominent place in the vote calculus (Miller and Shanks 1996).

In addition to this question about whether or not leaders matter, a tangential issue has been increasingly explored: the extent to which the importance of leaders in elections is growing. Scholars have pointed to the personalization of elections, arguing that party leaders matter more than they have in the past (Mughan 2000; Poguntke and Webb 2005). It is this second argument that provides the starting point for this chapter.

I have argued elsewhere (Bittner 2011) that leaders matter, based on a multicountry, multiyear assessment of the role of leaders, and in their introduction to this volume, Pruysers, Cross and Katz refer to the concept of 'personalism', the idea that individual candidates matter and that the personal is taken into consideration by parties, candidates and voters. Certainly, it seems safe to state that personality and 'the individual' candidate are important in the minds of voters, whether we base our analyses on a single election or multiple elections. Whether leaders have become *increasingly* important (*personalization* rather than personalism), however, is a question that can only be answered by looking at elections *longitudinally*, and I do so in this chapter.

To assess the extent to which elections have become more personalized over time, I look at elections in two countries: Britain and Canada.[2] Both are parliamentary democracies, in which voters do not directly elect the prime minister (in the way that they mark a ballot next to their choice for president), and these two electoral contexts provide a competitive environment in which *we would not expect leaders to matter much*, at least in comparison to presidential systems. Should leaders be of increasing importance to voters in these two established parliamentary systems, we will have a strong case for the personalization of electoral politics. I rely on data collected for the British Election Studies and the Canadian Election Studies over the last three decades to assess over-time trends in partisanship, ideology and perceptions of leaders. This chapter finds little evidence of personalization of politics; Canada in particular, I find, provides no support for the personalization hypothesis, although Britain's recent elections show a minor increase in the importance of leaders. I argue that in both countries, leaders have always been important, thus providing clear support for the 'personalism' hypothesis and showing, at best, mixed evidence of an increase in the importance of leaders.

THE INCREASINGLY IMPORTANT ROLE OF LEADERS IN ELECTIONS?

Scholars have, for some time now, assessed the role of party leaders in parliamentary elections, and although some suggest leaders matter very little once we account for other important factors (Blais et al. 2002), a sizeable amount of existing research suggests that leaders do have an important role to play in election outcomes (Bittner 2010, 2011; Johnston et al. 1992; Johnston 2002; Clarke et al. 1991; Lobo and Curtice 2014; Winham and Cunningham 1970; Brown et al. 1988). What is it about leaders that voters pay attention to?

Character and Competence: Voters' Perceptions of Leaders' Traits

Studies to date have primarily assessed the role of leaders in elections around the world in two ways: (a) through measures called 'feelings thermometers' in which voters are asked to indicate how warmly they feel towards party leaders on a scale (e.g., Aarts, Blais and Schmitt 2011) and (b) by asking voters to assess party leaders on a number of personality traits (e.g., Bittner 2011). Both measures are useful in different ways: the thermometer makes cross-national and over-time comparison much easier, given that survey questions are often different from election to election and that not all surveys ask questions about leaders' traits. The problem with these feeling thermometers, however, is that the actual 'meaning' of the questions may be confusing for voters, and the questions might be 'infused with party, group, and policy judgments' (Johnston 2002, 174). Even when we control for partisanship, attitudes and socio-demographic characteristics in our models, it might be difficult to capture 'real' feelings towards party leaders with these thermometers.

These are not the only ways that scholars have assessed the impact of leaders in elections: Mughan (2000) incorporates approval ratings from Gallup into his analyses, and scholars have also made use of open-ended likes/dislikes (e.g., Hayes 2009). Where possible, assessment of the role of leaders through personality traits is preferable because the meaning of traits is less ambiguous than thermometer ratings and other less-clear measures. Answering survey questions is complicated, and when we ask whether a given leader is 'intelligent' we are being much more specific and clear for a survey respondent, who can more easily understand and respond to a narrow concept such as intelligence than a wide and vague concept such as overall 'feelings'.

Studies of person perception suggest that voters assess candidates' and leaders' personalities in terms of two main categories, labelled 'character' and 'competence' (Bittner 2011). Character includes traits such as being trustworthy, honest, caring, empathetic and other related traits, whereas competence includes traits such as intelligence, strength of leadership, 'gets things done', and so on. Research finds voters notice and evaluate leaders on both of these dimensions and that these evaluations have clear electoral consequences; parties usually lose or gain between 2 and 5 percent of the vote based on perceptions of leaders (Bittner 2011). In addition, voters have expectations of leaders that divide along partisan lines. The competence dimension is seen to be a strength (and expected to be a strength) for conservative party leaders, whereas character is the stronghold of leaders of left parties (Bittner 2014). This independent impact of leaders on electoral outcomes suggests that parties ought to take leaders quite seriously and think strategically about how they campaign with the leader in mind.

The research is fairly clear that leaders matter in parliamentary elections and provides solid evidence in favour of the type of 'personalism' that Pruysers, Cross and Katz refer to in the introduction to this book. The question is, are they *increasingly* important?

Personalization of Elections: Are Leaders Increasingly Important?

Over the last few decades, scholars discussing voters and elections have pointed to changes in technology resulting in increased mediatization and coverage of the horserace (Mughan 2000); a decline of partisanship (Dalton and Wattenberg 2001); and the breakdown of traditional political cleavages (Franklin 1992). These three processes have, some argue, led voters to focus more on party leaders and personality than on party ties or policy platforms (Mughan 2000; Poguntke and Webb 2005; Wattenberg 1991). Labelling this process 'personalization' or 'presidentialization', scholars have made convincing arguments illustrating the increasing importance of leaders (e.g., Poguntke and Webb 2005; Rahat and Shaeffer 2007), whereas others suggest that the data are mixed at best, and that there is no personalization process going on (Adam and Maier 2010; Karvonen 2010; Kriesi 2012).

The media world as we see it (and consume it) today is very different from what it was fifty years ago, with the advent of television, the Internet and social media. Many scholars have observed that the nature of news reporting and consumption has changed and that how politics is covered has shifted accordingly. Numerous studies have pointed to the media's focus on the horserace (e.g., Gidengil et al. 2000; Mendelsohn 1993), as news stories report standings in the polls, comparing how the leader of one party fares in comparison to the fortunes of another. Mughan (2000) suggests that this has led to the increasing prominence and importance of leaders in the minds of voters because consumers of the media are faced with daily coverage of these individuals. More research is needed to track media coverage of leaders over time because it is possible that leaders have always been the focal point of media coverage and that as a result, voters have always had leaders top-of-mind when headed to the ballot box (see, for example, figure 12.1 in this volume).

Partisanship also has been seen to play a key role in the minds of voters (however subconsciously) since it was first discussed in the mid-1900s (Campbell et al. 1960). Much ink has been spilled over the nature and existence of partisanship and the extent to which it is solely a US phenomenon/concept (see Johnston 2006 for a comprehensive overview). This issue has not been put to bed, and scholars continue to debate whether and how individuals are influenced by partisanship when they vote. Some have argued that voters' attachments to parties have decreased over time (Dalton and Wattenberg 2000; Wattenberg 1991), and as a result, 'other' considerations (such as perceptions of leaders) have replaced partisanship in anchoring political behaviour. Elections have become more personalized, the argument goes, because voters no longer feel the attachment to party that they once did. Although scholars have assessed the role of partisanship around the world quite extensively (Blais et al. 2001; Jenson 1975; Johnston 1992; LeDuc et al. 1984; Wattenberg 1982), a more recent longitudinal analysis of Canadian and British partisanship in relation to the personalization hypothesis is needed. We lack up-to-date information about voter attachments over time.

Personalization is seen to be occurring because of changes in long-term forces, such as partisanship and also other traditional cleavages. Lipset and Rokkan (1967) pointed to the importance of the social bases of politics, which tied voters to parties and traditional bases of decision making, such as ideology and class. Scholars have argued that there have been important shifts in these traditional bases of decision making (Bartolini and Mair 1990), and that as a result of those shifts, the relationships between voters and parties are shifting, giving individual personalities more prominence (Poguntke and Webb 2005) and thus leading to a personalization of politics. There is mixed evidence of shifting cleavage structures, however, and as Franklin (1992) observes, there are many places around the world where traditional cleavages continue to play a key role in anchoring parties and politics. A longitudinal assessment of ideology is necessary to determine the processes that may have been at play over the long term.

Taken as a whole, the personalization literature is somewhat divided, and there is (at best) mixed evidence for the existence of personalization. A number of important studies have made strong arguments that leaders are more important over time (Poguntke and Webb 2005; Rahat and Shaeffer 2007); however there are a number of other scholars who remain sceptical (Bittner forthcoming; Karvonen 2010; Kriesi 2007; Adam and Maier 2010). Taken as a whole, the personalization hypothesis is one that needs further attention and systematic investigation. This chapter begins to unpack these complicated relationships by looking at two countries.

DATA AND ANALYSIS

Assessing an increase in personalization of elections requires longitudinal analysis, and although there are limits to historical data available today, it is possible to examine trends over time. This chapter assesses voters' perceptions of party leaders in Canada from 1984 to 2015 and in the United Kingdom from 1983 to 2015.[3]

The discussion that follows incorporates both bivariate and multivariate analyses. I begin by tracking perceptions of party leaders' traits as well as overall 'feelings' towards leaders over time, looking at perceptions of traits in two dimensions (character and competence) and feelings as measured by 'feelings thermometers'. In addition to canvassing attitudes towards leaders, I also track respondents' partisanship and ideological leanings (left-right self-placement) in both jurisdictions because of past research that credits the decreasing prominence of these two features of electoral politics, which have, scholars argue, been replaced by party leaders. Although these analyses provide us with interesting insights into patterns of perceptions over time, they do not tell us whether leaders 'count' more in the vote calculus over time.

To assess the role of leaders in comparison to other factors, I combine all years within each country and run two pooled multinomial logit analyses, in which vote choice for one of the three major parties is regressed on the 'usual' suspects (partisanship, socio-demographic variables and issue attitudes) as well as perceptions of leaders' traits. This is intended to ascertain whether different patterns emerge in both Canada and the United Kingdom: are leaders more important in one country or are they equally (un?)important in both? Finally, I disaggregate the data set once more and run a series of logistical analyses for each election in each country, again regressing vote choice on perceptions of leaders while controlling for other factors. I then graph the marginal effects of leaders' traits for each election over time to assess whether leaders have become increasingly important in the vote calculus. These analyses suggest that leaders have always been important in the minds of voters. Personalization, if it is taking place, is quite minimal.

ATTITUDES ABOUT PARTY LEADERS IN BRITAIN AND CANADA

First we track perceptions of leaders in Canada[4] and the United Kingdom, assessing evaluations of leaders' *character*[5] and *competence* over time.[6] Figure 3.1 shows average ratings of Canadian leaders' personality traits over time. These graphs compare the ratings of each of those leaders with the average across all party leaders (including leaders of minor parties from across the party system). The left-leaning New Democratic Party (NDP) party leaders have been evaluated most positively on the character dimension over time, whereas Conservative party leaders have been evaluated most positively on the competence dimension (although this is not universal across these elections).

This pattern can be seen again somewhat in the British data, as seen in figure 3.2: Lib-Dem leaders' character is generally perceived most positively, and at least in the earliest years of these data, Conservative party leaders were perceived most positively on the competence dimension. In the

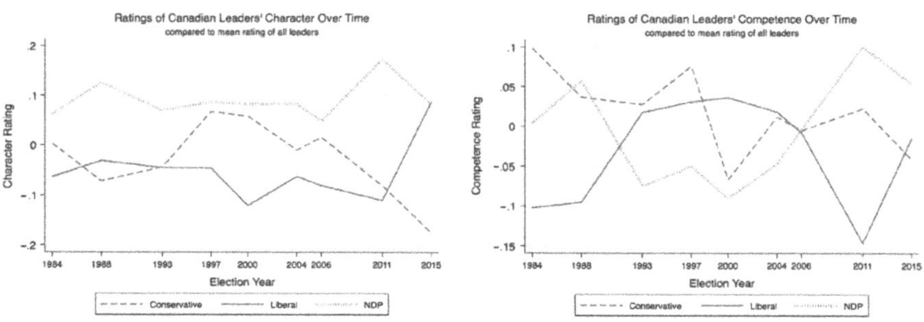

Figure 3.1 Perceptions of Canadian Leaders' Character and Competence, over Time.

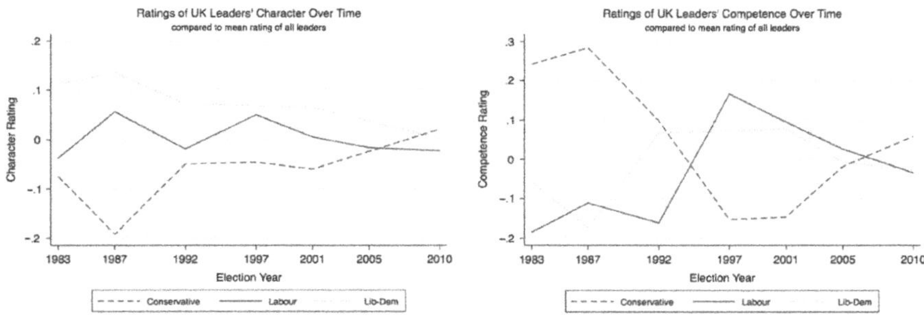

Figure 3.2 Perceptions of UK Leaders' Character and Competence, over Time.

late 1990s, the Labour party moved ahead on this measure until 2010 when the Conservative party leader was again seen to be most competent. Bittner (2011, 2015) identified this partisan stereotype, where frequently, over time and across space, left party leaders' character is perceived more positively and conservative party leaders' competence is perceived more positively (this pattern tends to hold for voters of all political leanings, not simply partisans of those two parties).

Furthermore, as the graphs in figure 3.2 illustrate, perceptions of British leaders on both dimensions have moved up and down over time but have been slowly merging together; in more recent elections, leaders are evaluated more similarly than they were in the past. It is not clear from these graphs why this might be the case or what the implications of this 'similarity' are for electoral outcomes (or the role of leaders in determining electoral outcomes). Certainly, these figures confirm 'personalism'; voters differentiate between leaders, across parties and over time, thus indicating that they are aware of, and do pay attention to, party leaders.

Figure 3.3 tracks voters 'feelings' towards party leaders over time, comparing average feelings towards leaders of the three main parties to the average for the leaders of all parties. Although I generally argue against the use of thermometer ratings (e.g., Bittner 2011), I include them here to compensate for the missing personality traits data across these two countries. Similar to the previous two graphs, what is fairly clear here is that voters do indeed see leaders differently, rating some leaders most positively in some years, and other leaders most positively in other years.[7] Interestingly, in 2015 thermometer ratings of the Scottish National Party (SNP) leader rose dramatically. It is a shame we do not have data tracking perceptions of traits in that election because it would be nice to be able to assess in what way feelings are linked to perceptions of character and competence.[8] What is clear is that in each election year, voters' feelings towards the party leaders change, although note that in 2010 British voters did not differentiate much between the party leaders (evaluations of all of them hover near the zero line, as was the case for perceptions of personality traits, as seen in figures 3.1 and 3.2).

Figures 3.1 through 3.3 provide us with evidence that voters pay attention to party leaders and that they have done so at least since the early 1980s in both countries. To further piece together this story about personalization, it is important to examine other behavioural 'sign posts' over time: what does party identification and ideological self-placement look like during this period? Figures 3.4 and 3.5 track partisanship and ideology over time, comparing the two countries.

Figure 3.4 tracks the proportion of voters claiming party identification for the three main parties, comparing those individuals to rates of non-partisanship over time, in both countries. The personalization literature claims that leaders matter more because voters are less tied to parties and ideology. As such, we ought to expect that the number of non-partisans should be increasing over time at the expense of partisans. Between 1984 and 2015, there is substantial fluctuation in the number of non-partisans and the distribution of partisans across parties. However, the start and end points are quite similar (although the proportion of Conservative partisans never returns to where it

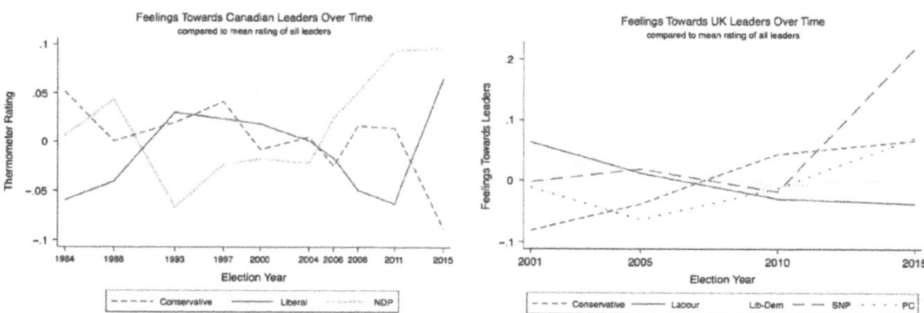

Figure 3.3 'Feelings' Towards Leaders in Canada and the United Kingdom, over Time.

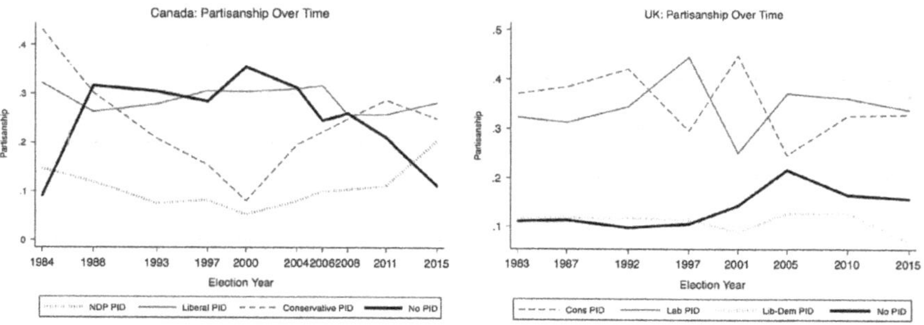

Figure 3.4 Party Identification in Canada and the United Kingdom, over Time.

began in 1984). Elsewhere (Bittner forthcoming) I have argued that the non-partisan line tracks closely with the massive changes that took place in the party system in Canada. These data suggest that having no party identification during this time is about the destruction and gradual come back of the Conservative Party, in addition to the Bloc Quéḃécois's appearance in the province of Quebec during that time, rather than about a partisan de-alignment (see Carty, Cross and Young 2000).

In the United Kingdom, there is a slightly different pattern. In 2001, the number of non-partisans increases by about 10 percent and then loses about half of this increase by the 2015 election. This pattern seems to coincide with a dropping number of Lib-Dem partisans, indicating that this party is losing supporters.[9] The United Kingdom demonstrates a 5 percent increase in the number of individuals claiming to be non-partisans in the last thirty years. These UK data do provide some support for a 'personalization' story because fewer respondents claim partisanship over time. It is conceivable that the decreased attachment to a party in this country may be associated with an increase in focus on party leaders among voters. Bivariate analyses alone, however, are not sufficient to make this claim.

Attachment to parties shifted over time in both countries, but Canadians began and ended this time period at approximately the same place, whereas British voters moved away from parties in slightly larger numbers. When it comes to ideological left-right self-placement, some movement is visible as well. I track left-right self-placement by partisan groups in figure 3.5, and this graph shows that although there is some movement, ideological self-placement remains broadly steady with start and end points closely matched. Of course, movement may have taken place before the early 1980s, but this cannot be determined from these data.

Ideology is coded such that the most right-leaning partisans are coded at 1 and the most left-leaning partisans are coded at 0; thus, it makes sense that

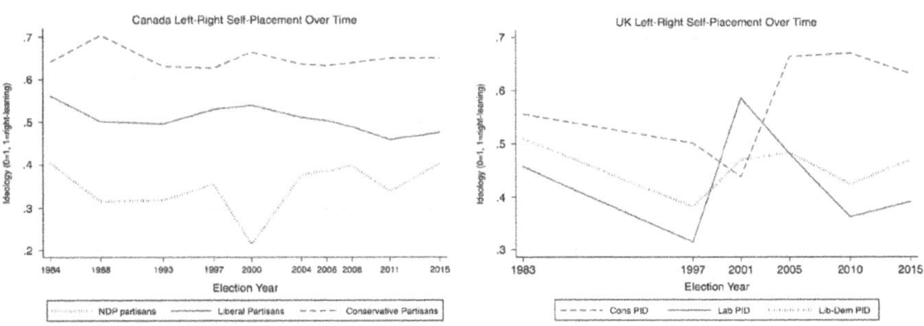

Figure 3.5 Left-Right Self-placement of Partisans in Canada and the United Kingdom, over Time.

Conservative partisans are at the top of the graphs (closer to 1), and NDP/Lib-Dem partisans are near the bottom of the graphs (closer to 0). These data suggest that Liberal partisans have moved slightly to the left over time, whereas Conservative and NDP partisans have fluctuated a little with time but remain today largely where they began in the early 1980s.

In the United Kingdom, the gap between those on the left and right has widened, notably because of the shift among Conservative partisans that took place after the 2001 election. Since 1983, Lib-Dem and Labour partisans moved to the left (although only slightly), whereas Conservatives partisans did a lot to widen the gap by moving to the right. What we don't know from these graphs is to what extent the partisans are the same people over time. Have individual Conservative identifiers become more conservative over time? Or did partisans who leaned more left move to another party (Labour? Somewhere else?), thus leaving the more right-wing partisans on their own in the Conservative Party? Does this move to the right have something to do with the UKIP party? Or something else? Yougov credits the party leaders for some of the ideological movement of the parties, charting the increasingly left-leaning leaders in the Labour party over time, from Blair to Milliband (Dahlgreen 2014). Is this how we can explain the drastic move to the right among Labour supporters in 2001? Perhaps Tony Blair's championing of 'New Labour' took hold among partisans? Enough of a hold to move them to the right of Conservative partisans? More research is needed to better understand the relationship among ideology, party and leaders in the United Kingdom. The figure fairly clearly indicates that partisans are more ideologically divided than they were thirty years ago; the gap between Conservative partisans and partisans of the other two major parties has grown.

Figures 3.1 to 3.5 do not provide substantial evidence in support of the personalization of elections, but the story of partisanship in the United Kingdom is potentially indicative of some personalization in that country. When we look at the impact of party leaders on vote choice, it continues to look like leaders have always mattered in these two parliamentary democracies. Personalism certainly exists, but the presence of *personalization* is less clear.

EFFECTS OF PARTY LEADERS ON VOTE CHOICE

To determine whether leaders influence vote choice, I ran a series of multivariate analyses and present the results graphically in figures 3.6 through 3.9. The first model was a multinominal logit model (data were pooled across all election years). The dependent variable was vote choice for one of the top three parties, coded 1 for Conservative Voters, 2 for Liberal/Labour voters and 3 for NDP/Lib-Dem voters (all other voters were excluded). This vote

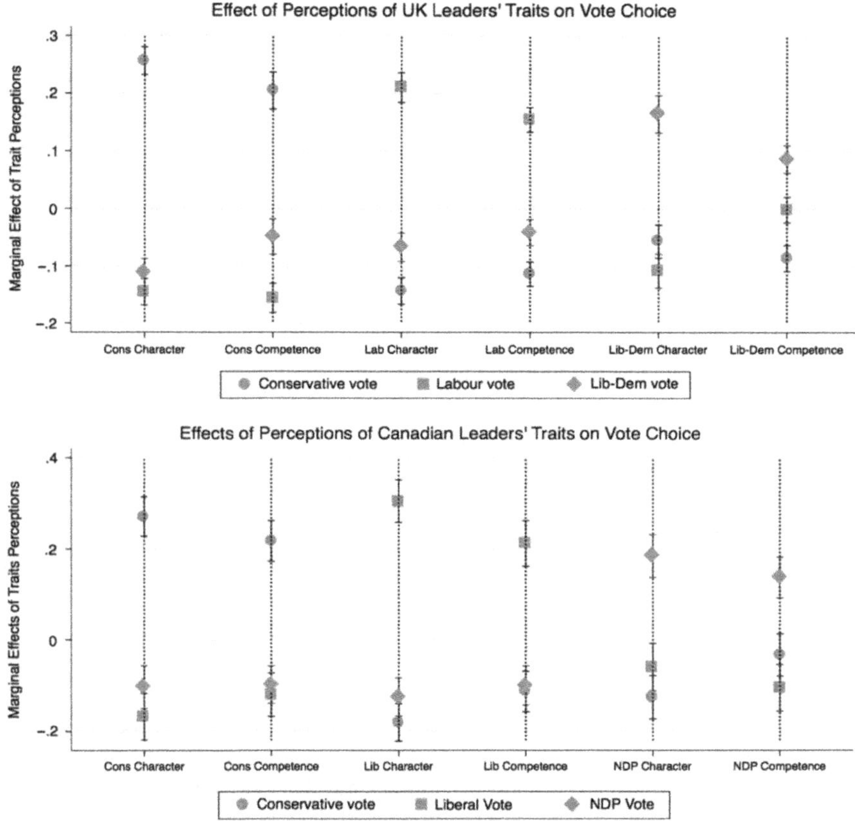

Figure 3.6 Effects of Perceptions of Leaders' Traits on Vote Choice in Canada and the United Kingdom, All Years.

choice variable was regressed on perceptions of character and competence of leaders of those three parties. The model also included control variables[10] for marital status, sex, education, employment status, age, party identification, left-right self-placement, issue attitudes on two dimensions (taxes versus spending and social conservatism as measured through attitudes towards abortion or same sex marriage) and election year.[11]

Figure 3.6 presents the marginal effects of traits perceptions for leaders of the three main parties on vote choice for one of those same three parties.[12] As the graph makes clear, evaluations of Conservative leaders' character and competence are most influential for those who vote Conservative, evaluations of Liberal/Labour leaders' character and competence are most influential for those who vote for that party and evaluations of NDP/Lib-Dem leaders' character and competence are most influential for those who vote for these parties. Also clear is that evaluations of leaders' character have a larger impact on vote choice overall than do evaluations of their competence. Finally, evaluations of the NDP and Lib-Dem party leaders' personality traits have the smallest impact on vote choice, which fits with past research that indicates that perceptions of leaders matter least for third or small parties (Bittner 2011).

The data presented in figure 3.6 clearly show that perceptions of leaders' traits have an influence on vote choice. What the graph does not show, however, is whether this effect has grown over time. Has there been a personalization of the vote?

To assess whether or not the effects of leaders have become more important over time, I disaggregated the data and ran separate logit models for each year, with vote for a single party (Conservative, Liberal/Labour, or NDP/Lib-Dem) as the dependent variable, rather than running multinomial logit models. These three vote choice variables were coded as dummy variables (vote for given party=1, vote for any other party=0).[13,14]

Figures 3.7, 3.8 and 3.9 track the impact of perceptions of a leader's character and competence on vote for his or her party in each election year.[15] Put simply, voters' perceiving party leaders positively on these two trait dimensions increases the likelihood that they will vote for their party.

Figure 3.7 tracks the relationship between perceptions of Conservative leaders' personality traits and the decision to vote for the party, and we can see that across both countries, positive evaluations of competence had a larger impact on vote choice than did positive evaluations of character. Further, it is notable that the impact of leaders has generally not become more sizable over time; impact of personality fluctuates from year to year, but a clear upward trend is not visible. In the United Kingdom, the 2005 and 2010 elections saw an increase in the effect of the Conservative leader's character in particular. The increase in the effect is suggestive that personalization

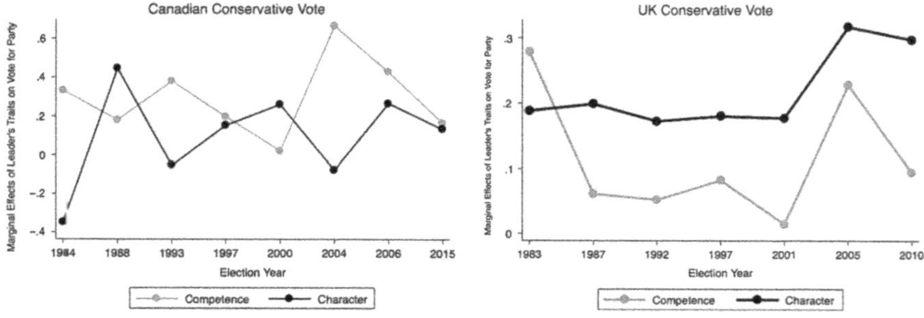

Figure 3.7 Effects of Perceptions of Conservative Leader's Traits on Conservative Vote Choice in Canada and the United Kingdom, over Time.

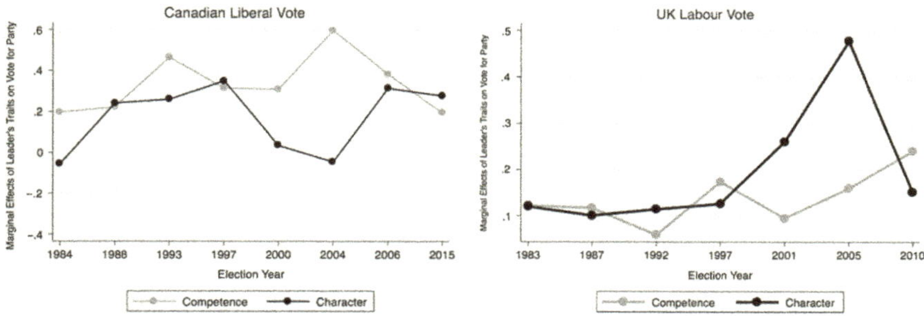

Figure 3.8 Effects of Perceptions of Liberal Party and Labour Party Leader's Traits on Vote Choice in Canada and the United Kingdom, over Time.

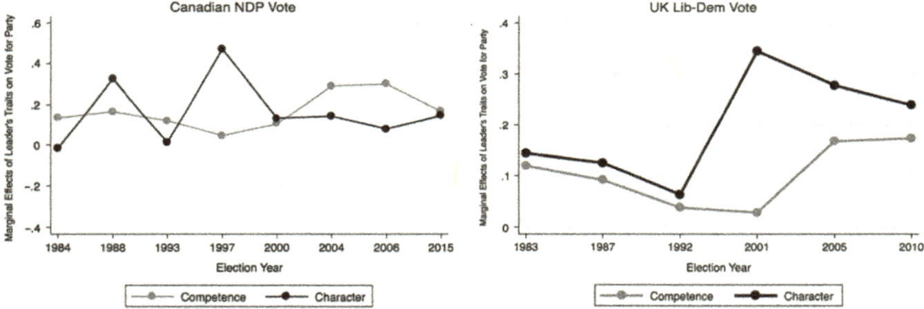

Figure 3.9 Effects of Perceptions of NDP and Lib-Dem Leader's Traits on Vote Choice in Canada and the United Kingdom, over Time.

might be taking place in that country, but given that we do not have data for 2015, it seems imprudent to talk about an increasing importance of traits in this country.[16]

These same patterns (fluctuation with little upward movement) are seen in figures 3.8 and 3.9 as well, suggesting that positive evaluations of Liberal/Labour and NDP/Lib-Dem leaders' personalities have an impact on the decision to vote for the parties. The Canadian trendlines show no upward trend at all, whereas the trajectories in the United Kingdom suggest that leaders' personalities *might* be more weighty in the vote calculus over time. Again, however, I urge caution in interpreting the UK numbers because we do not have 2015 data and therefore cannot track the relationship fully.

In the United Kingdom, we do see a slight increase in the effect of perceptions of personality traits over time, mainly because the 2001, 2005 and 2010 elections saw a spike in the impact of leaders (before that time, the impact was actually decreasing over time). Taken as a whole, there is scant evidence that personalization is taking place. Leaders have always been important in

Canada and Britain, and the effect of leaders fluctuates from year to year, as different leaders take the helm and run for office.

CONCLUSIONS

This chapter has assessed the extent to which there has been a 'personalization' of parliamentary elections. Assessing data from the British and Canadian Election Studies over the past thirty years (1983 to 2015), I find little to no evidence of a personalization of elections. Indeed, it appears as though voters have been evaluating leaders throughout this time period, providing substantial support for the concept of 'personalism' as identified in the introduction to this volume. The data suggest that evaluations of leaders' personalities have had an impact on vote choice in every election, although the magnitude of the effects of leaders varies from election to election. Data are missing from both countries, and as a result, these analyses must be interpreted with some caution. The British data point to the *possibility* of an increased personalization with a decrease in partisanship over time, a widening of the ideological gap between partisans over time and a slightly higher marginal effect of personality over time. We are missing the end point, however, without data about personality in the 2015 election, and as such, the most we can do is continue to follow British elections and cautiously interpret the data we do have.

What we *can* say definitively is that data suggest that leaders have always been important to voters in these two countries, and as has been argued elsewhere (Bittner 2011), there are a number of reasons to expect voters to consider party leaders in parliamentary elections:

1. Party leaders in Britain and Canada are competing for the top job. The leader of the winning party will become prime minister, and arguably, who has this job is important.
2. News media have placed leaders front and centre in horserace-style coverage of election campaigns (Mendelsohn 1993; Gidengil et al. 2000; Mughan 2000).
3. Human brains have limits, and psychologically it is 'easy' for voters to evaluate party leaders because it is similar to things we do on a daily basis outside of politics; we are constantly meeting new people and determining how we feel about them. Voters do not need to develop new skills to evaluate political candidates (Rahn et al. 1990).
4. Election campaigns are complicated, politics can be confusing and voters can take advantage of their feelings about party leaders to help them sort out what to do on election day (Sniderman, Brody and Tetlock 1991).

For similar reasons, it is reasonable to expect that local candidates also matter (Blais et al. 2003; Roy and Alcantara 2015), but of course we need to take into consideration the fact that name recognition and media coverage make a big difference in the minds of voters. Local candidates receive substantially less coverage than national leaders, and as such, are unlikely to have as much importance in the minds of voters, despite the fact that voters in both Canada and the United Kingdom are marking a ballot with local candidates' names on it. In this volume, Pruysers and Cross assess the role of local candidates and their relationship with the national party leader, as does the chapter by Chiru. They make a number of important observations about the role of personalism in politics and its multilevel nature by focusing their analysis on candidates and ordinary legislators.

Although local candidates may be less prominent in the minds of voters, certainly, personality is important in the minds of parties, and campaigns are run with parties in mind. As Pruysers and Cross (this volume) note, local candidates campaign by channelling and 'using' the name of their leader because they think it helps them to win votes. They also show that campaigns will wage attacks on the opposing party's leader more than they will on the opposing party itself. These findings point to the importance that parties place on leaders, and the perception that leaders can help both local campaigns as well as national campaigns. The data in this chapter provide additional support to the notion that leaders win and lose votes and that parties are right to consider leaders when planning their campaign activities.

In addition to campaign activity during election time, it is reasonable to expect that leaders have an important role to play in other aspects of governance (see both Malloy and Poguntke and Webb, this volume). Certainly, leaders play a prominent role on the international stage, whether negotiating treaties, shaking hands with other state representatives or making statements about a variety of pressing international issues. One needs only to look at the portrayal of Justin Trudeau and Donald Trump on the international stage to see how the media focuses on personality, looks and statements to understand the importance of the *person* in politics.

Simply put, *personality matters*. We can feel reasonably confident that leaders have always mattered in the minds of voters and that a process of personalization has not taken place. At the same time, in a world where our access to information about personality is only increasing, via, for example, Twitter, Instagram and Facebook (see Rahat and Zamir, this volume), it is conceivable that the role of personality might increase over time, and we must continue to track the relationship between leaders' personality and vote choice.

NOTES

1. Thank you to Bill Cross, Scott Pruysers, Richard Katz, Thomas Poguntke, Scott Matthews, David Peterson and Shannon Fraser for thoughtful comments and helpful suggestions on preliminary drafts of this chapter. Thanks also to Brooke Steinhauer for excellent research assistance. All errors are, of course, my own.

2. This chapter is a comparative extension of work that I have published elsewhere, which focuses solely on the Canadian case (forthcoming, *Electoral Studies*), and is part of a larger project that seeks to assess the role of personalization across many countries over time.

3. I start in 1984 (Canada) and 1983 (Britain) because although the Canadian Election Study (CES) included questions about leaders' traits in 1968, studies left out these questions in the 1970s. Rather than incorporating a large temporal gap into the analysis, I begin in the 1980s in both countries. Even with this later start date, however, there is still missing data for elections in both countries; the 2008 CES did not include questions about traits, and in 2011, some respondents were asked some questions about traits, but no respondents were asked about all traits, making assessment of this year's data difficult. The British Election Study (BES) included questions about leaders' traits starting in 1983, however in the most recent election (2015), traits questions were not included in the survey.

4. The Canadian data are also assessed in another paper, forthcoming in *Electoral Studies*. This chapter builds on those analyses, integrating British data. As such, the Canadian data presented in both papers are identical.

5. As noted previously, 'character' includes traits such as trustworthy, honest, caring, empathetic and so on, whereas 'competence' includes traits such as intelligence, strength of leadership and so on. A full list of all traits included in the surveys across all years and countries is available from the author on request.

6. Recall, 2008 is missing from the Canadian graphs and 2015 from the British graphs because the surveys did not include questions probing respondents for their perceptions of leaders' personality traits in those years.

7. Note that 2008 is included in the Canadian graph because we do have thermometer data in all of these election years. Note, too, that the British graph is truncated because we do not have these data prior to 2001.

8. The data for the SNP and Plaid Cymru are not presented in these figures because the graphs get crowded, but the data are available from the author on request.

9. Although not shown in the graph, the proportion of individuals claiming an SNP or Plaid Cymru identification does not shift much over the last ten years.

10. Complete models and lists of variables and coding available from the author on request.

11. The models were run only outside of the province of Quebec because of the different party system and related dynamics in that province. Assessing voters' choices in the Canadian multiparty system is conceptually difficult, particularly in relation to the different menus of options present in Quebec and the rest of Canada. Although omitting Quebec is not optimal, assessing the decisions made by all Canadian voters

together in a single model is not feasible either. Future analyses should assess vote choice in both parts of the country.

12. I used the 'marginals' package for STATA to run the model's post-estimations and graphed them using the 'marginsplot' command.

13. Models were otherwise the same, except issue attitudes and ideology were omitted from the model in an effort to boost the number of respondents included in each model (usually these questions were included in either the postelection survey or even the mail-back survey, therefore including them in the model massively eroded the N).

14. Recall (again) that 2015 is left out of the British graph and 2008 and 2011 are left out of the Canadian graph because traits questions were not asked in 2008, and in 2011 those who were asked about traits on one dimension were not asked about traits on the other; therefore, we cannot include perceptions of both dimensions in the same model.

15. As in the previous multivariate model, the 'margins' and 'marginsplot' commands were used with STATA to estimate the marginal effects of leaders' character and competence on vote choice. These analyses mirror and build on the analyses found in Bittner (forthcoming). Although evaluations of all three leaders were included in each year's model, I depict only evaluations for the leader of the party in question, because of (a) the substantially larger effect of evaluations of traits for the leader of the party and (b) the cleaner, easier to read trend lines.

16. In the 2015 British election, David Cameron's Conservative government increased the number of seats it held, whereas Nicola Sturgeon's SNP party went from six seats to fifty-six seats. These two parties won at the expense of the other two traditional parties, as the Labour party lost twenty-six seats and the Lib-Dems lost forty-nine seats.

Chapter 4

Personalism and Election Campaigning

National and Local Dynamics

Scott Pruysers and William P. Cross

Although political parties perform a wide range of functions (e.g., interest aggregation, mobilization and recruitment; see King 1969), perhaps the most important is the role that they play during elections. Indeed, the fact that parties *contest* elections is the defining characteristic that sets them apart from a variety of other political organizations such as interest or advocacy groups. In many electoral systems, campaigning occurs at multiple levels. Canada's single member plurality (SMP) electoral system, for instance, divides the country into 338 distinct 'electoral districts' (sometimes referred to as *constituencies* or *ridings*). Given that electoral victory is achieved in SMP (and in other systems such as the alternative vote, single transferable vote and, to varying degrees, in mixed-member systems) by winning in individual districts, parties often have an incentive to create active and strong local grassroots party organizations (Carty 1991; Carty and Eagles 2005; Carty, Cross and Young 2000; Cross 2004, 2016; Sayers 1999). As Koop (2011, 9) suggests, 'an impressive national campaign is useless if the party cannot win in more ridings than the other parties, and doing so requires both competent candidates and local organizations to support them'. Thus, in many countries there are *two* sets of election campaigns that occur simultaneously: a nationwide campaign that is dominated by party leaders, television advertising and party professionals on the one hand, and individual constituency campaigns in each district across the country on the other.

Given the multilevel nature of election campaigns, there are multiple arenas where personalized politics can manifest. Balmas et al. (2014) acknowledge this when they distinguish between 'centralized' and 'decentralized' forms of personalization. Although more detail is provided in the introductory chapter, centralized personalization is typically about party leaders and chief executives, whereas decentralized personalization is about candidates and other ordinary politicians. Despite the fact that personalization occurs at multiple levels, the literature has not developed evenly. Although there have been both conceptual (Balmas et al., 2014) and empirical (Cross and Young 2015; De Winter and Baudewyns 2015; Eder, Jenny and Muller 2015; Wattenberg 1995; Zittel and Gschwend 2015) examinations of decentralized personalization, the personalization literature remains firmly focused on party leaders and chief executives. Questions, however, remain regarding the extent of personalism that can be found at the constituency level, potential determinants of local campaign personalism and whether candidates are increasingly personalizing their campaign strategies.

The literature on centralized personalization is somewhat problematic as well, especially if we are interested in how parties engage in election campaigns. Although party leaders have received considerably more attention than their local candidate counterparts (see Zittel 2015), much of the literature has considered how frequently party leaders are discussed in the media (Foley 2000; Holtz-Bacha, Langer and Merkle 2014; Kriesi 2012; Mendelsohn 1996; Rahat and Sheafer 2007; Schulz and Zeh 2005) and how party leaders factor into the voting calculus of voters on election day (Bittner 2011; Johnston 2002; Mughan 2000). Although these are indeed crucial aspects of personalization, they do not consider how parties campaign or the strategic decisions they make regarding how visible the party leader should be versus the degree of emphasis devoted to the party brand (see Adam and Maier 2010). An important, though overlooked, question therefore, is how are parties and party leaders portrayed in *party* communications?

To address these limitations in the literature, this chapter explores both centralized and decentralized personalism during the 2015 Canadian election campaign. Doing so allows us to consider a number of previously unanswered questions. First, how personalized are party campaigns? By looking only at a single level (centralized or decentralized), most studies provide only a partial picture of the campaign or miss what the parties are doing entirely because of a focus on nonparty actors (media, voters, etc.). Examining both local and national campaign dynamics will therefore allow a more accurate depiction. Importantly, we are able to explore decentralized personalization over time by comparing survey results of local candidates in 2008 and 2015. We are also able to explore whether there are consistent patterns within parties. If, for example, the party is the central focus of the national campaign, is this also true for local constituency campaigns? Finally, we consider the level of variation that can be found between parties with regard to personalism, what might account for these differences and whether this variation is greater at one level than the other.

DATA AND CASE[1]

Canada provides an interesting case to explore the personalization of party campaigns for a number of reasons. First, its SMP electoral system allows us to consider both centralized and decentralized personalism in the same election and therefore hold constant the popularity of leaders and other contextual factors. Second, the stratarchical nature of Canadian parties (Carty 2002, 2004) allows the national and local campaign to work autonomously, providing local candidates considerable freedom in setting their campaign priorities and strategies. Finally, the party system is comprised of three main political parties that each place varying emphasis on party ideology, which may result in interesting differences across parties with regard to personalized politics. The Liberals, for instance, are a brokerage party that is characterized by ideological flexibility (Carty 2013, 2015), whereas the New Democrats are more ideologically rigid (Laycock and Erickson 2015).

To explore both centralized and decentralized personalism simultaneously, this chapter has marshalled a considerable amount of original data from a variety of sources. The analysis of centralized personalism includes more than 800 unique party communications sent during the 2015 Canadian election, including 58 television advertisements, 169 e-mail messages, and 601 press releases. In addition to exploring the extent of personalism in general, these data allow us to consider whether the practice of personalized politics differs by communication method. Furthermore, including multiple sources of data also allows us to consider dynamic forms of communication. Whereas television advertisements are largely static (mostly produced early in the campaign period), press releases and campaign e-mail communications are dynamic. Issued nearly every day, these forms of communication allow parties the ability to react to the current environment and change tactics from one day to the next (Pruysers and Cross 2016a, 545). Including these should provide a more complete and accurate picture of how the campaign unfolded.

To study decentralized personalism, by contrast, we draw on original survey data of candidates from two separate federal elections: 2008 and 2015. The 2008 candidate survey includes 338 responses from the Liberals and New Democrats, and the 2015 candidate survey includes 429 responses from the Liberals, Conservatives, New Democrats and Greens. The candidate survey data not only provide detailed information regarding the content and delivery of local campaign messages, as well as campaign volunteers and other candidate resources, but also allow for us to explore whether personalized local campaigning has become more common over the last decade.

PERSONALIZATION AND THE 'PARTY' CAMPAIGN

Before exploring how visible party leaders are in campaign communication, it is useful to consider the role of party leaders in Canadian elections more broadly. Among the most important institutionalized roles of party leaders is the election debate. Debates among party leaders were first introduced fifty years ago. Since then, there have only been three elections in which there was no debate among the leaders of the major parties (1972, 1974, 1980) and most have included several. Although debates among party leaders are not entirely uncommon in other parliamentary democracies, Canada was an early adopter. Although Canada first introduced these debates in 1968, Australia and New Zealand did not do so until 1984, Germany until 1972, and the United Kingdom 2010.[2] In fact, leaders' debates are so standard that the 2015 Canadian election saw the party leaders engage in televised (or online) debates on five separate occasions during the campaign. The first debate of the 2015 election, for instance, drew an audience of approximately 4.5 million viewers, with an additional 200,000 'video replays' in less than a week afterwards (Hutchins 2015).

Similarly, the leaders' tours, which see each leader travel the country numerous times over, are among the most carefully organized and expensive aspects of the election campaign. Strategically executed, these tours allow party leaders to mobilize voters in areas where local candidates may need additional support and allow strategists to target marginal ridings where additional seats can be won (Carty and Eagles 2005; Cross et al. 2015; Flanagan 2010). Leaders' tours are such a fundamental part of Canadian elections that the Canadian Broadcasting Corporation (CBC) catalogues the movements of each leader in an interactive map that allows readers to follow them on the campaign trail. The database contains information regarding what province and constituency the leaders are in each day, specific campaign stops and relevant policy announcements (see Gomez and Da Silva, 2015; Stephenson et al. forthcoming). This is in addition to daily articles focusing on the party leaders' whereabouts (e.g., CBC 2015). There is clearly a demand for information about party leaders during the campaign. Combined, the leaders' debate and tour provide an institutional framework for leaders to take centre stage during election campaigns.

What about leader visibility in the media? A number of empirical studies in recent years reveal the increasing importance of candidates and leaders in election news coverage in countries such as Germany, the United Kingdom, Israel and the United States (Dalton et al. 2000; Foley 2000; Rahat and Sheafer 2007; Schulz and Zeh 2005). Party leaders garner considerable media attention in Canada, receiving thousands of mentions throughout the campaign period. In fact, an examination of 13,210 news stories (across thirty-one distinct outlets) reveals that the three major party leaders were mentioned 59,460 times during the eleven-week 2015 campaign. Perhaps more importantly for the purpose of this chapter, mentions of party leaders equalled mentions of political parties. Total party mentions during the campaign period were 59,303, which were 157 fewer mentions than for the party leaders.[3]

It is important to note, however, that not all of the major party leaders received the same treatment in the media. Figure 4.1 plots total leader mentions minus their party mentions for each of the three major party leaders.[4] The results reveal that then Prime Minister Stephen Harper was mentioned considerably more often than his party in both regional and national media outlets. The opposite, however, is true for Tom Mulcair and the then largest opposition party, the New Democratic Party (NDP). The New Democrats were mentioned much more often than their leader, and this is particularly evident in regional media where the party received more than 3,400 additional mentions. This may reflect the party's more ideological roots and coverage of the party may be more policy based as a result. Alternatively, less emphasis on Mulcair could be the result of the NDPs historic third-party status or that voters were more familiar with Harper and Justin Trudeau, and therefore, coverage reflected this fact. As for the third-place Liberals, we find that national media outlets were slightly more likely to mention the Liberal

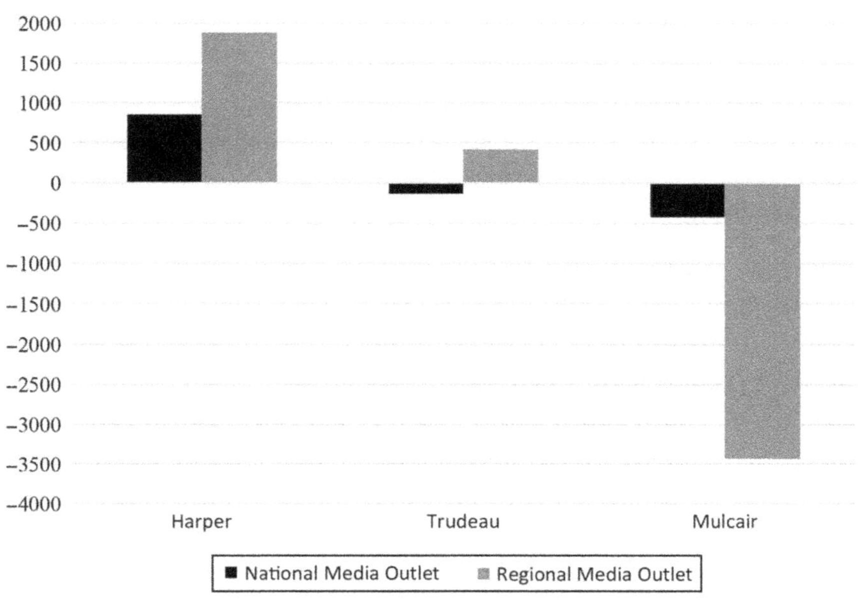

Figure 4.1 Total Media Mentions (Leader Minus Party).

Party than Trudeau, whereas regional media outlets were more likely to mention Trudeau over the Liberals.

Despite some possible overstatement, party leaders are important actors during Canadian elections (see Bittner 2011; see also Bittner, this volume). And this, of course, is not a new observation. Clarke et al. (1991, 89), for example, refer to party leaders as 'the superstars of Canadian politics'. Party leaders are important; this much is clear. What is less clear, however, is how parties portray themselves, how much emphasis they devote to their leader in campaign communications and whether this differs by party. To examine the prominence of party leaders in party-sponsored campaign communications, the analysis proceeds in two steps. First, we begin by considering how often parties reference their own leaders in television advertisements, campaign e-mail messages and party press releases, and how this compares to references to the parties in the same communications. After this, we consider how parties deal with opposing parties, and whether they attack rival leaders or rival parties, a measure we call *negative personalization*.

Television Advertisements

One way to explore how prominent and visible a particular party leader is during an election campaign is to look at television advertisements produced by the party. These advertisements are the single-biggest election expense in Canada and routinely account for nearly 50 percent of total campaign expenditures. The Conservatives, for instance, spent 41 percent of their total campaign expenditures on TV and radio advertisements in 2015 (Elections Canada 2016). Unlike other forms of party communication, these ads are viewed by millions of citizens and offer an 'unparalleled opportunity for parties to communicate with voters' (Cross et al. 2015, 106). As such, the messages that parties send via campaign advertisements are a crucial part of party competition and a core component of the party's strategy.

As table 4.1 demonstrates, party leaders were quite visible in television advertisements. Of the fifty-eight ads that the three major parties produced

Table 4.1 Leader Visibility in Television Advertisements

Party	*Number Featuring Leader's Image*	*Number in Which Leader Appears for a Majority of the Ad*	*N*
Liberal	17 (74%)	10 (44%)	23
Conservative	9 (43%)	7 (33%)	21
NDP	8 (57%)	6 (43%)	14
Total	34 (59%)	23 (40%)	58

NDP, New Democratic Party.

for the campaign, party leaders were visibly on screen for thirty-four of them (59 percent). This figure, of course, increases when we consider nonvisual mentions to a party's own leader or references to opposing leaders. Far from a universal trend, however, each of the major parties adopted a somewhat different approach to the question of leader visibility in their television advertising. The Liberals, for instance, focused heavily on their leader, Trudeau. He is featured visually in three in four Liberal television advertisements, and this number increases to eight in ten if we consider any mention of Trudeau rather than just a visual cue. In fact, the party's most iconic advertisement of the campaign is one that exclusively features Trudeau walking up an escalator speaking directly to the camera. This particular advertisement has been viewed more than three million times on the party's YouTube page and was easily the election's most-watched advertisement online. The party launched the campaign with a similar television spot titled 'Ready', in which Trudeau speaks directly to the camera and explains why he is prepared to be prime minister. Of the seventeen ads in which Trudeau was featured, he appeared on screen for a majority of the advertisement in ten (59 percent).

Neither the Conservatives nor the New Democrats took the same approach as the Liberals. In fact, despite serving as prime minister for nearly a decade (or perhaps because of that fact), Harper appeared in less than half of all Conservative Party television advertisements. Interestingly, although Harper only appeared in nine of twenty-one advertisements, he appeared on screen for a majority of the ad in seven of them. Thus, when Harper was in an ad he was typically the focus. Unlike the Liberals, however, the highest profile Conservative advertisements did not feature Harper and they did not make any mention of the Conservative leader. In fact, the ads with the most online views are exclusively about Trudeau. Although the New Democrats did not hide their leader, Mulcair was only featured in a slight majority of advertisements, 57 percent. This is somewhat surprising because Mulcair was relatively new and had never before campaigned as party leader. The party, however, did not use television advertisements as a method of familiarizing Canadians with Mulcair. Like Harper, when Mulcair was included in an advertisement, he was generally the focus, appearing for a majority in six of the eight ads in which he was on screen.

E-mail Communications

An increasingly common method for parties to communicate with supporters is online, especially via e-mail. Throughout the campaign the Liberals, Conservatives and New Democrats sent a combined 169 e-mails. Like television, e-mail allows parties to communicate, unmediated by the traditional media, to supporters. Moreover, as Williams and Trammell (2005, 560) suggest, e-mail messages can be easily 'forwarded to myriad nonsubscribers', which can help parties 'overcome the problem of selective exposure'. Thus, although the main method of receiving a party e-mail is to sign up with the party for updates, non-subscribers may be exposed in other ways via friends and family.

As table 4.2 reveals, leaders are well represented in routine campaign e-mail communications. Two of three messages that the parties sent during the campaign referenced their own leaders. Both Trudeau and Harper are mentioned in nearly three-quarters of party e-mails. Although substantially lower, Mulcair is mentioned in a slight majority of NDP messages. We can also consider who the e-mail was sent from. The Liberals stand out in this regard. While 2 and 6 percent, respectively, of Conservative and NDP e-mails were 'sent' from their respective leaders, one of five Liberal messages purportedly came from Trudeau.[5] It is also useful to know who is mentioned first: party or leader? In 55 percent of Conservative e-mail communications, Harper is mentioned before the Conservative Party, and this is slightly lower for Mulcair and the NDP (47 percent). The Liberals, however, stand out once again. Three of four Liberal messages mention Trudeau before the Liberal Party.

Press Releases

Although not necessarily meant for voters, press releases are directed to the media (DiStaso 2012). Specifically, they are a means of attempting to frame media coverage in a certain way and thus provide information to voters indirectly (Cross et al. 2015). If parties want the media talking about their leader, press releases should contain a considerable amount of focus on the leader. What is particularly interesting about press releases is that they are a dynamic form of party communication. These documents are produced every day of the campaign (often more than once), and therefore offer insight into a party's strategic decisions throughout the election.[6] TV ads, by contrast, are often produced before or early in the campaign period, often leaving little room for the party to adapt or respond to campaign dynamics. Thus, with

Table 4.2 Leader Visibility in Party E-mail Communications

Party	*Leader Mentioned*	*Leader Mentioned before Party*	*From Party Leader*	*N*
Liberal	43 (74%)	42 (72%)	12 (21%)	58
Conservative	44 (73%)	33 (55%)	1 (2%)	60
NDP	27 (53%)	24 (47%)	3 (6%)	51
Total	114 (67%)	99 (59%)	16 (10%)	169

NDP, New Democratic Party.

press releases, we can consider not only the emphasis given to leaders but also patterns over the course of the election campaign.

More than any other form of communication examined thus far, press releases contain a clear focus on party leaders (table 4.3). On average, three of four press releases produced for the campaign contain a reference to one of the party leaders. Moreover, the centrality and visibility of party leaders is demonstrated by the fact that they are mentioned in the lead paragraph in more than half of all press releases. This pattern is particularly evident among Conservative press releases where Harper is mentioned in 87 percent and is featured in the lead paragraph in almost as many (78 percent).

Parties and Leaders Compared

So far we have considered the emphasis that parties placed on their leaders during the campaign. Although useful, this only provides part of the picture. It is also useful to know how often campaign communications reference party labels and how this compares to mentions of the party leaders. We can summarize the level of personalism found in various party communications by reporting the leader-to-party ratio. That is, the number of communications that reference the party leader compared to the party itself (for a similar approach see Dalton et al. 2000). Values over one demonstrate a greater emphasis on the leader, whereas values lower than one reveal more of a focus on the party.

What we find is that leaders are well represented among campaign communications, even when compared to the parties that they lead. However, party leaders by no means eclipse their parties in visibility. The New Democrats, for instance, did not mention Mulcair in more television, e-mail or press release communications than they did the party. A leader-to-party ratio of 0.56 for e-mail communications, for instance, reveals that the party was far more visible. The closest Mulcair comes to overshadowing his party is in television advertisements where we find that for every ad that mentions the party, there is also one that mentions Mulcair. For the Liberals, we find more evidence of personalism. For example, a leader-to-party ratio of 1.13

Table 4.3 Leader Visibility in Party Press Releases

Party	*Leader Mentioned*	*Leader Is Mentioned in Lead Paragraph*	*N*
Liberal	183 (72%)	130 (51%)	255
Conservative	93 (87%)	83 (78%)	107
NDP	178 (75%)	111 (46%)	239
Total	454 (76%)	324 (54%)	601

NDP, New Democratic Party.

reveals that Trudeau was mentioned in more e-mail messages than the Liberal Party. Moreover, high leader-to-party ratios for television advertisements (0.95) and press releases (0.84) suggest a strong focus on the Liberal leader, despite the party being mentioned more frequently. As for the Conservatives, communications mentioning Harper outpace those mentioning his party in press releases (1.89) but not for e-mail (0.81) or television advertisements (0.61). Differences across the various communication methods likely reflect the intended audience. E-mails are sent to a more discrete and narrow group, largely made up of identified party members and supporters. It is possible that the party believed references to Harper, who was still relatively popular with Conservative voters, were likely to energize their base. This would help explain why the party placed more emphasis on Harper in their e-mail campaign than television advertising.

'Negative' Personalization

The analysis of centralized personalism thus far has examined how much emphasis the major parties placed on their own leaders. What about the attention devoted to competing leaders? In a recent article, we argue that personalization is more than just about how parties portray themselves and that there is a clear interparty element to the phenomenon (Pruysers and Cross 2016a). Political parties are increasingly going negative in their campaign advertisements (Buell and Sigelman 2008; Fowler and Ridout 2013; Geer 2006; Kaid and Johnston 1991; Krupnikov 2011; Lau and Pomper 2004), and this provides parties with another strategic choice regarding personalization: parties can choose to focus their attack on opposing parties or opposing party leaders. When attacks are directed at opposing party leaders, especially at higher rates than parties, we term this 'negative personalization'.

To look at negative personalization we compare how frequently an opposing leader is mentioned relative to his or her party. Here we find considerable evidence of personalism. The Conservatives, for example, referenced Trudeau in 62 percent of their television advertisements and press releases but only mentioned the Liberal Party in 38 and 36 percent, respectively. In a similar fashion, Liberal communications were significantly more likely to target Harper than the Conservative Party. Although Harper is featured in 65 percent of Liberal television advertisements and 69 percent of Liberal press releases, the Conservative Party is mentioned in less than 10 percent of Liberal TV ads and only 29 percent of Liberal press releases. Likewise, the Conservative Party is mentioned in 7 percent of NDP television spots, whereas Harper is targeted in fully half of these ads. Mulcair did not escape negative personalization either. Although the NDP was targeted in 27 percent of Liberal press releases, Mulcair was referenced in 44 percent. Figure 4.2 provides a clear

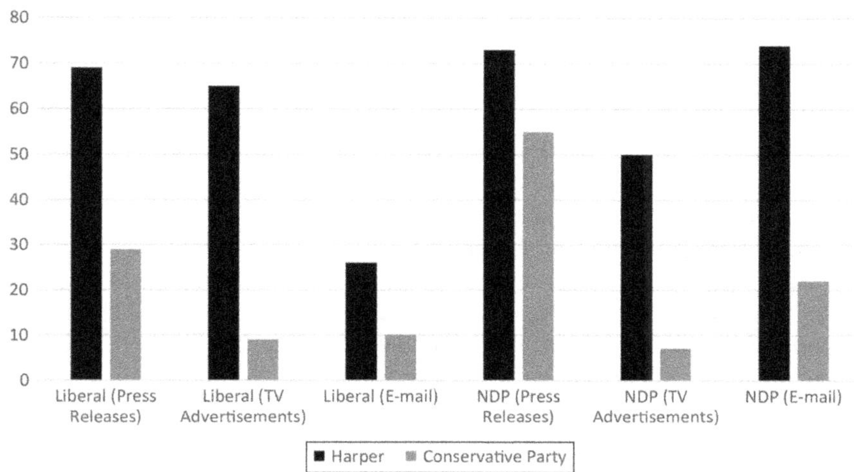

Figure 4.2 Negative Personalization Directed at Harper/Conservatives during the 2015 Federal Election (Percentage of Communications Reported).

visualization of the extent of negative personalization directed at Harper in Liberal and NDP television advertisements, e-mail communications and press releases. It should be clear that when parties engage in negative campaigning, it is opposing party leaders, and not opposing political parties, who are the main target.

Finally, we can also combine mentions to a party's own leader with mentions of opposing leaders to get a sense of how much party leaders in general were discussed throughout the campaign (and the same of parties). Of the fifty-eight television advertisements produced for the campaign, all but one mentioned at least one of the party leaders (98 percent) and only four failed to mention one of the three parties (93 percent). It is virtually impossible to watch any of the election advertising without hearing about a party leader. We find a similar trend among press releases as well. Here the vast majority of press releases reference at least one of the party leaders (96 percent) and one of the parties (94 percent). Although slightly lower than the other two communication methods, a majority of e-mails also mention at least one of the party leaders (80 percent) or one of the parties (83 percent). Leaders are therefore essential to the story that political parties are trying to sell to voters and the media.

PERSONALIZATION AND THE 'LOCAL' CAMPAIGN

Although both academic and journalistic emphasis is often devoted to the nationwide campaign, constituency campaigns play a crucial role in Canadian elections (Cross 2016; Pruysers 2015). As Carty, Cross and Young explain, 'It is on the ground in the constituencies, that much of the hard work of Canadian party politics takes place, for, at the end of the day, winning constituencies is more important than winning votes in the quest for power' (2000, 154). Moreover, Carty and Eagles (2005) find that local campaigns are not inconsequential to electoral outcomes; additional money and volunteers at the constituency level translate into additional votes. Although the electoral benefit is perhaps small, many electoral districts are won and lost by a few percentage points. A well-resourced and staffed local campaign can therefore make the difference between winning and losing in a district.[7] Given their importance to electoral outcomes, candidates may have an incentive to personalize their campaigns in an attempt to win additional votes.

In a regionalized SMP system such as Canada, however, it is sometimes difficult to distinguish localization of a candidate's campaign from personalization. Nonetheless, when a local candidate decides to deviate from the national campaign's script it is usually to highlight his or her own traits or positions on policy issues distinct from those of the party. In this section we explore the extent to which local campaigns were personalized, considering campaign content, delivery methods and candidate emphasis/visibility (Cross and Young 2015; Zittel and Gschwend 2008). Although we expect to find strong evidence of personalism, we expect that the degree will vary depending on the perceived relative popularity of both the party brand and leader as well as other contextual factors such as campaign resources.

Campaign Focus

In the previous section, we explored how much emphasis the nationwide campaign placed on party leaders and how this compared to the emphasis devoted to the party brand. When considering decentralized personalism, however, the strategic decisions are slightly more complicated. Unlike centralized personalism, where the decision is between emphasis on the leader or the party, decentralized personalism has three distinct components: local candidates can choose to emphasize themselves, their party or their leader. How much emphasis did local candidates place on their respective party leaders? When asked to quantify this on an 11-point scale (where 10 is as much attention as possible on the leader), we find that local candidates were more likely to emphasize their leader than not while campaigning in their local district (see table 4.4).

The mean score for the Liberals, New Democrats and Greens, for instance, is 6.7, 6.1 and 6.9, respectively. The Conservatives stand out in this regard with considerably less attention devoted to their leader as evident with a mean score of 4.3. This, of course, makes sense for at least two reasons. First, public

Table 4.4 Candidate Focus during Constituency Campaign (Means Reported)

	*Focus on the Party Leader**	*Focus on the Candidate vs. Party***
Liberal	6.7	5.3
NDP	6.1	5.7
Conservative	4.3	4.9
Green	6.9	7.2

*0, little attention as possible on the leader; 10, as much attention as possible on the leader.
**0, as much attention as possible for the candidate; 10, as much attention as possible for the party.
NDP, New Democratic Party.

opinion data reveal that Harper was consistently the least popular of the main party leaders (see, for example, Forum 2015). Second, although Harper was highly present in national press releases, he was somewhat hidden from voters in the party's television advertising. Thus, if any party's candidates were to avoid highlighting their leader it would be the Conservatives. It is interesting, however, that NDP candidates placed as much emphasis on Mulcair as they did. After all, he was often absent from national party communications (i.e., only appearing in half of all party e-mail communications).

Candidates were also asked to rate their campaign in terms of the emphasis they placed on themselves and their party on an 11-point scale, where 0 represents as much attention for themselves as a candidate, and 10 represents as much attention as possible for their party. On this balance between candidate and party, we find that candidates generally report placing more emphasis on their party than they did on themselves (table 4.4). Besides the Greens, however, this difference is rather small, and candidates did not place an overwhelming emphasis on the party relative to their own candidacy. In fact, the median response for the Liberal, Conservative and New Democratic candidates is 5, demonstrating a balance between 'candidate' and 'party'.

Campaign Tactics and Resources

Given that candidates do not overwhelmingly focus on their party relative to themselves and that they believe their individual candidacy is important to the outcome of the election in their district, we should expect to find evidence of personalized campaign tactics and strategies. In terms of their campaign communications we find strong evidence for personalized local campaigns (table 4.5). Although we find some variation between parties, the pattern is rather consistent. Outside of radio and television advertising, 70 to 80 percent of candidates in each party produced a variety of their own campaign materials independently of their party. As Cross et al. (2015, 111) note, this likely 'reflects a desire by these candidates to personalize their message instead of relying solely on those created and disseminated' by the party. The human

Table 4.5 Campaign Personalization (% of Local Candidates Who Produced the Following Independent from the Party)

	Campaign Poster (%)	*Ads in Local Press (%)*	*Flyers Leaflets (%)*	*Radio/TV Advertising (%)*	*Website (%)*
Liberal (2015)	81.2 (56)	82.6 (57)	88.4 (61)	65.7 (44)	78.6 (55)
NDP (2015)	74.0 (74)	74.5 (73)	89.0 (89)	49.4 (43)	62.6 (62)
Conservative (2015)	76.1 (86)	73.9 (82)	86.2 (100)	35.3 (36)	72.6 (82)
Green (2015)	62.6 (57)	38.4 (33)	63.4 (59)	16.9 (14)	54.3 (50)
Liberal (2015–2008)	+10.40	+10.60	+15.20	+10.30	+15.50
NDP (2015–2008)	+9.30	+20.40	+26.60	+4.10	+15.00

Note: Difference between 2015 and 2008 reported in percentage points.
NDP, New Democratic Party.

resources of campaigning are also highly personalized. A majority of volunteers on local Liberal and Conservative campaigns, for instance, are family and friends of the candidate. More importantly, these are reportedly individuals who would not have volunteered otherwise. What this suggests is that these people have little connection to the party but were mobilized to engage in campaigning because of their personal ties to the candidate.[8]

We find evidence that campaign messages were personalized around the individual candidate as well. The vast majority of candidates (eight of ten), for example, report raising specific issues in their campaign that were *not* raised by the national party campaign. In an SMP system such as Canada, these issues tend to be related to the candidate's electoral district (see Chiru, this volume). Furthermore, more than seven of ten candidates report that their own policy views (separate from the positions of their party) were important both in their initial nomination and in their canvassing of voters during the general election. Thus, it is apparent that both the content and form of campaign communication were highly personalized at the local level.

It is worth noting that decentralized personalization seems to be at least partly the result of the resources (or lack thereof) that are available. For the Greens, this leads to an interesting dynamic. On the one hand, because the party is rather small and poorly resourced, local candidates do not have the funds needed to produce independent and personalized campaign material. As a result, Green candidates are significantly less likely to create personalized ads for radio, television or newspapers than are Liberals, Conservatives or New Democrats. On the other hand, this same lack of resources necessitates that candidates run a personalized campaign in other ways. Nearly three of four volunteers (72 percent) for Green party candidates are friends and family of the candidate who were mobilized not to support the party but because of their personal connection to the candidate. This suggests that contextual factors are important when considering personalization (see also leader popularity in the previous section).

The survey data of local candidates also provide a unique opportunity to look for evidence of a change over time (see bottom two rows of table 4.5). Although data are only available for two time periods and for two parties, the evidence suggests that the level of personalization has been increasing over the last decade. The evidence is particularly compelling as we find a clear pattern in a single direction. When comparing Liberal responses from the 2008 survey to the 2015 election, for instance, we find a consistent 10 to 15 percentage point increase for each of the five local campaign indicators of personalization. For the New Democrats, we also see an increase across the board, although there is more variation. This ranges from a low of 4 percentage points in terms of the number of candidates who reported creating their own television or radio advertising to a substantial 27 percentage points for those who reported creating personalized leaflets or flyers. Likewise, although not included in table 4.5, the percentage of volunteers who were friends and family, as well as the share of vote attributable to their own candidacy, also increased during this time by 6.6 and 3.7 percentage points, respectively, for the Liberals and 5.7 for the New Democrats. Overall the evidence is rather clear; candidates are running increasingly personalized constituency campaigns.

Explaining Personalized Local Campaigns

Given the large number of candidates who contest general elections in Canada, we have an opportunity to explore the factors that account for more or less personalism at the local level; something we cannot do at the nationwide level as there are too few leaders. Cross and Young (2015) find that a number of factors related to the individual candidate (i.e., whether candidacy was motivated by a policy issue) help explain why some local campaigns are more personalized than others. We conduct a similar analysis here using the 2015 election data, which includes two additional parties (the Conservative and Green parties) as well as a number of additional potential explanatory variables (i.e., whether the nomination was contested).

Following Cross and Young's (2015) analysis of the 2008 Canadian election, we include a number of variables related to both the candidate and the electoral district, all while controlling for party. In terms of the electoral district, we include four factors that might help explain local campaign personalization. First, we distinguish between urban and rural electoral districts. Candidates in rural electoral districts are expected to run more personalized campaigns because the issues facing their constituency may be more easily articulated compared to larger cities, which encompass many districts. Second, we include a variable that captures the subjective competitiveness of the riding in terms of the candidate's perception of his or her chances to win the election. Our expectations in this regard are somewhat mixed. On the one hand, candidates with little chance to win may wish to personalize their campaign to distance themselves from an unpopular party in an attempt to win as many votes as possible by highlighting their own personal traits and accomplishments. On the other hand, candidates who are certain to win may be afforded the freedom to deviate from the party message without fear of losing the election. Third, we consider whether the candidate had to compete in a contested nomination before the general election. As Cross et al. (2016) suggest, candidate nominations are highly personalized events as these intraparty elections tend to downplay ideology and policy and instead highlight the personal characteristics and strengths of the candidates. We expect those individuals who had to win a nomination to also run more personalized election campaigns. Finally, we include a variable that captures the interparty dynamics between candidates. Candidates were asked what the principal aim of their main competitor was: to attract attention for themselves as a candidate or to attract attention for the party. Here we expect to find evidence of a contagion effect; when a candidate perceives that his or her opponent is running a personalized campaign, we expect them to respond in kind.

We also include five variables related to the individual candidate. First, we include the ideological distance between the candidate and the party. Candidates further from their party are expected to run more personalized campaigns, especially with regard to their campaign agenda and the raising of issues not covered by the central campaign.[9] Similarly, we consider the motivation for candidacy. Here we expect candidates who were motivated by a particular policy to adopt a personalized campaign strategy to promote their policy position. Furthermore, we expect that those who live in their constituency will be better equipped to raise local issues with credibility. Therefore, we suspect that these individuals will run more personalized campaigns. We also include the number of years that the candidate has been a party member. Our expectation is that new members, possible party outsiders, are more likely to personalize their campaigns compared to long-term party loyalists. Finally, we include gender as a control variable.

Table 4.6 includes the results of the logistic regression analysis where our dependent variables are personalized campaign means (personalized radio or television advertisements) and the presence of a personalized campaign agenda (raising of issues not covered by the central party campaign). Beyond the considerable party differences, we find three variables that are significantly related to the likelihood of a candidate producing his or her own radio or television advertising. Candidates who live in the electoral district that they are contesting, candidates who at the outset of the campaign thought they would win and those in rural ridings are significantly more likely to engage in campaign personalism. Three variables are also related to a personalized campaign agenda. As with campaign means, we find that candidates who thought they would win and those in rural ridings are significantly more likely to raise issues not covered by the central party campaign. Although we find evidence of a possible dynamic between competing candidates, it is not in the direction we expected. Rather than a contagion where candidates personalize their campaign when they think their opponent is running a personalized campaign, we find that candidates who perceive their opponent to be running a party-focused campaign are more likely to run a personalized campaign of their own. This may be a strategy to stand apart from the competition, and even 'humanize' their own campaign in relation to the 'party' candidate. In this sense they may be signalling that they will be a stronger representative of local voters, defending their interests even when at odds with their party.

Table 4.6 Determinants of Local Campaign Personalization (Logistic Regression Results)

	Campaign Means		*Campaign Agenda*	
	B	*Exp (B)*	*B*	*Exp (B)*
Residency in riding	.771	2.162**	–.193	.824
Candidacy motivated by policy	.069	1.072	–.083	.920
Ideological distance	–.049	.952	.000	1.000
Nomination (contested)	–.065	.937	.130	1.139
Chances to win	.374	1.454***	.373	1.452**
Opponent's campaign (party focussed)	.004	1.004	.069	1.071*
Rural electoral district	.632	1.881**	.646	1.908**
Length of membership	–.019	.981	–.003	.997
Gender (male)	.213	1.237	.265	1.304
NDP	–.641	.527	–.911	.402*
Conservative	–1.192	.304***	.771	.463
Green	–2.060	.127***	–.512	.600
Nagelkerke R square	0.252		0.084	

*p < .1.
**p < .05.
***p < .01.
Campaign means, did a candidate produce and pay for a local radio or television advertisement independent of the party?; Campaign agenda, did a candidate raise issues that were not raised by the national campaign?
NDP, New Democratic party.

Interestingly, we find no significant relationship between candidate gender and the propensity to run a personalized local campaign (see Thomas's chapter for a thorough discussion and gender and personalism).

CONCLUSIONS

This chapter sought to quantify the extent of centralized and decentralized personalism during the 2015 Canadian general election in an effort to more fully understand how personalized election campaigns are from the perspective of the main actors, political parties and their candidates. Although content analysis of news coverage and models of vote choice are central to the study of political personalization, they tell us very little about how parties actually campaign. We therefore focused our attention on the parties and candidates themselves. Importantly, we do so both locally and nationally.

In terms of centralized campaign personalism, the evidence is clear. Party leaders are central actors in Canadian elections; they appear in debates with their counterparts, they travel the country making dozens of campaign stops and they receive considerable media attention (often outpacing their party). The evidence presented here reveals that party leaders are also highly visible and are central actors in *party* advertising and communication. In fact, they appear in a majority of the 800-plus campaign communications examined.

Despite being referred to as the 'superstars' of Canadian politics, however, party leaders are not mentioned at every opportunity and they are not always the central focus of campaign communications. Political parties remain quite central and often appear more frequently than leaders. Thus, although the visibility of party leaders rivals that of political parties in some instances, it rarely ever eclipses the party. Where party leaders do consistently eclipse their party is in the negative advertising that routinely characterizes modern election campaigns. Parties are significantly more likely to attack an opposing party leader than they are an opposing party, and it is here that we find the greatest evidence of personalism.

When considering the decentralized form, we also find a considerable amount of personalism. The vast majority of candidates for the 2015 election produced campaign material independently of their party, a majority of volunteers provided their labour because of their connection to the candidate as opposed to the party and eight of ten candidates report raising issues not covered by the 'party' campaign. What's more, levels of decentralized personalization have increased, often substantially, since the 2008 federal election.

The high levels of personalism outlined in this chapter have a number of potential implications for political parties. First, the multilevel nature of personalization/personalism can challenge a party's ability to deliver a unified and coherent message during the election campaign. The evidence presented in this chapter reveals that strategies across the two levels are not necessarily consistent. New Democratic candidates, for instance, placed more emphasis on their leader than did Conservative candidates despite the fact that Harper was more visible than Mulcair during the nationwide campaign. The lack of consistency is because candidates have considerable autonomy over their campaigns as a result of the stratarchical bargain (Carty and Cross 2006; Carty 2004; Pruysers 2015) that provides local constituency associations with considerable freedom from the central party apparatus. As opposed to a more unified central party making decisions regarding campaign strategy at the nationwide level, there are hundreds of individual candidates making these decisions at the constituency level. Even if a leader is downplayed at the national level (for example, in television advertising), that same leader may receive a fair amount of attention at the local level because of a lack of coordination.

High levels of decentralized personalism also have potential implications for party discipline/unity. Individualized campaigns may strengthen the authority of ordinary Members of Parliament (MPs) within their parties and in the process of parliamentary decision making. As Zittel and Gschwend (2008, 998) suggest, 'candidates having campaigned in an individualised fashion, subjectively owing their election greatly to a personal vote, could become much more assertive towards the parliamentary party in the pursuance of constituency interests'. Our survey data demonstrate that candidates attribute a considerable amount of their vote share to their own campaign, independent of their party. Owing less of their electoral fortune to the 'party', these individuals might be less inclined to follow the party line, thus weakening party discipline and cohesion. Linking campaign personalization and parliamentary behaviour, Chiru (this volume) finds that local candidates who adopted individualized campaigns are significantly more likely to introduce constituency-related parliamentary questions in the legislature. Although party discipline might not suffer, the intraparty dynamics are nonetheless altered.

Legislators, however, are not the only actors whose behaviour is likely influenced by personalization. Not only are party leaders highly visible during election campaigns as our data demonstrate, but they also frequently tout their personal mandates from the tens of thousands of party members who directly chose them as leader (Stewart, this volume). The legislative behaviour of party leaders may also be changing as a result of centralized personalization because the increased authority and visibility encourages chief executives to engage in individualized behaviour, taking policy 'U-turns' independently of their parties, for example (Poguntke and Webb, this volume; see also Malloy, this volume). All of this, of course, speaks to how personalization can alter intraparty relations and change the dynamics between party actors, of which there are more than just leaders and candidates (see Gauja, this volume for a discussion of personalization and party members).

Personalized campaign communication, however, may also offer parties an opportunity. Kruikemeier et al. (2013, 54) argue that online personalized political communication increases citizens' political engagement by 'bringing politics closer to citizens'. Using an experimental design, the authors find that citizens who visited a website, which is more focused on an individual politician, reported feeling more politically involved than citizens who visited a website focused on a political party. Personalism, at least in the online space, can therefore help foster democracy by increasing citizen engagement with politics. Following this logic, television advertisements and e-mail messages that are leader- (or candidate-) centric may therefore help parties create a connection to voters and in turn combat feelings of antipathy towards traditional party politics.

NOTES

1. A few notes on data collection are warranted. Television advertisements were collected from party web pages as well as party-sponsored YouTube sites, and press releases were gathered from official party web pages. To collect e-mail messages, we signed up with each of the three major parties the day the writ was dropped. We limit

our analysis to those messages sent during the official campaign period. The 2015 candidate survey was conducted via an online survey tool between November 2015 and January 2016. Based on valid contact information, the response rate ranged from 23 percent for the Liberals to more than 40 percent for the NDP and Conservatives. The number of responses by party is as follows: Conservatives (138), Liberals (78), NDP (113) and Greens (100). For more information regarding the 2008 candidate survey see Cross and Young (2015).

2. Interestingly, there were no debates between party leaders during the 2017 UK election.

3. We thank Andrea Lawlor for sharing these data. They are examined more fully in the forthcoming volume from Stephenson, et al.

4. We distinguish between national media outlets that have a much larger audience (i.e., the *Globe and Mail* or *National Post*) and smaller local or regional outlets (e.g., *Windsor Star* or *North Bay Nugget*).

5. Likewise, although no Conservative e-mails contain Harper in the subject line, 6 percent of Liberal e-mail communications have a subject mentioning Trudeau.

6. Although party e-mails are equally dynamic, they are produced less frequently than press releases.

7. The evidence regarding a 'personal' vote at the local level is limited. Blais et al. (2003) find that although many Canadians (44 percent) form a preference for one local candidate over another, this is a decisive factor for only about 5 percent of voters.

8. Candidate selection in Canada's parties is highly decentralized and inclusive. Essentially anyone registering with the party a short time before the nomination vote is entitled to participate. The result is often significant recruitment of a candidate's friends and associates who may have little connection to the party (Pruysers and Cross 2016b; Cross et al. 2016).

9. It should be noted that the separate campaign agenda reported by candidates may often be 'local' in character (i.e., raising issues specific to the electoral district). As such, in an SMP system, localism may fuel personalism.

Chapter 5

Primaries and the Personalization of Party Leadership

David K. Stewart

> 'I don't care who does the electing, so long as I can do the nominating.'[1]

This perspective from Boss Tweed, of Tammany Hall and *Gangs of New York* fame, illustrates the significance of candidate pre-selection, showing that internal party decisions effectively determine and restrict the pool from which ordinary voters can choose their representatives and leaders. Throughout the twentieth century, classic work by scholars such as Michels (1915 [1959]) and Duverger (1951 [1967]) made clear the important role played by party leaders in democratic systems, implicitly at least, highlighting the processes through which these individuals acquire their positions. As Cross and Blais explain,

> Studying the selection and removal of party leaders is warranted both by the important role party leaders play in our democracies and because it addresses questions relating to the location and organization of power in political parties . . . leaders are the principal personalities in the democratic play (2012a, 1–2).

Kenig begins his classification of leadership selection methods by summarizing the significance of leaders:

> Party leaders are among the most important political figures in modern representative democracies. They play an increasingly important role in general elections and hold considerable power vis-à-vis their parties. . . .This phenomenon has been termed the 'presidentialization' or 'personalization' of politics (2009, 433).

There is a significant body of literature examining questions of leadership selection, and changes in the ways in which parties choose leaders has intensified interest in the subject. At a time when parties are losing legitimacy and having trouble recruiting members (Scarrow and Gezgor 2010; Allern and Pedersen 2007), they have at times seen thousands and even millions of people participating in the selection of party leaders.[2] This stands in sharp contrast to an overall trend in which 'party activism and membership have been declining across most of the democratic world' (Whiteley 2011, 36).

Evolution in leadership selection methods has taken place in an environment where the role and nature of leadership has also been in flux, albeit for a considerable time. In his classic mid-twentieth-century evaluation of parties, Duverger noted 'two essential facts seem to have dominated the evolution of political parties, since the beginning of the century: the increase in the authority of the leaders and the tendency towards personal forms of authority' (1951 [1967], 168).

McAllister, writing on the personalization of politics, more than fifty years later, makes similar points. As he explains, 'There is little doubt that politics has become more personalized over the past half century' (2007, 584). Moreover,

> The popular focus on leaders now appears commonplace across almost all of the major parliamentary systems, where parties once occupied center stage. The focus on leaders within parliamentary systems has become so marked over the past two decades that it has spawned a large literature that variously labels it the 'presidentialization of politics,' 'institutional presidentialization' and 'presidential parliamentarism' (571).

Indeed,

> leaders now hold their positions by virtue of a personalized mandate, rather than because of a support base within the party. This means that leaders can appeal to voters over the heads of the party, bypassing party factions and activists. . . . [O]nce a leader is popularly elected, the personalized mandate that he or she possesses will convey considerable policy autonomy, with little or no recourse to the party machinery (583).

Cross and Blais (2012b, 128) build on this, arguing that there is

> clear evidence of an ongoing shift in authority away from the parliamentary party towards grassroots members (Cross, 1996; Kenig, 2009a; LeDuc, 2001; Wauters, 2010). This is consistent with suggestions that declining rates of party membership (Mair and van Biezen, 2001) and public confidence (Dalton and Wattenberg, 2001) lead parties to provide more internal decision-making authority to their grassroots as an incentive to membership and to present a public image of being open and 'democratic'.

The increasing use of party member votes to choose leaders is also noted by Scarrow and Gezgor (2010, 826):

> as part of this trend, in the United Kingdom in 2005 members of the (opposition) Conservative and Liberal Democrat parties selected new party leaders in contests that very much resembled general elections, complete with broadcast debates between the leading candidates. Similarly, in Italy in 2005 Romano Prodi cemented his claim to lead his party by securing the nomination in a newly instituted party primary. In 2006, the French Socialists picked their presidential candidate in a closed primary that resulted in an upset victory for a candidate once regarded within her own party as an upstart challenger (Ségolène Royal).

Almost 200,000 Conservative members participated in the vote that made David Cameron the leader of the British Conservative party, while Jeremy Corbyn was initially elected by a British Labour electorate of more than 400,000. More than 4.4 million citizens participated in the Right and Centre primary in France in 2017, and in the 2005 Italian case noted previously, almost 4.5 million participated in a primary to designate the leader of the left coalition. The trend to increase involvement of citizens in the selection of leaders is noteworthy. Writing in 2016, Cross et al. note that parties are continuing to expand their selectorate and '[n]ot only have primaries become more popular over time, but selection by party members or voters also spans a wide array of countries, representing different types of party and electoral systems' (39). As Pilet and Cross conclude, there has been 'a significant, though not universal, trend towards more inclusive methods and towards a more systematic participation of party members' (2014, 226). Drawing on the work of Cross et al. (2016, 40), table 5.1 presents the overall change between 1975 and 2012 as well as the specific methods used in the parties they examined (forty-four in 1975 and fifty-nine in 2012).

With this in mind, it is important to consider the implications of different leadership selection methods on the campaigns, outcomes and tenure of party leaders. The goal of this chapter is to consider whether the choice of a selection method affects, in a significant manner, the personalization of politics.

Table 5.1 Leadership Selectorates 1975 and 2012

	Selectorate 1975	*Selectorate 2012*
Legislative Caucus	11 (25%)	6 (10%)
Party Delegates	32 (73%)	23 (40%)
Primary	0 (0%)	23 (40%)
Mixed	0 (0%)	5 (9%)
Other	1 (2%)	2 (3%)
N	44	59

Source: Adapted from Cross et al. (2016, 41–42).

As Rahat and Sheafer (2007, 65) make clear, 'political personalization should be seen as a process in which the political weight of the individual actor in the political process increases over time, while the centrality of the political group (i.e., political party) declines'. Institutional personalization, by contrast, 'is the adoption of rules, mechanisms, and institutions that put more emphasis on the individual politician and less on political groups and parties' (66). Although party leaders are the focus of this analysis, personalization can occur at multiple levels, including, for instance, candidate selection.

This chapter discusses the different methods of choosing party leaders that have been adopted by parties and attempts to provide an assessment of the impact of selection models on personalization. With changes in leadership-selection methods producing much wider electorates and thus requiring different sorts of campaigns, assessing relationships between these new methods and personalization is important. Although the emphasis is on Canadian parties, references to other parties are also made. Rahat and Sheafer highlight the spread 'of primaries in the US as a main factor in the transformation from party centered to candidate centered politics' (2007, 66). The expanded voice of party members in leadership choices represents 'an institutional change—the opening up of candidate selection methods (institutional personalization)—is the first link in the chain of personalization (s)' (70). The discussion therefore begins with a review of the US primary model.

THE PRIMARY MODEL: US PRIMARIES

Writing in 1984, DiClericio and Uslaner noted correctly that '[a]mong the democracies of the world, the United States stands alone in according its citizens a significant role in determining who their choices shall be for the highest office in the land' (6). This is no longer the case because 'a variety of parties outside the United States allow non-members to participate in leadership and candidate selection' (Kenig et al. 2015, 152). It is nonetheless useful to reflect on the implications of the US primary model for presidential nomination developed in the 1970s, particularly because the term *primary* has evolved from US usage.[3]

Primaries became more significant as a result of a lack of faith in political elites. Primaries were intended to reduce the control of the political elite by allowing ordinary voters a more direct voice in the designation of candidates for public office. At the presidential level, primaries have been so successful in that endeavour that there has been some pushback. DiClerico and Uslaner argue that

> one of the most persistent indictments against the reformed nominating process was its failure to provide a meaningful role for party and elected officials,

> thereby leading to a loss of quality control over candidates as well as diminishing the need for contenders to court the support of those who share in the governing process (1984, 33).

Donald Trump's candidacy illustrated this concern and the critiques he raised about the legitimacy of a 'brokered' convention stand as a classic rejection of it. From his perspective, making the decision at a convention is simply wrong. However, Kenig et al. note that the US parentage of primaries actually downplays the fact that actual choice of leaders is made formally at a nominating convention at which delegates cast the decisive votes (2015, 156). The strong role for super delegates in the Democratic nomination process represents a reaction against the weakening of party elites and an indication that even in its home base, primaries reflect substantial rule variation.

The movement to primaries reveals issues that need consideration in terms of the personalization of politics. First is the impact of ideology and the notion that primary voters may actually be more ideological than general election voters. To again cite DiClerico and Uslaner, 'Because the broad center of moderate and independent voters seldom vote in the primaries, the decisions are abdicated to small groups of motivated extremists of the left or right' (1984, 26). The implication is that the method of selection enfranchises a somewhat different, and perhaps more extreme, selectorate. As Cain, Lewis and Rivers note,

> Primary voters in American primary elections tend to be more partisan and ideological than general election voters. Moreover, since primaries pit candidates from the same party against one another, partisan appeals are necessarily ineffective, forcing candidates to try and distinguish themselves on some other basis, such as ideology or policy (1988, 2).

This intersects in a curious way with the literature on personalization. Personalization suggests a movement away from ideology to competition driven by less policy-oriented considerations (see for instance, Bennett 2012). Bennett suggests that the absence of ideology facilitates personalization of politics. As he explains,

> as ideology has faded, neoliberalism has emerged as the default ideology of our time. . . . As a result, many voters were deprived of meaningful election choices on what was formerly known as the Left, and younger citizens often developed aversions to politics and government altogether (2012, 26).

Given the convergence to a neoliberal ideology, both partisan appeals and ideology are ineffective means of differentiating candidates during primary elections. As a result, the personal characteristics and accomplishments of individual candidates take on additional importance, contributing to the personalized nature of primaries.

Primary participation is also much more of an individual activity. In selection processes involving party delegates, there are often rules regarding representation on the basis of gender or age. In those cases, delegates may see themselves as representing a particular group rather than just themselves. This is part of the change in the nature of party membership that Gauja explores in chapter 7 of this volume.

The other key implication of the lessened influence of the party elite is the increased possibility of nominees coming from outside the mainstream political process. Bennett notes that this has long been a possibility: 'Personalized politics has long existed, of course, in the form of populist uprisings or emotional bonds with charismatic leaders' (2012, 22). Without a substantial gatekeeping role for party elites, competitive campaigns on behalf of outsiders are more promising. Writing about the 2016 US primaries, Freedland (2016) noted that 'both Trump and Sanders are outsiders to the parties they seek to lead: not long ago neither were even members'. The degree to which campaigns from populist outsiders can be accurately captured by the term *personalization* is an open question, but primaries offer opportunities for participation from voters unhappy with the political system and primaries with limited barriers to voter participation likely facilitate populist eruptions within parties. Indeed, the election of Jeremy Corbyn as the leader of the British Labour party exemplifies that this is not simply a US phenomenon. As leadership candidates attempt to build their electoral support among new types of voters, it seems likely that their campaigns and eventual support will be more personally based with an increased emphasis on their own individual attributes.

METHODS OF LEADERSHIP SELECTION

As the process for choosing party leaders has broadened, there have been a number of attempts to classify the different methods used. One of the first was by LeDuc (2001), who presented a continuum based on inclusiveness that ran from open primaries on the inclusive end to the parliamentary caucus at the exclusive end. Arraigned between them were closed primaries, local caucuses, party conventions and an electoral college.

In 2009 Kenig offered a similar model with the range, again, running from inclusive to exclusive and cycling through the electorate, party members, selected party agencies, parliamentary party group (PPG), party elite, and a single individual. More recently Kenig and his colleagues (2015, 151) offered a modified version of this which identifies what they term a 'primary zone' of leadership selection involving party supporters defined either as voters or members. Selection by party delegates, the PPG, the party elite or a single leader remain the other options. Their analysis draws attention to the various terms that have been used to describe systems allowing party members to vote directly for leaders and suggests that primary can be used to describe selections involving voters, supporters or party members.[4]

A review of the different methods of selection reveals the incredible layers of complexity involved in describing a particular model. Among the parties that allow members to vote directly for the leader, there are wide variations including differences based on the value attached to each vote, the number of voting locations, the methods by which the ballots are cast, the utilization of electoral colleges and an even wider variation in minor rules. In her fascinating look at leadership selection Fieschi argues that 'the rules appear to be under near-constant revision (if only because parties never seem satisfied with them)—for the "pillars" of parliamentary democracy to be permanently on the verge of being tinkered with is puzzling' (2007, 484). As Carty and Blake concluded in an early discussion of Canadian use of these models 'there is little consensus on how such systems ought to be organized and operated' (1999, 213).

Kenig's review of the literature in this area draws attention to the impact of the specific rules. As he explains:

> The different methods for selecting a leader may bear significant political consequences. For instance, they may affect the types of candidates competing and persons selected . . . determine the level of competitiveness in the contest . . . and dictate to what extent the incumbent leader is secure in his/her position (2009, 434).

This chapter now moves to a discussion of the various models as they relate to notions of personalization. In this analysis, attention will be limited to three models: selection by legislative caucus,[5] selection by party convention, and following the Kenig et al. 2015 classification, selection by primary. Pilet and Cross have demonstrated the decline in selection by legislative caucus and show that '[t]he picture that we observe in 2012 is therefore the co-existence of two dominant selectorates: party members and party conventions' (2014, 228). Nonetheless, the logic of selection by legislative caucus is important and the decline in such selections offers insight into the implications of personalization. With a movement away from colleague-based selection, leadership campaigns are more likely to be based on the readily identifiable individual characteristics of the candidate instead of firsthand assessments of leadership qualities, factional membership or even electability.

Selection by Legislative Caucus

Of the models to be discussed, selection by parliamentarians is the simplest to describe and has become well known from the Australian experience. Essentially, the elected members of a party choose their leader and can unseat a leader at almost any point. Tiffen (2015) describes Australian leadership changes as 'frenetic . . . Labor MPs deposed a first term prime minister, Kevin Rudd, who went on to resume the leadership three years later. Now the Liberal party has emulated its opponents by launching its first leadership spill against a newly elected prime minister'. The process involves significant peer review and keeps the leader dependent on his or her colleagues for position retention. Although there may be ideological or factional or electoral concerns involved in the process (see Cross and Blais, 2012a, 129–36), this method has only an indirect relationship to personalization. Legislators, of course, want to maximize their electoral support and protect their own status and are therefore likely to favour the candidate best positioned to do so. However, these decisions are contingent and are made with a strong personal base of knowledge about the possibilities.

There are also models that mix primaries with a decisive role for the legislative caucus. Labour parties in Australia and New Zealand now utilize an electoral college that preserves a strong role for caucus. In Australia, the votes of members are weighted at 50 percent with the other 50 percent coming from the caucus. In the case of the only leader elected under this model, the losing candidate obtained almost 59 percent of the membership vote but lost because the support for his opponent within the caucus was even higher. In New Zealand the caucus vote is weighted at 40 percent, and in Ireland, Fianna Fail also gives the caucus 40 percent of the votes and Fine Gael reserves fully 65 percent of the weight for their legislators. In a somewhat different vein, the British Conservative caucus provides members with a choice between two candidates chosen by the caucus, whereas the Labour party requires that nominations be supported by a specific percentage of the party's parliamentary caucus to enter the race, a provision that in the past has kept some candidates out of the contest (Heppell 2010). In May 2016, the Irish Labour party members were denied a leadership primary when no member of the legislature would second the nomination of a potential candidate. There was some backlash to this with the *Irish Times* reporting:

> The grassroots are totally unhappy. . . . We are unhappy because we are denied the opportunity to select the leader of our party. It is bad for democracy, it is bad for us, and it will leave a very sour taste. Some members have already resigned from the party, and I am sure others will go (*Irish Times* 2016).

Perhaps the party elite learned a lesson from watching the 2015 British Labour race unfold. Jeremy Corbyn won an easy victory in the party primary, but only after having grave difficulty in securing the level of parliamentary support necessary to make it on the ballot. As the BBC explained,

> The reason he did so was that a number of MPs—including some with diametrically opposed views—'lent' him their votes. At the time, they argued Labour needed the widest possible debate after its election defeat and it would be wrong if the left of the party was excluded. . . . One of them, former acting party leader Margaret Beckett, ruefully owned up to being a moron (BBC 2015).

It is intriguing to consider the implications of this parliamentary-determined primary field. Parliamentarians can keep candidates from entering the contest and have the ability to designate a short list from which voters must choose. A rule of this sort in the United States giving such authority to members of Congress might well have kept candidates such as Donald Trump, Ted Cruz and Bernie Sanders out of the presidential-nominating process. Providing such authority to elected officials at the top may impede the 'personalization' of leadership. However, it is important to keep in mind that elected officials want to be reelected and may well see the personal appeal of candidates with limited backgrounds in the party or government as likely to enhance their prospects. Nonetheless, superficial knowledge stemming from media coverage, social media or candidate rhetoric is unlikely to play a major role in these decisions.

Selection by Party Convention

In this model, the selection of a party leader is not made by elected officials but is a decision reached by party 'activists' in a common setting. The use of a convention eliminates the ability of elected officials to determine their own leader. Courtney's 1995 analysis of the movement away from caucus selection to convention selection in Canada revealed two critical changes. First, the process opened up the position to individuals who were not actually members of the legislature and diminished the importance of an extensive parliamentary career as a stepping stone to obtaining the leadership. Second, the relationship between the leader and elected party members was altered because the leader no longer depended on his or her legislative colleagues to remain in office. What the caucus had not created, it could not remove. Indeed, as the Canadian experience with conventions evolved, the ability of the convention to remove leaders, even in the face of legislative support became institutionalized. In broadening the group of potential leaders and in enhancing the leader's independence from caucus, conventions contributed to the growing personalization of party leadership.

The move to conventions was based on concerns about the 'representative' nature of the caucus, but it preserved a relatively strong voice for party elites, especially elected officials. Representativeness was often assessed on a regional basis because it was quite possible for important electoral regions to have a limited legislative presence in a particular party. The broadened base of the selectorate then could conceivably provide a better representation of the country and select a leader with broader appeal. The voice of the party elite was intended to provide some form of oversight, usually by guaranteeing representation from so-called ex-officio delegates from the party or the legislature. This helped to ensure that the decisions of ordinary delegates were leavened and influenced by this disproportionate voice for the party elite.

The compelling nature of arguments based on representativeness has spilled over into the primary zone because a number of primary models involve the weighting of votes based on region or constituencies. This ensures that candidates have support from a number of areas and cannot win an election simply by maximizing support in their home area. Similarly, some primaries attempt to retain a voice for significant groups within the party by utilizing an electoral college that guarantees a certain percentage of the total vote to specific groups. Usually these are members of the legislature, but on occasion can be key groups such as labour unions. Ed Miliband's narrow victory in the 2010 British Labour election was largely the result of support from affiliated members as his leading opponent secured majorities from the parliamentary party and ordinary party members. Similarly, in the 2014 New Zealand Labour party primary, Andrew Little won a narrow victory despite his opponent winning majorities from caucus and the general membership. By winning more than 75 percent of the affiliated vote, he managed to obtain 50.5 percent of the final vote.

Convention models are most appealing when one assumes that the delegates attending these gatherings are long serving and dedicated party activists who have the long-term interests of the party at heart and are deeply engaged in a deliberative process. As conventions evolved, these assumptions became much harder to sustain. Leadership candidates saw that their chances of victory were enhanced by electing delegates predisposed to supporting them, rather than simply trying to persuade activists of their suitability for the position. As a result, long-serving and dedicated party officials could often be swept aside by new members in the quest to elect supporters of particular candidates (Stewart 1997). Instead of a deliberative choice being made by long-time activists, the convention could simply become the ratification of results from the delegate selection meetings dominated by candidate organizations. In such cases, the convention has in effect ceased to be the site of decision making for the leadership. The logic of conventions suggests that candidates will prefer to elect delegates committed to them rather than being forced to persuade delegates at the convention of their suitability. In reality, this will produce delegates elected based on the candidate's personal campaign efforts with loyalty to the candidate becoming critical to selection.

Selection at a party convention however does ensure access to similar information. These relatively small gatherings offer the opportunity to hear each candidate speak, discuss their qualifications with other delegates and to build coalitions. Courtney suggests that 'convention coalition-building has contributed to the development of basically centrist, consensual political parties and leadership in Canada' (1995, 285). Moreover, he argued that: 'One of the strengths of a convention system dominated by party regulars mindful of the party's long-term interests is that it 'militate[s] against the choice of an extremist candidate' (86). Finally, he viewed positively the fact that the 'vast majority of those who have served as delegates . . . overwhelmingly have had several years of experience in the party' (287). With candidate organizations invading local delegate selection meetings, this view came increasingly to reflect an idealized model rather than reality. Moreover, as mentioned previously, delegates might have group-based approaches to representation, for instance related to gender, age or electoral district.

Despite the past involvement of delegates in the party, one of the factors involving selection by delegates is the nature of the choices made by delegates. Elected officials have something personal at stake in the selection of the leader, but this is not quite the same for delegates. Delegates traditionally have been long-standing party members and a study of Canadian party members by Young and Cross found that 'ideological or policy related commitment to the party is by far the most important reason for joining' (2002, 549). Choice by convention affords the distinct possibility that the choice is made by a more ideologically driven group and may result in the election of more extreme candidates than would selection by the legislative caucus. Indeed, in a review of leadership decisions made by major Canadian parties in the early 1980s, Johnston found that 'the decisive factors in both Liberal and Conservative delegates' behavior seemed to be ideas about policy' (1988, 215). Cross and Blais note that convention delegates might be more 'ideologically extreme' and that 'electability might be less of a factor among the activists as, for the most part, their jobs are not dependent on the electoral success of their party. While activists surely prefer their party to be in government, they may not be as willing as MPs to sacrifice ideological concerns for electability' (2012, 151–52). In this sense, personal considerations relating to the candidate may take second place to policy considerations.

Selection by Primary

The broadening involvement of ordinary members, supporters or voters in the selection of party leaders obviously changes the nature of the process. Using the Kenig et al. definition that 'primaries are those selection methods in which the cumulative weight of influence of party members, supporters and / or voters, is equal to or greater than all other more exclusive selectorate(s) combined' (2015, 152) provides a useful device for assessing the potential implications of this model for personalization of power. As leadership candidates attempt to build support with a wider electorate and distinguish themselves from their opponents, an emphasis on individual attributes seems likely to grow.

In assessing the impact of primary models, the focus will be largely on the Canadian experience. As Cross and Blais explain

> While none of the Westminster parties have moved to primaries of the US sort, in which party membership is not a requisite for leadership voting, some of the Canadian parties have come close. They have done so by allowing any interested voter to join the party up to the last hour, typically well into the leadership campaign and just prior to voting, and still be eligible to participate (2012, 169).

Late and easy entry of participants limits the ability of candidates to determine the electorate and to reach out to all voters. Candidates may not know who voters are in many cases, and there are likely to be substantial elements of the selectorate who are uninvolved and untouched by candidate mobilization efforts.

Participation in a primary differs dramatically from participation in a convention. In one of the rare studies of voters in a party primary, Stewart conducted a survey of Conservative primary voters in the province of Alberta and found that voters had a limited 'party pedigree. Only 5 per cent of these voters had ever held an elected party position and fully 55% of them joined the party for the first time in the year of the vote. . . . More significantly, a majority of the participants (55%) admitted to joining the party *just to vote for the leader*' (1997, 114–15). Almost one in five took out membership on the day of the second ballot, only about one-fifth were members of the federal party, and less than one-fifth worked for the party in the previous election campaign (115).

Studies of voters in the 2015 and 2016 British Labour primaries reveal similar results. In a study that compared members who joined after May 2015 with more long-standing members, the Economic and Social Research Council (ESRC) Party Members Project found new members were much less likely to have attended a public meeting, distributed leaflets, displayed general election posters or canvassed for the party (ESRC Party Members Project 2016). Examining the 2015 and 2016 British Labour primaries also reveals the involvement of voters who were not completely supportive of the party in the recent past. Almost one-fifth of the new voters supported the Greens in the 2015 general election. Concerns were raised about Conservative supporters participating to ensure the selection of an unelectable Labour leader, but studies looking at the political values of participants suggest that they were overwhelmingly left wing and anti-austerity (Bale 2016).

In the Canadian province of Alberta, the decision of who was to lead the party was made by voters with a limited background in the party. Moreover, the decisions were made in the absence of much in the way of direct contact with campaigns:

> most voters did not meet a single candidate during the campaign, attend any of the regional all candidate forums, or participate in other campaign events. Less than half the voters reported being contacted by workers . . . and only one in four utilized the toll-free information lines provided by many candidates (Stewart and Archer 2000, 60).

In short, unlike caucus or convention selections, primaries facilitate 'participation by those whose acquaintance with campaigns and the candidates came through the media rather than through personal knowledge or meetings. In this respect, the process appears to resemble an election more than a leadership convention' (65).

To a large degree this confirmed some of the fears expressed by opponents of primary elections. Courtney warned that this model

> would represent the ultimate act of individualization of Canadian leadership selection politics . . . [and that it will] come at the cost of the acquired value of political experience—whether acquired in caucus or in the party apparatus—of those working most closely with the leader, the prospective leaders, and the party (1995, 292).

Individually based evaluations of leadership candidates seem almost certain to grow with the wider electorates enfranchised by primaries further contributing to personalization. Courtney warns that '[t]he switch could ultimately prove problematic for the health of local political organizations and the larger political community in Canada' (1995, 292).

Undoubtedly primaries change parties and the nature of leadership politics. It is, however, difficult to determine whether this makes it more likely for decisions to be made based on personal characteristics or nonpolicy-related matters. Stewart and Archer found that policy considerations were important because '[a]ttitudinal differences clearly affect support coalitions' (2000, 58). Young and Cross's investigation into the reasons Canadians offered for joining parties revealed that 'belief in the party's policies is the reason for joining given the greatest weight by party members' (2002, 557). Their survey was conducted at a low point of the electoral cycle, that is a period in which there was no general or party election ongoing, but it does suggest that broadening the involvement of ordinary members in a selection process does not eliminate the salience of policy concerns.

Indeed, Carty and Cross suggest that one of the ways in which party members can change party policy is indirect—through a change in personnel. They argue that leadership elections 'represent contests over competing orientations on important social, economic and constitutional issues' (2006, 100). Understanding this feature of primaries is critical in coming to terms with personalization.

Even policy considerations become personalized with candidates defining particular and potentially divergent directions. In a discussion of one of the earliest Canadian examples of a primary, the selection of Mike Harris as Conservative leader in Ontario, Whitaker (2001) noted the importance of the policy package presented by leadership candidates. He suggested that the primary opened up 'an opportunity for ideologically committed right wingers to seize the party franchise. . . . With Harris as leader, the moderate policy orientation of the past could be discarded and replaced with a hard right neoliberalism' (18). In Alberta, a decision of the Progressive Conservative party to move away from primaries was inspired in part by concerns that primary voters were insufficiently ideological. One former candidate suggested that such races 'appear to have transformed the PC party into a centre left coalition party' (Morton 2013), while another indicated somewhat cryptically that 'I think it's time we stopped electing premiers and started electing the leader of our party' (Bellefontaine 2016). The general point is that outsiders and candidates not favoured by party regulars were advantaged by primary selections and that policy views matter. Such considerations are also likely to be at play in candidate selection more generally.

Cross and Blais suggest that primary voters 'are less likely to be motivated by policy concerns than are activists who find their way to national conventions', but policy positions and ideology 'do provide the framework within which they are contested and do have an effect on voting behaviour' (2012a, 153–54). Such cleavages 'can create natural blocs of supporters for leadership candidates' (147). Because primary voters are less policy driven, the role of policy in primaries is tied up with impressions regarding the preferences and values of the candidates. Cross et al. expand on this, suggesting that in some ways primary voters are more similar to legislators than they are to convention delegates. As they explain:

> Unlike parliamentarians who are often willing to sacrifice ideological concerns for electability, party activists are generally more extreme in their views and more concerned with policy than with immediate electoral success. . . . [T]he available evidence suggests that primary voters cast their ballots according

to similar considerations as the PPG. The literature suggests that membership votes often come down to questions of electability (2016, 137).

The 2015 and 2016 British Labour leadership races suggest the need to be careful in assessing the more pragmatic approach of primary voters. Jeremy Corbyn's victory is partially attributed to 'his anti-austerity message' and of his embrace of 'supporters of other parties, most notably the Greens but also far left groups' (BBC News 2015). His victory is also attributed to the decision to allow anyone who was willing to pay a three-pound fee to participate in the election, which again suggests that his 'outsider' campaign was facilitated by the primary model.

This highlights the importance of assessing the mobilization strategies used by candidates in primary campaigns. Carty and Cross describe the memberships of Canadian parties as small (2006, 103) and argue that participants 'constitute a constantly swirling membership' (104). Carty and Blake show that 'parties have seen these contests as ideal opportunities to reactivate the interests, energies and often memberships of partisans who have let their organizational ties lapse or to mobilize new groups into the party' (1999, 217). Despite the interest of the party, they maintain that 'it is the campaigns of competing candidates that mobilize supporters and bring them into the party. As a consequence, highly competitive contests typically see more signing up of new members; those in which the outcome is in little doubt generate less growth' (217).

Primaries facilitate party transformation as candidate-based support coalitions can overwhelm long-term members and define the party's image and future. Once again the victory of Jeremy Corbyn is illustrative. As Rentoul (2017) explains, Corbyn 'recruited a new party to outvote members of the old'. The number of full members of the Labour party increased from 190,000 in May of 2015 to 515,000 in July of 2016 and 'those who were members before May 2015 voted predominantly for Owen Smith, whereas the new members opted mainly for Jeremy Corbyn' (ESRC Party Members Project 2016). Corbyn's campaign and victory also point to the importance of group-based voter mobilization and social media in primary campaigns. Social-media campaigns were an essential part of Corbyn's campaign and clearly focused on him directly. It was not however solely his campaign efforts that mobilized new voters. As Poletti (2016) explains, 'Of the new members, one in ten (10.4%) consider themselves a member of Momentum, the association supporting Corbyn's leadership'. Group-based mobilization has also been identified as part of the 2017 Canadian Conservative leadership race with advocacy groups credited with registering thousands of potential voters (Mazeruuw 2017). Voters mobilized by such groups likely have different concerns and desires than the voters who take it on themselves to participate.

Whitaker (2001), in his evocative description of what he terms 'virtual parties',[6] builds on the candidate-driven nature of such competitions. As he explains,

> voters mobilized by candidates in a primary-type contest are not socialized into the party. . . . They simply pay for a membership and cast a vote for their candidate in much the same isolation that characterizes voting in general elections. They miss the social matrix of the party, and miss learning its norms and practices, its sense of collective memory and shared identity (17).

Whitaker goes on to suggest that '[v]irtual parties form up around particular leaders, in the first instance at the time they challenge for control of the party at a leadership contest. Winners then usually take all' (2001, 19). This exemplifies how the primary model of selection can transform the party and reconstitute it in the image of the winner. It is, of course, not simply primaries that afford such opportunities. Carty, in an analysis of Canadian leadership conventions, suggested that 'parties choose leaders in the hope that they will give them new policies and a new persona' (1988b, 73–74). Nonetheless, with their openness, party primaries make it easier to personalize policy and redefine the party for the broader electorate. In this sense, parties utilizing primaries are often viewed as 'empty vessels', open to being taken over by individual candidates (consider, for example, Corbyn in the United Kingdom). In chapter 4 of this volume, Pruysers and Cross identify some of the complexity involved in multilevel elections but note that leaders at least rival parties in visibility.

Carty and Cross provide confirming evidence of the importance of mobilizing new members. They suggest that leadership campaigns typically start with candidates' teams recruiting members into the party on the ground—many of them completely new to the party. The vast majority of these instant members take no further part in party activities and withdraw from it immediately following the leadership contest. 'The real job of winning the leadership contest must be done on the ground by mobilizing supporters' (2006, 104). Cross et al. elaborate on this, noting the transitory nature of such memberships. As they explain: 'membership numbers tend to soar in the lead-up to primary elections only to fall off once they are over. This is a result of members joining only to support an individual candidate; such personalized recruitment does not engender a longer term commitment' (2016, 187). Although focusing on candidate selection, Cross and Pruysers (2017) reveal that party members who supported a losing candidate in the intraparty election are significantly more likely to report that they will not renew their memberships, suggesting that their attachment and commitment is highly personalized around the individual candidate and not the party. Once again, Gauja's work in this volume on the changing nature of party membership involvement is pertinent.

Cross and Blais further highlight the importance of recruitment and indicate how much the party may change in the course of a leadership election. They note that 'the number of party members eligible to vote can increase as much as 100 per cent between the launch of a leadership campaign and voting day' and that leadership campaigns are very much focused on 'identifying potential supporters and signing them up as members' (2012a, 139). Parties are transformed by the 'gate crashers' and 'tourists' (see Stewart and Archer 2000[7]) who seize the opportunity afforded by primaries for a direct voice in determining political leaders and an indirect voice in policy direction. The 'new' party is defined, as least in the short term, by the winner and, if it is not completely virtual, it is certainly very much personalized. Parties, much like rivers, undergo constant reformation as new members cycle in and out. It may be impossible to step in the same party twice.

This potential redefinition of the party and its image points out the importance of one of the features of primaries not developed in this analysis, namely the degree to which the desire of voters to participate in a party primary is likely influenced by the competitive position of the party.[8] A primary involving hundreds of thousands of essentially self-recruited voters will differ substantively from a primary enfranchising a few thousand voters largely signed up by the candidates. In such models, outsiders who are highly critical of the party whose leadership they are contesting may find that populist campaigns based on themselves personally promise the potential of success. It seems likely that the primary model makes such campaigns more promising. As Freedland indicates 'What connects many—not all—of these figures is a rejection of the political system as it currently stands. The new populists don't simply say that the ruling party has failed and now the opposition should have a turn. They insist the entire system is broken' (2016).

The primary implications identified by Stewart and Archer indicate that under this model

> Individual leadership candidates put in place their own personal election machinery, maintain their own lists of potential voters, and cultivate an allegiance in the first instance to themselves and only secondarily to the party. . . . [moreover] Campaigns become based to a greater extent on mechanisms of mass marketing and less on direct personal contact; they become focused on recruitment of new party members, including many who may have an ephemeral connection to the party, rather than on the conversion of existing party members to one of the candidates (2000, 168).

Their conclusion has direct implications for personalization as they argue that '[t]he move to direct election of party leaders will contribute both to an increased importance of leaders, as they become less dependent upon their caucus colleagues for support, and also to increased instability of party loyalties' (170). Accordingly, as Poguntke and Webb suggest, [t]he tendency towards personalized leadership is likely to lead to a concentration of power resources in the leader's office' (2005, 9). In short, primaries contribute, at least indirectly to the personalization of politics. The relationship between primaries and personalization is not direct or even intended, but primaries can facilitate personalization in systems where personalized competition was not previously the norm.

This is not to say that all aspects of primaries contribute to a greater concentration of authority in the hands of successful candidates. Bringing in new people with a limited background and commitment to the party may help a candidate win the leadership, but such support does not provide day-to-day support or provide the same kind of base in times of trouble that a loyal coterie of parliamentary supporters will bring. Malloy's chapter in this volume illustrates the complex nature of the relationship between the leader and the parliamentary party and makes clear the importance of the leader's approach to this relationship.

Primaries, or even conventions, can saddle legislative parties with a leader with whom there is no affective relationship and whose qualities threaten the party elite in ways that are both material and ideological. Primary elected leaders have few resources to call on in internal party battles. This is not an issue in the US model because all candidates have to be renominated, and there is no formal role for presidential nominees after losing an election. In parliamentary systems, however, there is an on-going role and party leaders must pay some attention to their elected colleagues (see Cross and Blais 2012a; see also Malloy, this volume). In some cases the broader membership can be mobilized by leaders intent on retaining their position. The example of Jeremy Corbyn is illustrative as is that of Pedro Sanchez in the Spanish Socialist party. The party elite essentially forced Sanchez to resign, but the vigorous grassroots campaign he waged saw him returned to the leadership. It is also important to note that although the party has become more personalized, the desire for broader participation ensures wider involvement in candidate designation and contributes to ongoing policy debate. Once again the chapter by Pruysers and Cross in this volume usefully highlights the candidate issue.

In all likelihood, candidates who won their leadership via what Morley (1992) calls a 'conquest' model must demonstrate the promise of electoral success to retain support.[9] Following the loss of an election, the tenure of primary produced leaders may well prove to be 'nasty, brutish and short'. Cross and Blais argue that, despite the move to a broadened electorate, 'leaders are unable to stay in power long once they have lost the confidence of their parliamentary colleagues' (2012a, 179). The case of Corbyn, however, questions this conclusion since he was able to survive an overwhelming vote of no confidence by his parliamentary party.

Katz and Mair have shown that the evolution of party membership has affected the relationship between the leader and the party as 'an atomized membership is less likely to provide the basis for the mobilization of challenges' (1995, 21), and leaders may therefore appear more secure. However, the shortened tenure of leaders associated with primary selection found by Pilet and Cross (2014, 237) suggests a complicated relationship between the party and the leader. The leader is able to assert plausible claims to a wide mandate that provides short-term protection from challenge. If, however, this mandate is secured in large part on the basis of claims of electability (see Cross et al. 2016), failure to obtain satisfactory election or even polling results can render the position of the leader untenable. Because one of the components of personalization is an increase in the electoral significance of the leader (see Bittner, this volume), the prospect or reality of unsatisfactory results may lead parliamentary colleagues to push their leader towards the door. The transitory nature of party participation demonstrated by primary voters makes them both an unreliable source of security for the leader and an unlikely source for punitive actions directed towards the parliamentary group for a lack of support.

Poguntke and Webb make clear that the personalization and concentration of power is to some degree contingent. They suggest

> a shift towards personalized leadership which may be very strong as long as it is successful electorally, but which is likely to be vulnerable in times of impending or actual electoral defeat. In other words, we would expect party leaders to be less likely to survive electoral defeat than has been the case in the past (2005, 10).

Thus, although leaders may bask in the light of enhanced personal power initially, their power is dependent on generating electoral success. This need for success is likely to be stronger in nonideological parties. In a discussion of the Canadian Liberal party, Cross and Young note that 'the nature of the party's brand has shifted periodically, often taking on the characteristics of its leader . . . [and] suspect that the appeal of personalization may be stronger in a party that bases less of its electoral appeal on ideology (2015, 310–11). Leadership of such parties is likely to be less secure.[10]

CONCLUSIONS

Cross et al. maintain that '[o]ne of the most immediate and identifiable consequences of primary elections is the emphasis that these intra-party contests place on candidate-centred politics. Primaries promote personalization' (2016, 183). There is no doubt that primary selections contribute to the personalization of power. However, this is by no means uni-causal nor is it absolute. Previously in this chapter attention was drawn to Duverger's mid-twentieth-century description of the growing concentration of power. This concentration took place long before primaries became relevant, even in the United States. It is also important to consider concurrent trends that contribute to the personalization of power. These include a decline in the relevance of ideology, the emergence of a neoliberal policy consensus and the decline of parties as organizations. The latter in fact was part of the reason for the move to primaries. In this regard, the weakening of parties as organizations might be viewed as one of the original causes of increased personalism, rather than one of its main effects.

In terms of understanding personalization as it relates to privatization, it is also important to consider the increase in the number of women contesting leadership positions. Trimble (2005) has shown that media coverage of such politicians is more personal in nature and part of the process of personalization observed may be related to this factor. Following a study of a woman contesting the Canadian Conservative leadership in 2003, Trimble concluded

> Belinda Stronach endured constant press inspection of her physical personal and private life throughout the Conservative leadership race. That a third of the newspaper stories about the leadership race mentioning her candidacy discussed her appearance is both remarkable and disheartening (2005, 18).

Thomas's work in this volume on personalization and gender reveals that more attention is needed to its gendered effects.

Direct personal knowledge and involvement with leadership candidates has declined over time, making leadership elections, in some respects, more impersonal in nature. Instead, following Richard Fenno's (1978) description of how representatives establish connections of trust with their constituents, candidates need to establish their qualifications (understanding and experience), identification (I'm one of you) and empathy (I understand and care about your situation) via surrogates, the media or social media to an audience with no real personal knowledge of them. Candidates must work hard at developing their personal appeal for audiences who have no direct connection with them. Personalized politics thus develops in the absence of personal interaction with the candidates.

As well, there are indications that the tenure of primary produced leaders is less secure, perhaps indicating some lessening in personal authority in the long term. Factors such as party type, competitive situation and the leader's ability to inspire loyalty are also important as is the nature of the selection model. It is also clear that more empirical work on the impact of different leadership selection models is needed. The existing literature leaves open questions such as:

Are voters less likely to be ideologically driven depending on method used?
Do mobilization strategies differ by model?
Are 'conquest'-based candidacies more likely in some models?
Does the media cover the leadership contest differently?
Does the selection method affect leader security?

In this chapter, an attempt has been made to offer some preliminary answers to these questions, but more empirical and comparative work is needed to provide comprehensive answers. The chapter suggests that the move from party conventions to primaries has contributed to increased personalization. This is not only related to the personalization of policy but is also related to the facilitation of populist campaigns that are more personal in nature. In general, primaries contribute to personalization by emphasizing individual over group participation, by hollowing out the party and personalizing membership around the winning candidate and by allowing leaders to claim a personal mandate from thousands (sometimes millions) of voters. However, it is important to note that the personalization of politics was becoming a more prominent part of conventions, and it is almost certain that the personalization of parties would have continued to grow even without primaries. Primaries have therefore hastened, but did not create, personalization.

The battle to elect convention delegates has been well described by Carty (1988a) as 'trench warfare', and the outcome of such battles meant that 'conventions no longer ensure that decisions will be made by long-time party activists and parties may find themselves vulnerable to organized interests. . . . The battle in the trenches for delegates also has devalued the deliberative nature of conventions' (Stewart 1997, 127–28).

Even before the emergence of primaries, studies of Canadian deliberative conventions suggested that '[w]hen most Canadians think about politics, leadership dominates their perspectives. For most Canadians the leader is the party' (Goldfarb and Axworthy 1988, ix). One unsuccessful convention candidate lamented that parties were being reduced to vehicles for the selection of leaders, and writing in the early twentieth century, Andre Seigfried maintained that

> it is of the first importance to the success of a party that it should be led by someone who inspires confidence and whose mere name is a programme in itself. As long as the Conservatives had Macdonald for their leader, they voted for him rather than for the party. So it is with Laurier and the Liberals of to-day. If Laurier disappeared, the Liberals would perhaps find that they had lost the real secret of their victories (1966 [1907], 136).

A stronger description of personalization is hard to find, and it predates Canadian primaries by almost eighty years.

NOTES

1. As quoted in Susan Welch et al. *Understanding American Government* (2010, 208).
2. For example, around 50 million Americans voted in the 2016 US primaries and almost 7 million people voted in the 2016–2017 primaries in France.
3. It is important to stress that the US model retains a significant convention portion and combines primaries and caucuses. It was not until 1972 that a majority of convention delegates were elected in primaries.
4. Kenig et al. further unpack the notion of primaries, distinguishing between pure and mixed primaries, and in the pure primary category explaining differences between open, semi open and closed models (2015, 152–53). This is an important factor in considering the impact of primaries, but it is not developed in this analysis. In the discussion to follow little attention will be paid to weighting, financing or the electoral systems used.
5. The term *legislative caucus* is used instead of parliamentary party group. This is also the case in table 5.1.
6. 'Virtual parties form around politicians seeking the leadership of parties, as relatively small entourages or coteries of political strategists, marketing and communications experts, "spin doctors," PR flacks and "policy wonks." If successful, the same coterie then in effect colonizes the party and runs its subsequent election campaign. The party, as such, serves as little more than a convenient franchise' (Whitaker 2001, 17).
7. Gate crashers are voters who decide to participate at the last moment, whereas tourists are those who participate in the primary but have no ongoing interest in being associated with the party. It is relatively easy for tourists to participate in primaries, but it is also the case that candidates in conventions were actively recruiting tourists to participate in delegate selection meetings.
8. As an example, participation in the British Liberal Democratic primary dropped by more than 7000 in 2015 as compared with 2007.
9. In a study of the Canadian New Democratic Party, Morley (1992, 133–34) outlined a 'conquest' model for securing party leadership. In this model

> A new leader may come to his or her post, after a mighty struggle with political rivals to grasp the prize. . . . [there is] no consensus in the organization as to who should be the

> new leader, . . . office holder and other key activists are split in their support . . . bitterness between the contenders and a deeper bitterness among their supporters . . . [and] the new leaders will place key supporters in important executive and administrative positions.

Primaries may be more likely to produce this sort of result.

10. The fate of Canadian New Democratic Party (NDP) leader Thomas Mulcair illustrates the importance of party competitiveness and the focus on ideology. Before 2015, NDP leaders were relatively free of fear of removal from power following one bad election result. Following an election in which the party presented a more moderate image and expected to gain power, Mulcair became the first party leader to actually lose a leadership review. Mulcair was elected by party members but ousted by the presumably more ideologically focused convention delegates.

Chapter 6

Personalized Politics Online

Gideon Rahat and Shahaf Zamir

In just two decades, the World Wide Web has become a pivotal arena of human activity, especially in developed postindustrial democracies. While in 1995, Internet usage in twenty-five democracies ranged from 0.4 to 13.9 users per 100 people and in 2005 from 25.2 to 87.0, by 2014 those figures were 62.0 to 98.2 (World Bank 2015). Technological developments, from infrastructure to interface, make the Web increasingly simple and accessible. With that has come an endless proliferation of mobile phones and tablets and a daily hike in the number of people opening social-media accounts. Especially prominent in this context are, of course, Facebook and Twitter, which entered public life by 2006. In short, the Internet has become central to the everyday life of many, maybe even of most citizens, and thus has become crucially relevant for politicians and for political activity, particularly in democracies.

Politics online developed in parallel to the general development of the Web. In the Internet's early days, the online presence of political actors was mainly anecdotal and aimed at gaining exposure in the traditional media for being innovative. Then, it became a political forum per se, though initially via websites that had limited interaction with users (Gibson, Ward and Lusoli 2002; Gibson and Rommele 2005). Since 2006, online politics has settled most significantly in social-networking sites. This allows the creation of direct unmediated interactive contact among parties, politicians and citizens, radically transforming the nature of political campaigns (Vergeer, Hermans and Sams 2011). For parties and politicians, being online became a must. And it shows (see table 6.1).

This chapter looks at personalized politics online.[1] It presents a cross-national comparison of parties' and politicians' presence and activity on the Web and citizens' consumption of this activity, especially on Facebook and Twitter. It also explores the content of such activity through the analysis

Table 6.1 Share (in Percentages) of Parties, Party Leaders and Prominent Politicians That Had Websites, Facebook and Twitter Accounts as of February 2015 (in brackets, the Number of Cases)

	Websites			*Facebook Accounts**			*Twitter Accounts*		
Country	*P*	*PL*	*PP*	*P*	*PL*	*PP*	*P*	*PL*	*PP*
Australia	100 (4/4)	100 (4/4)	100 (8/8)	100 (4/4)	100 (4/4)	100 (8/8)	100 (4/4)	100 (4/4)	100 (8/8)
Austria	100 (4/4)	25 (1/4)	15 (2/13)	100 (4/4)	75 (3/4)	46 (6/13)	100 (4/4)	50 (2/4)	38 (5/13)
Belgium	100 (5/5)	60 (3/5)	93 (14/15)	100 (5/5)	100 (5/5)	87 (13/15)	100 (5/5)	100 (5/5)	100 (15/15)
Canada	100 (4/4)	100 (4/4)	89 (8/9)	100 (4/4)	100 (4/4)	89 (8/9)	100 (4/4)	100 (4/4)	78 (7/9)
Czech Rep.	100 (4/4)	75 (3/4)	83 (10/12)	100 (4/4)	100 (4/4)	75 (9/12)	100 (4/4)	50 (2/4)	75 (9/12)
Denmark	100 (5/5)	40 (2/5)	53 (8/15)	100 (5/5)	100 (5/5)	93 (14/15)	100 (5/5)	60 (3/5)	60 (9/15)
Finland	100 (8/8)	100 (8/8)	100 (24/24)	100 (8/8)	100 (8/8)	96 (23/24)	100 (8/8)	88 (7/8)	79 (19/24)
France	100 (3/3)	67 (2/3)	56 (5/9)	100 (3/3)	100 (3/3)	100 (9/9)	100 (3/3)	100 (3/3)	100 (9/9)
Germany	100 (6/6)	100 (8/8)	88 (15/17)	100 (6/6)	100 (8/8)	76 (13/17)	100 (6/6)	75 (6/8)	29 (5/17)
Hungary	100 (4/4)	40 (2/5)	43 (3/7)	100 (4/4)	100 (5/5)	86 (6/7)	100 (4/4)	0 (0/5)	14 (1/7)
Iceland	100 (4/4)	50 (2/4)	33 (4/12)	100 (4/4)	100 (4/4)	92 (11/12)	100 (4/4)	75 (3/4)	42 (5/12)
Ireland	100 (4/4)	50 (2/4)	67 (8/12)	100 (4/4)	50 (2/4)	75 (9/12)	100 (4/4)	100 (4/4)	83 (10/12)
Israel	88 (7/8)	13 (1/8)	13 (3/24)	88 (7/8)	100 (8/8)	79 (19/24)	63 (5/8)	88 (7/8)	42 (10/24)
Italy	100 (5/5)	80 (4/5)	83 (10/12)	100 (5/5)	100 (5/5)	67 (8/12)	100 (5/5)	100 (5/5)	75 (9/12)
Japan	100 (4/4)	100 (4/4)	83 (10/12)	100 (4/4)	75 (3/4)	42 (5/12)	100 (4/4)	100 (4/4)	67 (8/12)
Luxembourg	100 (5/5)	50 (3/6)	31 (5/16)	100 (5/5)	83 (5/6)	50 (8/16)	100 (5/5)	67 (4/6)	56 (9/16)
Netherlands	100 (6/6)	33 (2/6)	17 (3/18)	100 (6/6)	67 (4/6)	50 (9/18)	100 (6/6)	100 (6/6)	72 (13/18)
New Zealand	100 (4/4)	20 (1/5)	55 (6/11)	100 (4/4)	100 (5/5)	100 (11/11)	100 (4/4)	100 (5/5)	82 (9/11)
Norway	100 (6/6)	33 (2/6)	25 (5/20)	100 (6/6)	100 (6/6)	90 (18/20)	100 (6/6)	83 (5/6)	95 (19/20)
Poland	100 (4/4)	75 (3/4)		100 (4/4)	50 (2/4)		100 (4/4)	100 (4/4)	
Portugal	100 (4/4)	0 (0/4)		100 (4/4)	75 (3/4)		75 (3/4)	25 (1/4)	
Spain	100 (3/3)	67 (2/3)	56 (5/9)	100 (3/3)	100 (3/3)	78 (7/9)	100 (3/3)	100 (3/3)	100 (9/9)
Sweden	100 (8/8)	33 (3/9)	38 (9/24)	100 (8/8)	89 (8/9)	88 (21/24)	100 (8/8)	78 (7/9)	83 (20/24)
Switzerland	100 (5/5)	83 (5/6)	60 (9/15)	100 (5/5)	67 (4/6)	47 (7/15)	100 (5/5)	83 (5/6)	40 (6/15)
United Kingdom	100 (3/3)	33 (1/3)	89 (8/9)	100 (3/3)	100 (3/3)	56 (5/9)	100 (3/3)	100 (3/3)	78 (7/9)
Total	99 (119/120)	57 (72/127)	56 (182/323)	99 (119/120)	90 (114/127)	76 (247/323)	97 (116/120)	80 (102/127)	68 (221/323)

P, Parties; PL, Party Leader; PP, Prominent Politicians.

*The data on Facebook pages do not include pages that were only informative but did not contain any shared information supplied by the politicians or the parties. These pages are not active user pages and probably were not created or maintained by the party or politician or their representatives.

of the Israeli case. It addresses two questions: first, does the online world encourage personalized politics, or does it perhaps create a new opportunity for the empowerment of political parties? Second, is online personalized politics mainly about party leaders or also about the empowerment of other politicians? In answering these questions, this chapter highlights multiple different layers of personalism and reveals that a variety of actors engage in personalized politics online.

OFFLINE AND ONLINE PERSONALIZED POLITICS IN THE CONTROLLED MEDIA AND IN VOTERS' BEHAVIOUR: A COMPARISON

The analysis of the presence and activity of parties and politicians online (the *supply side*) is an analysis of the controlled media.[2] That is, the content of the websites and social-networking sites of parties and politicians is under their control. These platforms allow political actors to address the public directly, without any (online or offline) mediation by journalists. Politicians see the Web as an efficient campaign channel that allows them to directly communicate with and mobilize voters, to build a modern image and to increase their own visibility (Karlsen 2011). The *supply side* of online personalized politics can be seen as part of the campaign behaviour of parties and candidates, and as such analysing it adds to the existing knowledge on the personalized politics of political campaigns (see also Pruysers and Cross and Chiru, this volume). It is, however, different in representing a form of personalized politics that also persists between elections.

In terms of control, the websites and social-networking sites of politicians resemble traditional partisan media outlets, paid advertisements and other types of campaign propaganda. Online communication also shares features with traditional mass media, such as the dissemination of written, verbal and visual pronouncements. However, it differs in its capacity to meld these features, and in its potentially much larger volume, higher speed, the option of establishing two-way and multiple communication channels and the ability of each online participant to become a publisher and to control his or her own publications (Gibson and Ward 2000).

Online-controlled media may also have an effect on news in the uncontrolled media (online and offline television, radio and newspapers), which may be seen as more important or as important. Journalists increasingly follow the presence of parties and politicians online and report accordingly (Vergeer, Hermans and Sams 2011) and politicians are conscious of this (Karlsen 2011).

Studies of offline-controlled media imply that we should expect to find high levels of personalized politics online. The literature on political campaigns indicates that the modern televised campaign puts the party leader at the forefront (Butler and Ranney 1992). Additionally, some studies (Cross and Young 2015; Zittel 2015) also show that there are personalized elements in the campaigns of individual candidates.

The analysis of the consumption of the output of parties and politicians online is an analysis of personalized politics in voters' behaviour. Unlike the studies that examine the impact of leaders' evaluations on the vote (Bittner this volume and 2011; Garzia 2011, 2014; Lobo and Curtice 2015) or the analysis of the use of the personal vote (Renwick and Pilet 2016), this topic is not directly about voting decisions. Although the identity of the users is unknown and may include youth with no voting rights and people from other countries, the political actors refer to and address them as potential voters, supplying them with political information and campaign messages. In addition, we mainly look at the behavioural patterns of citizens (or future citizens), whose main activity in democracy is that of voting, and it is about the consumption of material that intends to mobilize them in support of the suppliers, parties and politicians. The expression of this support is mainly through voting although a minority of online 'consumers' may be more politically active.

Studies of personalized politics and voters' behaviour are divided in their analysis concerning the impact of leaders on the vote (compare, e.g., Holmberg and Oscarsson 2011 to Bittner 2011). Yet most recent studies (e.g., Garzia 2014; Lobo and Curtice 2015; Bittner, this volume) attribute a significant impact to the voters' evaluation of leaders. Following this, we also expect to find personalized politics on the *consumption side* of online politics.

The Study of Personalized Politics Online

Online politics is winning increasing scholarly attention (Vergeer 2012). Within this field, personalized politics is sometimes addressed as one element out of several (e.g., Schweitzer 2012; Vaccari 2013) and is sometimes the focus of research (e.g., Hermans and Vergeer 2012). Like the study of personalized politics and personalization offline (see, for example, Adam and Maier 2010; Karvonen 2010; Pruysers, Cross and Katz, this volume), the online version is characterized by a gap between the theoretical expectation of finding high levels of personalized politics and the generally mixed, if not negative, empirical findings.

We understand personalized politics to centre on the prominence of individual politicians in comparison to political groupings. For example, Pruysers and Cross's (this volume) analysis regarding local campaigns finds that most candidates have their own websites, independent of their party's site. Yet many studies of online personalized politics focus on individual politicians without comparing them to their parties (Dolezal 2015; Enli and Skogerbø 2013; Hermans and Vergeer 2012; Karlsen 2011; Kruikemeier 2014; Lilleker and Koc-Michalska 2013). From our perspective, such studies ignore the 'other half' of the personalized politics story, the political parties. Without comparing parties to individual politicians and without measuring the ratio of their prominence, we cannot be sure if politicians are indeed more prominent than parties. That is, it may be that the volume of activity and consumption of both is high. If this is the case, then we cannot talk about predominantly personalized politics.

Some studies of online politics have directly compared parties and candidates. They identified (as in studies of offline politics; see, for example, Karvonen 2010) high variance in the levels of personalized politics between (Kruikemeier et al. 2015) and within (Livak, Lev-On and Doron 2014) countries. Reviewing these studies, we found some that claim that parties have the upper hand in the online world, whereas others identify clearly personalized politics and still others present a more nuanced picture (Vaccari 2013; Livak, Lev-On and Doron 2014; Larsson 2016; Small 2010; Hermans and Vergeer 2012; Karlsen 2011; Kruikemeier 2014; Schweitzer 2012; Jackson and Lilleker 2009). No one general conclusion can be drawn, and for good reason: such studies examine different platforms (e.g., websites, Facebook and Twitter), different countries and sometimes different political actors.

No study has yet covered as much cross-national ground as this chapter does. It looks at the supply side (existence of websites, Facebook pages, Twitter accounts and Facebook and Twitter activity), but it also examines the relatively neglected consumption side, that is, the extent to which citizens are connected to these sites. Moreover, it is the first work to compare party leaders to other prominent politicians. In addition, it looks beyond the election period. Twitter and Facebook activity does not disappear after elections (even if its intensity diminishes).

RESEARCH QUESTIONS AND HYPOTHESES

Do Online Platforms Encourage Personalized Politics or Rather Empower Political Parties?

The online world is a relatively new arena of democratic politics. It was created at a time when processes of party change and the personalization of politics in the offline world were already under way. Does this world empower parties and help them revive, or does it rather empower individual politicians?

Most scholars accept the notion that personalized politics is enhanced in the online world. Many see the platforms (especially Web 2.0 with its social-media features) as especially fitting for the enhancement of personalized politics because they allow unmediated direct interactions between politicians and citizens (Enli and Skogerbø 2013; Gibson and Ward 2009; Kruikemeier et al. 2015; Vergeer, Hermans and Sams 2011). The affordability of online platforms is another reason to expect that individual politicians, who typically do not have the considerable resources that parties often have, will be better off with these new tools (Calise 2011; Enli and Skogerbø 2013). In addition, one expects individuals to be more open to innovations than bureaucratic party organizations (Vaccari 2013; Small 2010). It can even be claimed that technology returned one of the properties of the premodern campaign, the personal interactive element, though in a new form (Vergeer, Hermans and Sams 2011).

However, the same online tools may also be used by parties (Bennett 2012; Ohr 2011; Vergeer 2012) and may thus help them to revive and enhance their status vis-à-vis individual politicians. They can use them to centralize their organizational control (Gibson and Ward 2009; Karlsen 2011). With their advantage in terms of staff and resources, they can better develop, activate and exploit the tools available in the online world (Druckman, Kifer and Parkin 2009; Vaccari 2013). Parties can tap these tools to revive some of their traditional functions: to rejuvenate forms of membership (Scarrow 2015), supply information directly to activists, members and supporters and improve and coordinate their organization and activities (Rommele 2003). Also, new intraparty realms for direct democracy and deliberative democracy can be developed. If television, as a visual medium, enhanced personalized politics by making it easier to present a persona rather than an abstract entity (McAllister 2007), the online world may allow parties, as abstract entities, to revive. In the online world, even abstract entities (parties) can have direct and unmediated connections with citizens (members, supporters, etc.).

The research question was posed in a dichotomous manner, yet as several scholars note, both sides, parties and individual politicians are expected to have some advantages and some disadvantages in the online world (Gibson and Ward 2009; Larsson 2016; Ohr 2011; Vaccari 2013; Vergeer 2012). Indeed, studies of personalized politics online identify variation in levels of personalized politics (Dolezal 2015; Hermans and Vergeer 2012; Karlsen 2011; Kruikemeier et al. 2015; Lilleker and Koc-Michalska 2013; Livak, Lev-On and Doron 2014; Vaccari 2013). They attribute these to such factors as the influence of the different electoral systems and political cultures at the country level, the type of selection methods and party ideology at the party level and gender and seniority at the individual level.

Following this discussion, and keeping variance in mind, we can suggest all three possible hypotheses: personalized politics may be enhanced online, may decline or maybe parties and politicians will both successfully use the opportunities found in the online realm and thus would maintain the offline balance in their powers. In short, we expect variation, but we are also interested to see if the general balance tips towards parties or individual politicians.

Who Benefits: Leaders or Other Politicians?

Beyond consideration of individual versus party is the question of which individuals within the party capitalize on personalization. As suggested throughout this volume, there are different levels of personalized politics; Pruysers and Cross explore local candidates, Chiru considers Members of Parliament, Gauja examines party members, Malloy and Puguntke and Webb consider party and governmental leaders, and so on. Here we examine whether personalized politics is dominated by the party leader or shared with other prominent party politicians.

Indeed, the reasons to expect personalized politics online are relevant to both party leaders and other politicians. But should we expect leaders to be more prominent than other important politicians, as in the offline world, or does the Web offer opportunities to equalize their status?

This question touches on a primary theme in research concerning online politics: Is the online world a continuation or a reflection of the 'real' world, or can it actually create change in the balance of power between political actors (Gibson and Ward 2009; Larsson and Kalsnes 2014; Samuel-Azran, Yarchi and Wolfsfeld 2015; Vaccari 2013)? The 'normalization' approach expects those who are powerful offline to be similarly powerful online. This approach is empirically supported by studies that suggest, for example, that large parties are more prominent online than small parties, and studies that demonstrate that the same citizens who participate offline tend to participate online and that parties and politicians use the Web for top-down controlled communication rather than for genuine interaction (Lev-On and Haleva-Amir, 2018; Gibson and McAllister 2015; Enli and Skogerbø 2013; Gibson and Ward 2009; Small 2010; Schweitzer 2012). Following this logic, we may expect that leaders, with their superior status and resources, would be more prominent online than offline.

The competing approach to 'normalization' is (depending on the context) the 'innovation' or 'equalization' approach. It sees the online world as an autonomous new arena. It claims that the new opportunities that Web 1.0, and especially Web 2.0, supply to political actors change the balance of power among them. That is, individual politicians who are not party leaders can potentially compensate for their relative weakness in the offline world by using the tools and opportunities of the online world. Those who are likely to take advantage of online opportunities are those who suffer from offline deficits. Some studies present findings that support this approach, for example, studies that demonstrate that power relations offline are significantly different from those online (e.g., large and small parties have a somewhat more equal status on the Web; see, for example, Gibson and McAllister 2015); that young citizens, who are inactive offline, tend to participate online; or that parties and politicians utilize the Web for direct unmediated two-way communication (Vaccari 2013).

Following these approaches, two competing hypotheses can be proposed: the 'normalization thesis' leads us to expect higher levels of personalized politics in the case of party leaders, whereas the 'equalization' or 'innovation' thesis suggests that party leaders and other politicians will stand on more equal ground in the online world.

METHODOLOGY

Our cross-national study is based on a database that covers aspects of online politics in twenty-five democracies: fifteen relatively old, established European democracies (Austria, Belgium, Denmark, Finland, France, Germany, Iceland, Ireland, Italy, Luxemburg, Netherlands, Norway, Sweden, Switzerland and the United Kingdom); five non-European veteran democracies (Australia, Canada, Israel, Japan and New Zealand); two early (Portugal and Spain) and three late (Czech Republic, Hungary and Poland) third-wave European democracies. The research population includes, in each country, all parties that won 4 percent or more of the vote in the two most recent general elections to the lower houses before February 2015 (a total of 120 parties); their political leaders as of early 2015 (a total of 127 because several parties have coleaders); and in twenty-three of the twenty-five countries, three prominent politicians other than the leader from each party. The identity of these politicians was determined through an expert survey.[3] The research population thus comprises three types of political actors: parties, their leaders and three other prominent politicians from each party. Thus, we distinguish between the very top of the party (the leader) and other prominent party figures.

Our first examination of the supply side is the very presence of the actors online: did they have a website, Facebook page or Twitter account in the first months of 2015? Next, we examine online activity. In the case of Facebook, we counted the number of times that each actor updated its Facebook page within a given month (January 15–February 14, 2015) to measure supply (personalized online-controlled media); the number of page fans in a given day in February–May 2015 was coded for a measure of consumption (personalized online voters' behaviour). For Twitter, the average number of Tweets per month (supply, personalized online-controlled media) and the number of followers (consumption, personalized online voters' behaviour) were coded.[4] Then the ratios for both supply (updates/Tweets) and consumption (fans/followers) between parties, on the one hand, and individual politicians, on the other, were calculated. For each party the leader-to-party ratio and the prominent politicians-to-party ratio (average for the prominent three) were calculated. The higher values were put in the numerator. Finally, a minus sign was assigned when the value for parties was higher and a positive value when the value for individual politicians was higher. Thus, the resulting personalized politics index for each case ranges up from 1 or down from –1. Then, the average and median values for each country were calculated (for more details see Rahat and Kenig, forthcoming).[5]

To interpret the values of the index, a cutoff point was defined. It differentiated between values that express personalized politics and those that do not. Values equal to or higher than (-2) were defined as indicating personalized politics and values lower than (-2) signified that parties have the upper hand. The logic of this cutoff point is simple and is based on the notion that the party, which is a group that includes a leader and additional politicians, can be expected to be at least twice as active (updates/tweets) or 'consumed' (fans/followers) as its leader or any other individual politician.

An analysis of parties' and politicians' posts was used to 'zoom in' to their online activity. Because such an examination is costly, we limited it to the analysis of Facebook posts of Israeli parties, leaders and three prominent politicians within a given month (January 15, 2015–February 14, 2015).[6] Israeli politics is highly personalized both online (as we will see) and offline (Balmas et al. 2014). It is thus interesting to see whether the high levels of personalized politics are moderated or remain high when taking a closer look at the content of the posts. A party leader or any politician may have his or her own Twitter account but nonetheless focus on the party platform, branding, etc. In that case, personalized activity and its consumption would also benefit the party. Indeed, the relationship between personalized and partisan politics is not always zero-sum.

The levels of personalized politics of the Israeli posts were assessed as follows. In the analysis of those presented by parties, we measured the shares of posts that mentioned the party leader and of posts that mentioned any other politician from the party. For posts presented by party leaders, we measured the share of posts that mentioned the party by name or by its logo. Regarding posts by the three prominent politicians, we calculated the average share of posts that mentioned the party by name or logo.

FINDINGS OF THE CROSS-NATIONAL COMPARISON

Supply (Controlled-Online Media Personalized Politics): Presence in the Online World

A first sign of the relative status of parties and politicians in the online world is their presence. Table 6.1 presents data on the online presence of parties (P), party leaders (PL) and the other three prominent politicians from each party (PP).

It is clear that parties have a greater online presence, particularly in the number of websites. All parties but one (Israel's ultra-religious Shas) had websites, whereas less than 60 percent of politicians had personal websites. In twenty of the twenty-five countries, the share of parties that had websites was higher than the share of individual politicians. In five countries, there was 100 percent presence of parties and their leaders. Of these, in Australia and Finland, all actors had complete online presence. Thus, regarding websites, parties are doing better, and never worse, than individual politicians.

With Facebook, parties still have the upper hand, but the gap is much narrower than for websites. Virtually all parties (again excluding Shas) have Facebook accounts, as do 90 percent of party leaders and 76 percent of prominent politicians. In nine of the twenty-five countries, a higher share of parties had Facebook accounts than individual politicians. In twelve countries, all parties and party leaders had Facebook accounts, meaning they had equal presence. In three countries, all actors had 100 percent presence, whereas in Israel, party leaders had 100 percent presence, parties 88 percent and prominent politicians 79 percent. Thus, the gap between parties and individual politicians is not only lower than for websites in general, but in the case of party leaders it does not exist in most countries (sixteen out of twenty-five).

Twitter falls somewhere in between websites and Facebook. Although almost all (97 percent) parties had Twitter accounts, 80 percent of party leaders and 68 percent of the prominent politicians had them. In twelve of the twenty-five countries, a higher share of parties had Twitter accounts than individual politicians. In eight countries, all parties and party leaders had Twitter accounts. In four countries, all actors had 100 percent presence. In Israel 88 percent of the party leaders had Twitter accounts, as did 63 percent of parties and 42 percent of prominent politicians. Thus, the parties' edge is more evident than in the Facebook platform, but still in almost half the countries (twelve of twenty-five) party leaders are on par with parties.

From these data we see that in general parties are more present online than individual politicians because they have more websites and social-media pages. The gap is larger when it comes to websites. Websites might be a thing of the past, and Web 2.0 might well reflect the latest trends. Indeed, a candidate survey in Norway found that candidates saw social media as more beneficial than personal websites (Karlsen 2009). A study of the Israeli case that compared 2010 and 2015 found a decline in the number of members of parliament who had personal websites and an increase in those with Facebook and Twitter accounts (Zamir and Rahat 2017). Looking at national patterns, we find many cases where parties and their leaders are on par on social media. Parties are less present only in one case, are on par in about half (or less in the case of websites) and are more present in the rest. Overall, in terms of presence, parties have the upper hand.

Supply (Controlled-Online Media Personalized Politics): Parties' and Politicians' Activity in the Online World

Table 6.2 presents another aspect of the supply side, the levels of online activity. It shows the average and median values of the national ratios of Facebook updates in a given month, in terms of the parties-to-leaders ratio (columns two and three) and the parties-to-prominent politicians ratio (columns four and five). It also presents the average and median values of the national ratios of Tweets in a month, in terms of the parties-to-leaders ratio (columns six and seven) and parties-to-prominent politicians ratio (columns eight and nine).

A comparison of the values that appear in the last two rows of table 6.2, total averages and medians for all cases, demonstrates that parties are somewhat more active online than individual politicians: twelve out of sixteen values are below our cutoff point, pointing to partisan prominence. Of the 190 values that appear in the table, 101 (53 percent) are below the cutoff point, whereas 89 (47 percent) indicate personalized politics. The values of the total medians are not far from the cutoff point (range –1.5 to –2.7). The overall picture thus illustrates some leverage for parties. Yet there is high variance and high range: there are countries in which seven out of eight of the values attest to personalized politics (Austria, Canada, Luxemburg and New Zealand), and in others, all values are about nonpersonalized politics (Iceland, Portugal and Switzerland).

When comparing total averages and medians (last two rows of table 6.2) of the online personalized politics index of party leaders to that of prominent politicians, seven out of eight values suggest more activity from prominent politicians than of party leaders. This is translated into four out of eight values above the cutoff point for prominent politicians and none for party leaders. Out of the ninety-eight values of the party leader-to-party ratio, forty-five (46 percent) point to personalized politics; of the ninety-two values of the prominent politicians-to-party ratio, forty-four (48 percent) point to personalized politics. In ten countries, it is higher for party leaders; in eight countries,

Table 6.2 Supply Side: Ratio of Parties' and Politicians' Facebook Posts and Twitter Tweets*

	Facebook Updates in a Given Month				*Tweets per Month*			
	Party Leader-to-Party Ratio		*Prominent Politicians-to-Party Ratio*		*Party Leader-to-Party Ratio*		*Prominent Politicians-to-Party Ratio*	
Country	*Average*	*Median*	*Average*	*Median*	*Average*	*Median*	*Average*	*Median*
Australia	**0.2**	**0.4**	**–0.1**	**0.0**	–3.5	–4.7	**–1.3**	**–1.5**
Austria	**–0.6**	**–1.6**	**–0.5**	**–1.6**	**2.6**	**2.6**	**–1.5**	–2.1
Belgium	–8.6	–3.5	**–0.5**	**–1.7**	–84.4	**–1.9**	**–0.5**	**–1.2**
Canada	**–1.0**	**–1.2**	–2.3	**–1.6**	**0.3**	**0.2**	**1.7**	**1.4**
Czech Rep.	–26.6	–8.1	–2.6	–2.6	–2.4	–2.4	**–1.0**	–3.4
Denmark	**–0.6**	**1.2**	–2.2	**–1.5**	–3.0	–2.2	**–0.1**	**2.7**
Finland	–20.1	–2.8	–4.6	–3.6	–4.7	–5.7	–4.2	**–1.8**
France	–3.4	–3.6	–6.0	–5.3	–5.4	**–1.4**	–11.4	–3.5
Germany	–5.4	**–0.3**	–3.8	**–1.4**	**–1.6**	–2.3	–2.8	–3.4
Hungary	**–1.9**	–2.0	–4.6	–4.5			**–1.9**	**–1.9**
Iceland	–7.7	–8.6	–13.9	–3.6	–45.4	–8.1	–5.7	–4.8
Ireland	–8.2	–8.2	**–1.9**	–2.4	–27.9	–14.1	–4.5	–3.5
Israel	**–0.3**	**–1.1**	–2.2	–2.0	**–0.6**	**0.1**	**0.8**	**0.8**
Italy	**–1.6**	**–1.6**	–2.2	**–1.9**	–7.8	–4.6	–5.2	–4.6
Japan	**–1.9**	–2.7	–3.2	**–1.0**	–3.7	–3.1	–5.1	–3.6
Luxembourg	**–0.6**	**–0.4**	**0.3**	–2.3	**–0.3**	**1.1**	**0.1**	**1.0**
Netherlands	–9.0	–2.7	–12.1	–2.8	**–0.2**	**1.2**	–2.9	**–1.4**
New Zealand	**–1.1**	**–1.8**	**–1.2**	**–1.8**	–2.2	**–1.8**	**–0.7**	**–1.7**
Norway	**–1.7**	**–1.7**	–2.7	–2.0	**–1.3**	**–1.7**	**–0.7**	**–1.7**
Poland	–2.1	–2.1			**–1.9**	**–1.9**		
Portugal	–106.6	–21.0			–5.1	–5.1		
Spain	–3.9	–3.3	–3.0	**–1.4**	**–1.6**	**–1.2**	–2.1	–3.3
Sweden	–3.7	**–1.3**	–11.0	**–1.5**	**0.4**	**1.3**	**3.8**	**2.0**

Switzerland	–25.6	–7.0	–10.1	–7.5	–4.3	–2.8	–3.3	–3.6
United Kingdom	**–1.4**	–2.6	–9.8	**–1.5**	–3.7	–3.3	**–0.7**	**–1.5**
Total Average	–9.7	–3.5	–4.4	–2.4	–8.7	–2.6	–2.1	**–1.8**
Total Median	–2.1	–2.1	–2.7	**–1.9**	–2.7	–2.1	**–1.5**	**–1.8**

*__Bold__ means personalized politics: The value is higher than the cutoff point of –2 (i.e., the parties have less than twice the updates/likes than the politicians).

Notes: (1)The ratios of prominent politicians-to-party ratio are based on the average values of three prominent politicians in each party. Prominent politicians without accounts were not included in this calculation. (2) Parties in which the leader or party did not have an active account were not included in the calculation of the average/median of their country. (3) Facebook topic pages containing information mainly from Wikipedia were not considered because they do not allow active updating. (4) In Hungary only one prominent politician had a Twitter account. The values for Hungary for Twitter that appear in the table are thus based on the ratio between this prominent politician and his party. (5) Data for Poland contain only information about party leaders. Only one Polish party leader had an active Twitter account. The values concerning Twitter in Poland that appear in the table are based on the ratio between this party leader and his party. In addition, only two Polish leaders had active Facebook accounts. The values for Facebook updates in Poland that appear in the table are based on the ratio between these party leaders and their parties. (6) Data for Portugal contain only information about party leaders. Only one Portuguese party leader had an active Twitter account. The values for Twitter updates in Portugal that appear on the table are thus based on the ratio between this party leader and his party. (7) The values for the prominent politicians-to-party ratio on Twitter for Israel are based on two parties. In the other Israeli parties, prominent politicians or the parties did not have an active Twitter account. Similarly, the values of party leader-to-party on Twitter for Israel are based on ratios of four parties; in the other parties, the party or the leader did not have an active account. (8) The values of the leader-to-party ratio for Twitter in Austria and the Czech Republic are based on only two parties in each country. In the other Czech and Austrian parties, the leaders did not have a Twitter account. (9) The values of the leader-to-party ratios for Facebook updates in Ireland are based on only two parties; in the remaining Irish parties, the leaders did not have a Facebook account.

it is higher for prominent politicians; in four countries, the numbers are even. In general, levels of prominent politicians' online personalized politics are somewhat higher than those of the party leaders. That is, online tools are used to equalize the status of prominent politicians vis-à-vis their parties' leaders. We also checked if there is a correlation between the levels of activity of leaders and other politicians and found moderate and significant correlations between the medians of Facebook updates and tweets of the party leaders and prominent politicians (Pearson's $r=0.51$ $p<0.05$; Pearson's $r=0.50$ $p<0.05$).

Consumption: Online Personalized Voters' Behaviour

Table 6.3 presents the consumption side, that is, the levels of online personalized politics in voters' behaviour. It outlines the average and median values of the national ratios of Facebook page fans in a given month, in terms of parties-to-leaders ratio (columns two and three) and parties-to-prominent politicians ratio as of the first half of 2015 (columns four and five). It also presents the average and median values of the national ratios of Twitter followers in that period, in terms of parties-to-leaders ratio (columns six and seven) and parties-to-prominent politicians ratio (columns eight and nine).

The values in the last two rows of table 6.3, total averages and medians, demonstrate that consumption of politicians online is higher than that of parties: eleven out of sixteen values are above our cutoff point and suggest personalized politics. Of the 190 values that appear in table 6.3, 117 (62%) are above the cutoff point, whereas 73 (38%) are below it. The values of the total averages and medians range from 5.5 to –13.9. There is high national variance and high range: there are countries in which seven out of eight values testify to personalized politics (Australia, Belgium and Israel), and in others, only two out of eight values (Germany, Ireland and Sweden), or one of four (Poland) are about personalized politics. Thus, in general, there are signs of personalized voters' behaviour, but cross-country variance within a rather wide range is also evident.

When comparing total averages and medians (last two rows of table 6.3) of party leaders to other prominent politicians, in eight out of eight comparisons, we witness higher consumption for party leaders than for prominent politicians. This is translated into seven out of eight values above the cutoff point for party leaders and four of eight for prominent politicians. Of the ninety-eight values of the party leaders-to-party ratio, seventy-seven (79 percent) point to personalized politics; of the ninety-two values of the prominent politicians-to-party ratio, forty (43 percent) point to personalized politics. In nineteen countries, there are more values that testify to personalized politics of party leaders; in only two countries are there more values

Table 6.3 Consumption Side: Ratio of Parties' and Politicians' Facebook Fans and Twitter Followers*

	Facebook Fans				*Twitter Followers*			
	Party Leader-to-Party Ratio		*Prominent Politicians-to-Party Ratio*		*Party Leader-to-Party Ratio*		*Prominent Politicians-to-Party Ratio*	
Country	*Average*	*Median*	*Average*	*Median*	*Average*	*Median*	*Average*	*Median*
Australia	**–0.6**	**–0.4**	**–1.1**	–2.8	**1.1**	**1.3**	**1.5**	**2.0**
Austria	–2.8	–2.2	–11.8	–12.4	**3.8**	**3.8**	**–1.0**	**–1.5**
Belgium	**–1.6**	**–1.6**	–4.8	**–1.5**	**1.4**	**1.4**	**2.5**	**1.9**
Canada	**0.4**	**0.2**	–7.5	–7.0	**4.7**	**3.3**	–4.4	–4.4
Czech Rep.	–2.9	–2.8	–7.7	–9.3	**1.5**	**1.5**	–2.8	–2.4
Denmark	**1.0**	**1.1**	**–1.8**	–2.1	**1.9**	**1.3**	–5.3	**–1.8**
Finland	**–0.8**	**–1.7**	–5.6	–3.8	**4.1**	**1.9**	–2.4	**–1.2**
France	**0.8**	**2.9**	–2.1	**–1.8**	**2.9**	**5.1**	**0.7**	**1.1**
Germany	**0.4**	**–1.5**	–6.5	–3.8	–4.1	–2.9	–3.4	–2.4
Hungary	–2.0	**–1.3**	–8.8	–11.7			**1.3**	**1.3**
Iceland	**0.1**	**0.1**	–3.7	–3.6	**0.7**	**3.0**	**0.6**	**1.4**
Ireland	–7.7	–5.7	–3.3	–3.1	**0.2**	**0.2**	–3.5	–3.4
Israel	**21.4**	**8.7**	–13.1	**0.2**	**40.3**	**37.5**	**0.1**	**0.1**
Italy	**6.8**	**5.2**	–3.1	–2.3	**10.8**	**9.9**	**0.2**	**2.1**
Japan	**–1.2**	**–1.7**	–6.7	–7.2	**0.5**	**0.2**	**–1.8**	**–0.7**
Luxembourg	–35.6	**–1.1**	**–0.4**	**1.2**	**5.9**	**1.1**	**14.1**	**1.5**
Netherlands	–12.0	–5.0	–69.4	–30.6	**17.3**	**3.8**	–2.2	**–1.2**
New Zealand	–2.4	**1.0**	–93.4	–6.5	**8.3**	**8.2**	**–1.0**	**0.1**
Norway	**0.7**	**1.6**	–8.0	–8.3	**3.2**	**2.6**	**–1.9**	**–1.8**
Poland	–8.4	–6.8			**22.2**	–2.0		
Portugal	–5.1	**1.7**			**1.9**	**1.9**		
Spain	**–0.6**	**–1.1**	–2.0	–2.1	**1.0**	**1.2**	**–0.6**	**–1.2**
Sweden	–5.6	–2.9	–12.9	–12.7	**–0.4**	**–1.5**	–2.8	–2.2

(continued)

Table 6.3 Consumption Side: Ratio of Parties' and Politicians' Facebook Fans and Twitter Followers* (continued)

	Facebook Fans				*Twitter Followers*			
	Party Leader-to-Party Ratio		*Prominent Politicians-to-Party Ratio*		*Party Leader-to-Party Ratio*		*Prominent Politicians-to-Party Ratio*	
Country	*Average*	*Median*	*Average*	*Median*	*Average*	*Median*	*Average*	*Median*
Switzerland	–55.5	–3.8	–5.3	–5.6	**–0.5**	**0.3**	**–0.1**	**0.1**
United Kingdom	**–1.0**	**–1.2**	–39.6	–50.2	**3.8**	**2.6**	**0.2**	**–1.7**
Total Average	–4.6	**–0.7**	–13.9	–8.1	**5.5**	**3.6**	**–0.5**	**–0.6**
Total Median	**–1.2**	**–1.2**	–6.5	–3.8	**2.4**	**1.7**	**–1.0**	**–1.2**

***Bold** means personalized politics: The value is higher than the cutoff point of –2 (i.e., the parties have less than twice the updates/tweets/fans/followers than the politicians).

Notes: (1) The ratios of prominent politicians-to-party are based on the average values of the three prominent politicians in each party. Prominent politicians who did not have accounts were not included in this calculation. (2) Parties in which the leader or party did not have an active account were not included in the calculation of the average/median of their country. (3) Facebook topic pages were included because they contained accessible information on the number of fans of politicians and parties. This information enabled us to examine the way that Facebook users chose to consume information about parties and politicians even if they did not have active pages. In personal Facebook profiles, we examined the number of Facebook 'followers' or 'friends' because fans' were not an option. (4) In Hungary only one prominent politician had a Twitter account. The values for Twitter in Hungary that appear on the table are based on the ratio between this prominent politician and his party. (5) Data for Poland contain only information about party leaders. Only one Polish party leader had an active Twitter account, yet other Polish party leaders had nonactive accounts that had been followed by thousands of users. Therefore, values for Twitter in Poland on the consumption side contain the ratio between four party leaders and their parties. (6) Data for Portugal contain only information about party leaders. Only one Portuguese party leader had an active Twitter account. The Twitter values of Portugal that appear on the table are thus based on the ratio between this party leader and his party. (7) The ratios prominent politicians-to-party for Twitter in Israel are based on ratios of two parties. In the rest of the Israeli parties, prominent politicians or the parties did not have an active Twitter account. In addition the leader-to-party ratio for Twitter in Israel are based on ratios of four parties. In the rest of the Israeli parties, the party or the leader did not have an active account. (8) The leader-to-party Twitter values of Austria and the Czech Republic are based on ratios of only two parties. In the rest of the Czech and Austrian parties, the leaders did not have an active Twitter account.

attesting to higher levels of personalized politics of other prominent politicians; and only in two countries are the numbers even. In general, levels of online personalized politics of party leaders are much higher than those of other politicians. That is, consumption online reflects the superior status of party leaders vis-à-vis other prominent politicians.

Table 6.4 presents summary data (averages and medians) for supply and consumption. First, in twelve of sixteen comparisons, the values of consumption lean more towards personalized politics than those of supply. In addition, only four values regarding supply are above the cutoff point, and eleven for consumption are above it. Personalized politics is clearly more evident when it comes to consumption. Second, prominent politicians seem to work harder in the cases of both Facebook and Twitter. That is, levels of online personalized politics (controlled media) are higher among prominent politicians in comparison to leaders. But when it comes to consumption (voters' behaviour), levels of online personalized politics are much higher for leaders compared to prominent politicians.

It might be expected that supply (updates/tweets) and consumption (fans/followers) will correlate. That is, efforts (measured as intensity of updates/tweets) will be rewarded (measured in number of fans/followers). He or she who presents more posts and tweets will have more fans and followers. Yet the eight possible correlations we examined were weak and insignificant. It might be that those who are less popular try harder because they wish to attain the level of the more successful actors. Indeed, a study of politicians' activity on Facebook and Twitter in Sweden and Norway in a nonelection period found that the most active actors were the 'underdogs', younger, and less-experienced backbenchers (Larsson and Kalsnes 2014). Yet, we did not find any moderate and significant negative correlation either. However, we checked correlations at the country level, and it might be the case at the level of the party and individual politicians that clearer patterns emerge.

We also looked at the composition of the group of the top-twenty actors in terms of the amount of Facebook page fans and Twitter followers, out of the total population: 120 parties, 127 party leaders and 323 prominent politicians from the twenty-five countries. Fifteen of the twenty leading actors were party leaders and two were prominent politicians. Two of the three parties in the top-twenty list are clearly highly personalized parties (M5S and Jobbik). In the case of Twitter, only one personalized party (M5S) was found in the top twenty, and most of the politicians on the list were also party leaders (fifteen out of nineteen). This seems to imply that although personalized politics is not a predetermined consequence for all actors in all countries, the top political online realm is more personalized in terms of consumption.

Table 6.4 Supply and Consumption: Ratios of Parties and Politicians Facebook Updates/Fans and Twitter Tweets/Followers: Summary Data for Twenty-Five Democracies*

	Facebook				*Twitter*			
	Party Leader-to-Party Ratio		*Prominent Politicians-to- Party Ratio*		*Party Leader-to-Party Ratio*		*Prominent Politicians-to-Party Ratio*	
	Average	*Median*	*Average*	*Median*	*Average*	*Median*	*Average*	*Median*
Total Average Supply	–9.7	–3.5	–4.4	–2.4	–8.7	–2.6	–2.1	**–1.8**
Total Average Consumption	–4.6	**–0.7**	–13.9	–8.1	**5.5**	**3.6**	**–0.5**	**–0.6**
Total Median Supply	–2.1	–2.1	–2.7	**–1.9**	–2.7	–2.1	**–1.5**	**–1.8**
Total Median Consumption	**–1.2**	**–1.2**	–6.5	–3.8	**2.4**	**1.7**	**–1.0**	**–1.2**

***Bold** means personalized politics: The value is higher than the cutoff point of –2 (i.e., the party has less than twice as many updates/tweets/fans/followers than the politicians).

PERSONALIZED POLITICS OF FACEBOOK POSTS: THE ISRAELI CASE

Pruysers and Cross (this volume) reveal that 'party' communications can be highly personalized around the leader. The reverse could also be true for 'leader' communications. That is, posts and updates from a given party leader can be party-centric, rather than leader-centric; although the fact that politicians rather than parties become the main carrier of the message is a sign for personalization, the message may still be partisan or personalized or some mix of both. What are the politicians posting about? Themselves? Their party? Only by examining the content of the online activity can we get a complete picture of online politics and the degree of personalism. This section examines Israeli political actors' Facebook posts. The dates studied (January 15–February 14, 2015) were quite close to the election date (March 17, 2015). The parties' online activity can thus be perceived as part of the election campaign. This could have made it more partisan in the context of the Israeli closed list electoral system. Yet, high levels of personalized politics are evident in Israel also in the context of electoral politics (Balmas et al. 2014). Indeed, in a comparative perspective (tables 6.2 and 6.3), Israel (even at the time of partisan elections) is highly personalized in terms of supply and even more so in terms of consumption.

Looking at the supply side of the posts, we sought to examine, on the one hand, to what extent parties related to their politicians in their posts, and on the other hand, to what extent individual politicians related to their party.

Figure 6.1 shows the share of posts in which Israeli parties mentioned their politicians (leader, other politicians or both).[7] Thus, the first measure is for personalized politics in general, the second is for party leaders and the third is for prominent politicians.

Evidently, there are differences in the levels of personalized politics between the parties (the range is 78 to 38 percent). The differences between levels of personalized politics of leaders compared to other prominent politicians also vary. In some parties, the leader's share is higher than all other politicians' combined. Especially prominent is the 'leader party' Yesh Atid, which mentioned its leader in 55 percent of the party posts compared to only 19 percent of posts that mentioned its other politicians. Meanwhile, in some other parties, the other politicians' share is higher than that of the leader. In another 'leader party', Yisrael Beyteinu, only 20 percent of the posts mentioned the leader, whereas 38 percent mentioned other politicians from the party list that he nominated. The Joint List is an extreme example because it did not mention its leader (Ayman Odeh) ever. The most personalized party in terms of its posts, the Likud, mentioned its other politicians more than it mentioned its leader, Prime Minister Benjamin Netanyahu.

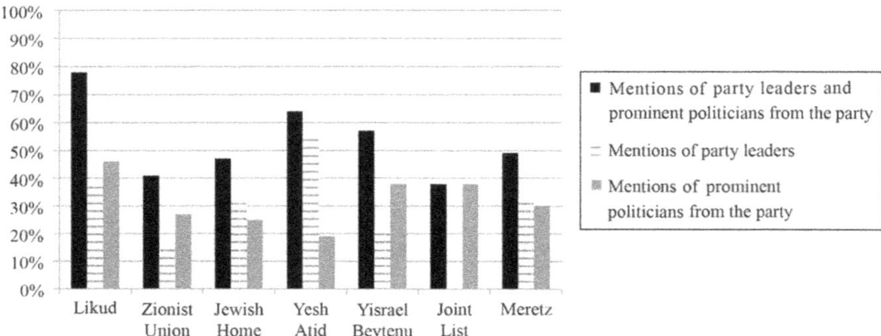

Figure 6.1 Mentions of Party Leaders and Prominent Politicians in Posts Presented by Israeli Parties (Percentage of Posts).

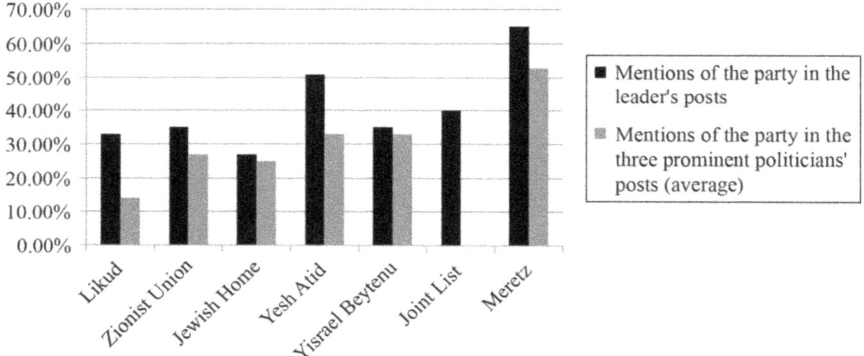

Figure 6.2 Mentions of Party Name or Logo in Facebook Posts Presented by Leaders and Prominent Politicians in Israel (Percentage of Posts).

To summarize, there is clearly interparty variance in the general levels of personalized politics and in its focus.

Figure 6.2 presents the partisan content of posts of individual politicians, party leaders and three prominent politicians.[8] Interparty variance is evident once again. Party leaders are found to be more partisan than other politicians. This would be a surprise if we expected weaker politicians to use their party affiliation as a resource more than the stronger politicians (the leaders). Our interpretation of these findings is that in the context of highly personalized politics in Israel, the politician whose status is defined by his position as the party leader is more likely to mention it than other politicians. The party may be identified with the leader, whereas other politicians have to tout their uniqueness compared to their fellow partisans.[9]

CONCLUSIONS

High variation in the national levels of online personalized politics demonstrates that it is not a necessary development. There is no technological determinism at play here and both parties and individual politicians can exploit the opportunities of the online world. However, the lack of correlation between supply and consumption seems to imply that attempts to be active online do not necessarily result in higher consumption.

Although in terms of presence and activity parties usually have the upper hand, in terms of consumption personalized politics is more evident, especially for party leaders.[10] Interestingly, the presidentialization thesis (Poguntke and Webb 2005; see also their contribution in this volume; Webb, Poguntke and Kolodny 2012) finds support in terms of consumption but not of supply.

There is an element in the findings on personalized politics that may nevertheless be evidence of the power of parties; if the online activity of party leaders is consumed much more than other prominent politicians, this suggests that there is something that their status in the party gives them. This interpretation may be further supported by the finding that party leaders tend to mention their parties in their posts more than other politicians. We may further argue that the party is the factor that makes a specific politician the most consumed by the public. Because politicians come and go while parties stay, we may claim that they still have the upper hand.

Yet, this perspective emphasizes only one side of the story. For highly personalized parties, the party is a vehicle for the leader, not vice versa. But beyond these cases, at a time when the party-society linkage is weakening, the strength of party leaders may not always reflect the strength of parties, but rather the fact that parties, as state-regulated organs, are a necessity for any ambitious politician.

NOTES

1. 'Personalization' refers to a process and as such should be empirically studied as a development over time, generally requiring at least two points in time. However, in the case of online politics, we may be justified in looking at a single point in time because this is a world that was recently created, starting from point zero. Still, following the approach of the editors of this volume, we frame our research here as personalized politics and not as political personalization (see Rahat and Kenig, forthcoming, for an expanded approach).

2. The use here of the term 'controlled' media, rather than 'paid' media used by Rahat and Sheafer (2007) and Balmas et al. (2014), should be credited to Karlsen (2011).

3. We asked each country expert to identify three prominent politicians from each party. Most did so; sometimes we got more and often fewer names. The experts explained the deviations and we accepted their reasoning. We ended up with names of 323 prominent politicians who were not the parties' political leaders.

4. One can consume Twitter page content without being a follower. However, being a Twitter follower as well as a Facebook fan is a sign that the user is interested in a specific topic, person or organization. Furthermore, by following or becoming a fan, the user makes his or her interest publicly known, thus expressing his or her consumption habits to other users. Therefore, following or becoming fans is not only the most available proxy for online consumption, but it is also the most appropriate one.

5. National averages, and medians when having an even number of cases, may still have a value between 1 and (–1).

6. The posts were downloaded through the Netvizz App in Facebook connecting the API server. Though the dates are the same as in the first section, some posts of politicians and parties (Likud, Benjamin Netanyahu and Naftali Bennett) were deleted or disappeared in the months before we conducted the analysis and thus could not be downloaded and analysed. The three prominent politicians of the Joint List (Masud Ganaim, Jamal Zahalka and Ahmad Tibi) held personal Facebook accounts; therefore their posts could not be downloaded and analysed. All the politicians of the ultra-religious parties (except Shas leader Aryeh Deri) did not have active Facebook accounts and therefore were not part of the analysis.

7. The ultra-religious parties were not included in this analysis because one of them posted only two updates during the examined period and the other (Shas) did not have a Facebook page. In addition, the three prominent politicians of the Joint List had private profiles and could not be analysed here.

8. UTJ politicians and Shas' prominent politicians are not on Facebook and therefore were not included in the analysis. In addition, the Joint List's three prominent politicians had private profiles that could not been analysed.

9. A comparison of the number of mentions of individual politicians by the parties and the number of party mentions by individual politicians found no clear general pattern. A comparison of the average number of likes of the posts presented by each type of political actor found, similarly to the previous section, that personalized politics is more evident on the consumption side and that consumption is higher for leaders than for other politicians.

10. When examining Twitter, however, it is even the case for other politicians (although at a lower level).

Chapter 7

Party Organization and Personalization

Anika Gauja

Like the contributions by Stewart and Rahat and Zamir in this volume, this chapter focuses on the 'party face' of personalization. Specifically, it examines the intersection between personalization and party organization, exploring the causes and mechanisms of personalized politics within parties and the implications of a more personalized mode of politics for how parties organize and for party democracy more generally. As noted in the introductory chapter to this volume, most existing studies of personalization focus on political elites (party leaders, politicians, candidates, etc.) at different levels of the party. As will be explained, in so far as they are applied to parties as organizations, these accounts find overwhelming evidence of a transfer of power to party elites at the 'centre' or national level of the party (centralized personalization), or at the peripheries (decentralized personalization). This can occur through changes to conference arrangements, candidate selection processes, leadership-selection contest rules or policy-development processes, providing the institutional bases for party personalization to occur.

To push the debate on party personalization further, I suggest that we also need to understand how personalization is occurring from the 'bottom-up'. That is, to shift our focus from party elites to members and supporters to better appreciate how these institutional changes are accompanied by—or in many cases facilitated by—more individualized, or personalized, forms of partisan participation. In some ways, this can be seen as a complementary analysis to understanding decentralized forms of personalization, where power is dispersed from the leadership group to individual candidates (Balmas et al. 2014; also see the Introduction to this volume). However, my argument differs from a decentralized account of party personalization in one important respect: I argue that personalization is a concept that can be applied beyond candidates, leaders and parliamentarians as *political elites* to party members and supporters as *political participants*. Hence, if we talk about personalization at different levels (or layers) of the party, this account of personalized party politics would sit at the very bottom of the personalization hierarchy.

I have developed this perspective drawing on insights from several different literatures, including social-movement studies and media and communications scholarship and integrating these accounts with the existing literature on party personalization and intraparty democracy. The consequences of personalization for party organizations are potentially profound. In some ways, a more personalized style of politics creates a new way of organizing for parties and presents a myriad of lower-cost opportunities for individuals to engage with these institutions. In this sense, personalization is not always antithetical to the party. However, it also comes at the risk of undermining the traditional institutions of intraparty democracy and decision making, including the power of organized subgroupings, the 'common identity' of the party organization and its ability to engage in collective action.

The chapter is set out in three sections. The first canvasses the diversity of ways in which the term *personalization* is used in different fields of inquiry and how this structures the way in which we conceive of the relationship between party organization and personalization. Analysing the dominant 'top-down' model of personalization, this section of the chapter presents the current picture of party organization by examining the empirical evidence that is used to substantiate the claim that party organizations are changing and that their role in modern democracies is gradually being eroded. The second section presents an alternative/complementary 'bottom-up' view of personalization that focuses on citizen participation and engagement. It provides additional indicators for assessing the impact of personalization on party organizations, concentrating on the increasing individualization of party membership through evolving channels of communication and participation, as well as the phenomenon of 'multispeed membership' (Scarrow 2015) and alternative modes of partisan affiliation. The third section presents some contemporary examples of the ways in which political parties are mediating more personalized relationships with their members and supporters and discusses the implications that this mode of personalization might hold for party organization and representative democracy.

PARTY ORGANIZATION AND PERSONALIZATION: A TOP-DOWN PERSPECTIVE

Although there appears to be some agreement about the genesis of personalization, in that it reflects a myriad of complex factors including the erosion of traditional political cleavages, a changing communication environment, the internationalization of politics and the growth and increasing complexity of the state (see for example, Passarelli 2015, 10; Karvonen 2010, 1; Poguntke and Webb 2005, 16), how it is manifested in contemporary politics and how it incorporates party organization into the analysis differs considerably, depending on one's analytical approach.

For those writing in the frame of electoral studies or on campaigning, where the primary role of parties is to mediate between candidates and voters, personalization is all about candidates and leaders. McAllister (2015, 337), for example, argues that the key consequence of personalization is that leaders have become much more prominent and that 'considerable popular attention is directed towards the personalities of the leaders'. For Karlsen and Skogerbø (2015, 428), the emphasis is on candidates, who build their own campaign organizations, and become—rather than the parties they represent—'the focus of the campaign communication'. For political communications scholars, personalization refers not only to a shift in the focus of media coverage, but also in what it emphasizes. In a personalized media environment, coverage 'goes beyond the visibility of individuals, instead referring to an increasing focus on their "character" or "personalities"' (Holtz-Bacha, Langer and Merkle 2014, 156). This may, as Thomas discusses in her chapter in this volume, also involve a process of 'privatization' in which the individual is examined in an increasingly 'nonpolitical' light with a focus on personal life, appearance, etc.

For those interested in political systems, personalization is inherently connected to the broader phenomenon of 'presidentialization', which reflects structural shifts in political institutions (Poguntke and Webb 2005, 5). Like the examples cited, the presidentialization thesis has at its core a focus on leaders and expresses a 'tension between political parties and individual leaders', with 'political power resources and autonomy' shifting to the latter at the expense of the former (Pogtunke and Webb 2005, 7).[1] Therefore, as a concept, personalization has institutional, media and campaign elements, which all point to a stronger focus on candidates or politicians instead of political parties and collective identities (see Balmas et al. 2014; Kriesi 2012, 826; Karvonen 2010, 4).

What is common to all these accounts of personalization is that they (a) signal a shift to the increasing visibility and power of political elites and (b) that they are presented as antithetical to the traditional roles of political parties as the primary collective organizations in systems of representative government. This has potentially serious implications for political parties. If we think about organization in terms of the structures that facilitate the performance of key party functions such as interest aggregation, policy development, candidate selection and political communication and education, then the prognosis for parties is not particularly bright. For example, Balmas et al.

(2014, 47) argue that 'personalization implies a decline in the role of parties' because of the following trends:

> People identify with personalities rather than parties; individual politicians, rather than parties, become the representatives of specific policies; interest aggregation occurs more on an *ad hoc* basis rather than within parties; individuals rather than parties communicate with the public; policy emerges from an interaction between individuals in government rather than as a product of debate and deliberation within the party; and, to a certain extent, candidates and leaders select parties rather than the other way round.

Poguntke and Webb offer a slightly different take on the organizational implications of presidentialization that is based on relationships of power within the party rather than functions of the party and suggest that organizational changes are all underpinned by 'a shift in intra-party power to the benefit of the leader' and 'growing leadership autonomy from the dominant coalitions of power within the party' (Poguntke and Webb 2005, 5). Although not quite as circumspect about the future of party organizations—'they have maintained their central role as a mechanism for elite selection'—presidentialization does nevertheless imply the 'weakening of party as a collective actor in modern democracies' (Webb and Poguntke 2005, 352; see also Poguntke and Webb, this volume).

Empirical Evidence of 'Top-Down' Personalization

Previous scholarship has suggested numerous ways in which we might find evidence of the impact of personalization on political party organizations. Individual behaviour that downgrades the importance of party, whether it is leaders seeking autonomy or voters making personal evaluations, would constitute personalization as antithetical to collective identity (see Balmas et al. 2014, 40). An empirical strategy might also focus on identifying changes in intraparty rules, processes and structures, along the lines suggested by Poguntke and Webb (2005, 20). For these authors, the following changes to party organization are particularly important:

- The institutionalization of direct leadership elections
- Rule changes that give leaders more formal powers
- The growth of leaders' offices (in terms of funding and personnel)
- Increasing autonomy in policy development
- The increasing use of plebiscitary and professional modes of communication to connect with voters and members.

A substantial body of existing research suggests that the organizational rules and processes of political parties are indeed changing in the ways described. These changes are so pervasive and ubiquitous that Webb and Poguntke state in the concluding chapter of their comparative edited volume that

> Developments in the party face of presidentialization can be reported very straightforwardly: none of the country experts doubts that the leaders of (potentially) governing parties have enjoyed a growth in intra-party power and/or autonomy, or these were already comparatively high at the start of the period analysed and have remained so, in each and every case (2005, 343–44).

As each of the thirteen countries covered in the volume (Poguntke and Webb 2005) provides evidence of these changes, it is not necessary to repeat the individual country observations here. However, it is worth noting that this empirical checklist continues to be reflected in more recent developments, including parties' increasing experimentation with primaries (see for example Cross et al. 2016), the increasing policy autonomy of elites (Gauja 2013) and professionalized, data-driven, centralized, communication techniques (see, for example, Kreiss 2012, 2016).

There is, nevertheless, a significant degree of variation among parties in the extent to which they have institutionalized rules that provide for more 'leader-centric' forms of intraparty democracy, such as the formal adoption of plebiscitary, rather than assembly-based forms of decision making (see Poguntke et al. 2016, 671–73). The essential difference between these two forms of intraparty democracy is that assembly-based intraparty democracy is a collective enterprise, with decisions being reached in a meeting of members or delegates that is connected with a discussion about the substance of a decision (Bolin et al. 2017, 160–61). By disconnecting the group discussion and decision, plebiscitary democracy is a far more individualized process, whereby decision makers will act often in isolation to 'vote' on intraparty matters, such as policy and personnel selection. A recent study utilizing data from the Political Parties Database Project found that although 55 percent of the 122 parties analysed allowed for plebiscitary decision making (Poguntke et al. 2016, 672; Bolin et al. 2017, 161), there are still significant differences within countries, which will need to be tracked as more longitudinal data from the project become available.

Another way of conceptualizing the organizational impact of personalized politics is to examine the importance of organized groupings within political parties. These groups, whether they are internal subgroups such as youth wings and women's networks or external interest groups with formalized links into the party (for example, unions), all represent organizational expressions of collective identity. In a climate of personalized politics with a greater emphasis on leaders, candidates and individualized forms of participation, we would expect the formal significance of these groups (e.g., their institutionalization in party rules and voting processes) to be limited. However, it may also be the case that informally such groups continue to matter, insofar as they may be relied upon by a highly personalized leadership for support or to build coalitions within the party. Such a leader might pick and choose among groups, claim to represent groups within the party and personify their concerns. The key point to note here is that although groups may continue to exercise power through informal or noncodified channels within the party, this power is intimately tied to the leader, whether it is derived from the leader's approval or used as a means of supporting him or her.

A recent study conducted by Allern and Verge (2017)—again utilizing data from the Political Parties Database—investigated the comparative state of parties' links to groups, differentiating between external interest groups (nonparty organizations) and party suborganizations (party organizational units) and focusing on the extent to which they enjoy formal status and representative rights within a party's formal rules. Notable to their findings is that affiliated nonparty organizations are found only within five of the nineteen countries contained in the database. Only 8 percent of parties have affiliated nonparty trade unions, and 3 percent have affiliated business peak associations (Allern and Verge 2017, 117). Comparing this to the analysis of a previous data set covering only Western Europe, the authors conclude that although the 'use of this formal linkage mechanism has declined in some cases . . . it should be noted that it has always been a rare phenomenon' (Allern and Verge 2017, 117).

A greater proportion of the parties in the Political Parties Database have intraparty suborganizations (80 percent), but these are limited to a fairly small number per party (only 20 percent of parties mention more than two-party organizations in their statutes). The most common of these subgroups are women's groups (41 percent) and youth wings (78 percent). Of those parties included in the database, only a small percentage have economic/functional groups (2 percent), farmers' groups (6 percent) or groups organized along ethnic/linguistic (6 percent) or religious (3 percent) lines. Overall, the authors conclude that 'alternative party sub groups organized along non-economic or demographic lines, such as issue based groups, have not flourished . . . most parties are not organized as federations of party-based interest groups' (Allern and Verge 2017, 118–19).

Although there is scope to undertake further research into groups that are not formally recognized by parties in their rules and constitutions, these findings suggest that, with the exception of women's groups and youth wings, institutionalized collective groupings within parties are not common. While it is impossible in the absence of longitudinal data to conclusively link this to personalization as a trend, it is an organizational configuration that is consistent with a personalized form of party politics, insofar as there are few formal intraparty groupings that could mobilize to counter elite power and leaders' appeals to individual party members. Although women's groups and youth wings are common, as members are brought together by age and gender without any other connection or commitment to each other, it is difficult to see how these groups might provide a meaningful basis for collective action and organization as a counterpoint to more autonomous and powerful party leaders.

So if evidence of political personalization within party organizations is so widespread, where does the debate go from here?

PERSONALIZATION AND INDIVIDUAL PARTICIPATION: A 'BOTTOM-UP' VIEW

As I have suggested, the dominant view of personalization adopted by scholars working across political parties, electoral systems and institutions is one that focuses on political elites: leaders, candidates and politicians (see for example, Karvonen 2010, 5–14). This is the case whether we are concerned with their behaviour, media constructions, voter evaluations or the institutions or decision-making processes that support their power. What is missing from this analysis, however, is an understanding of how personalization impacts the party organization as seen from the 'bottom-up'—one that focuses on the roles, participation and power of party members and supporters.

Although such an approach may seem counterintuitive given the way in which personalization as a concept has traditionally been used in party scholarship, there is no reason why personalization, defined as 'the increasing importance of individual actors over time' (see the Introduction to this volume) cannot be applied as a useful heuristic to examine the changing nature of party membership, the ways in which citizens engage with parties and participate in their key functions and decision-making processes (leadership and candidate selection, policy development and campaigning). In moving beyond personalization as a process to personalism as a state (one of the key themes of this book), this frame, or shift in focus, provides a way in which we can also undertake a more nuanced and holistic evaluation of the consequent relationships of power resulting from increasingly personalized, or individualized, forms of engagement.

Insights into the changing nature of political participation by media and communications and social-movement scholars provide an alternate way of thinking about personalization, which complements much of the recent research into partisan affiliation, participation and the changing nature of party membership (Achury et al. 2017; Gauja 2015a, 2017; Faucher 2015a;

Scarrow 2015). In these fields, personalization is synonymous with individuation/individualization and is associated much more with the political behaviour and participatory preferences of citizens rather than elites, who typically seek 'more flexible' associations with causes, ideas and political organizations, and 'more personalized brands of politics organized around individual lifestyles and social networks' (Bennett and Segerberg 2013, 5–6; 2011, 771). Although this perspective has something in common with the 'privatization' of politics argument (as discussed by Thomas, this volume), in this context, appeals to the personal experiences of individuals are not removed from politics, rather they are inherently connected to the process of mobilizing for political action. Although citizens may have turned away from traditional political institutions, they 'continue to experience common interests and political concerns (hence the impetus to join in action with others)' (Bennett and Segerberg 2013, 6; see also Bennett 2012). In many ways, this view challenges the belief that participation and political experience is only significant if it can be represented as a collective interest (Coleman 2005, 275).

In this account of personalization, organizations—including political parties—do not necessarily cease to play a role in politics, but rather must find ways to engage individuals 'in very personal ways: as consumers, animal and nature lovers, Facebook friends, Twitter followers, and self-styled global citizens who often prefer more direct ways of acting politically than voting or becoming formal members of organizations' (Bennett and Segerberg 2013, 5). By drawing on the personal when campaigning, recruiting supporters and seeking policy engagement, political parties could be seen to facilitate a process of 'personalized' or 'individualized' collective action. The normalization of digital technologies and increasing use of social-media platforms (see Vromen 2017) is key here: both in driving demand for personalized online participation and providing political organizations, including parties, with the technologies through which this can occur. Bottom-up personalization, in this way, does not necessarily sit in opposition to the party as a whole, rather, it can be conceptualized as a new way of organizing.

This approach to personalization speaks to the key debates surrounding intraparty democracy and the changing nature of political parties as organizations in several ways. The first point of engagement is with the thesis of party decline in advanced democracies. Is bottom-up personalization occurring as a consequence of party decline, or it is contributing to it? Have more personalized norms of political participation, through their demands for issue-based, individualized, ad-hoc and nonideological actions undermined the traditional role of political parties as interest aggregators and mediators between civil society and the state?

The second point of connection is to the adaptive capacities of political parties to be able meet these shifting participatory demands (Gauja 2017).

In particular, the phenomenon of personalization from the bottom-up raises the issue of parties' ability to incorporate 'new forms of political participation' (Faucher 2015a) within existing party structures and traditional arenas for the expression of intraparty democracy, such as party conferences and representative committees. Is incorporation even possible? Or, are we witnessing a much more fundamental shift in party structures through the individualization of personnel selection, policy development and communication and campaign functions?

The final way in which studies of personalization intersect in social-movement literature and party scholarship literature is in their shared concern for the implications of individualization on the collective identity of the party/movement and its ability to convey a coherent 'brand' or champion a shared cause. For social-movement scholars and political sociologists, the difficulties come with fragmentation and the loss of control this can generate over a movement's 'political capacity', its mobilization efforts and agenda-setting capabilities (Bennett and Segerberg 2011, 773–74; Beck and Beck-Gernsheim 2002). For party scholars, fragmentation not only undermines collective identity, but brings the possibility of increased elite control if the authority produced by a collective membership and organized subgroupings within the party is undermined (Katz and Mair 1995, 2009).

Personalization, therefore, when conceptualized in terms of individual partisan engagement, also prompts us to think more critically about what political grouping(s) these processes relate to. As a new form of organization, individualized practices face significant challenges in maintaining organizational coherence and could undermine existing organized groupings within the party, but it is not necessarily the case that bottom-up personalization stands in opposition to the idea of the party as mediating agent in society-state relations.

EMPIRICAL EVIDENCE OF BOTTOM-UP PERSONALIZATION

What are the empirical indicators of more personalized forms of partisan engagement with party organizations? Building on the work of Bang (2011), Bennett and Segerberg (2011) and Li and Marsh (2008), I suggest several markers that revolve around flexibility in three key elements: the way in which issues and causes are defined, how support is expressed and how affiliation is practised:

- More personalized forms of communication from the political party with potential policy participants. Rather than appealing to broad ideological

commitments and causes, the way in which campaigns and participatory opportunities are presented will include opportunities for customization and personal engagement with issues and actions.
- By the same token, citizens are encouraged to suggest problems and issues for resolution (without a clear or imposed definition by the party) in the relative absence of ideological cues and bases for action.
- Political activity may be construed in party discourse (websites, pamphlets, etc., comments by leaders and party elites) as fun and exciting, rather than appealing to an individual's sense of civic duty.
- Party branding is minimized and emphasis is placed on the issues as a lived experience.
- Participation does not involve long-term commitment, but rather opportunities for ad-hoc engagement, including more flexible forms of affiliation (Gauja 2015b, 94).

These additional indicators of party personalization supplement, rather than replace the broader institutional markers of top-down party personalization as described previously. They also sit below the distinction between centralized and decentralized modes of political personalization, which as I already argued, emphasizes the role of political elites rather than participants. Indeed, the empirical characteristics associated with each layer of personalization, taken together, provide a valuable frame of reference in evaluating the implications of personalization for party change and democracy.

Personalization and Changing Parties: Empirical Illustrations

In this section of the chapter I provide several illustrative examples of bottom-up personalization relating to the key party functions of campaigning and communication, membership and affiliation, policy development and leadership selection. These examples are not intended as a systematic analysis, but rather as illustrative examples of the range of processes and party adaptations that could be considered under the heading of bottom-up personalization.

Campaigning, Communications and Digital Media

As Rahat and Zamir's chapter in this volume highlights, it is just as important to analyse the extent and impact of personalization online, as it is offline. And increasingly for political parties, as well as for the analysis of their organizations, maintaining the separation between these two arenas is becoming less relevant because online spaces not only provide opportunities for partisan participation, but they also increasingly structure how party membership (and supportership) is delivered and experienced (Gerl, Marschall and Wilker 2017; Gibson, Greffert and Cantijoch 2017; Bailo 2015; Scarrow 2015).

Digital-media technologies are not only important in terms of their increasing use, but also the ways in which these tools shape organizational relationships within political parties. As Bennett and Segerberg (2011, 771) argue, 'communication technologies aimed at personalizing engagement with causes facilitate organizational communication and coordination at the same time as they enable flexibility in how, when, where, and with whom individuals may affiliate and act'. For political parties, the impact of these technologies goes well beyond the Twitter accounts and Facebook pages of leaders and politicians, to Facebook groups (see for example Marichal 2012, 13), and much more sophisticated systems of enabling engagement and decision making through websites, blogs, action items such as online petitions, donations, the creation and addition of user-generated content, policy-development platforms and communicative networks.

In this mode of organization, communication takes on a significance that goes beyond the simple receipt and broadcasting of information. In the complex modern media environment, where it is often difficult to distinguish information provision from interactivity, many scholars have adopted the view that communication is constitutive of organization (see Bennett and Segerberg 2013, 42). Although within the realm of party scholarship, communication recipients may be seen as 'low intensity participants', this is a contested view in the social-movements literature, where in a more fluid environment 'communication mechanisms establish relationships, activate attentive participants, channel various resources, and establish narratives and discourses' (Bennett and Segerberg 2013, 42; see also Marichal 2012, 111–13), which in turn, shape participation.

One example of this has been the gradual uptake of social-networking sites and online platforms to provide the basis for a different kind of online organizational infrastructure. NationBuilder, an online community-organizing software platform that enables parties to build campaign sites and websites that incorporate communications, fund-raising and volunteer management/profiling functions, is an excellent illustration of the trend towards party-mediated, online, personalized political action. As McKelvey and Piebiak (2016) note, NationBuilder is the 'leading non-partisan platform used [by political parties] in the United States, Canada, the United Kingdom, and Australia'. Key features of NationBuilder sites include the ability to link to social media, to specific issue campaigns, to enable users to easily donate or volunteer and to create databases of user activity. Membership of the party is downplayed and supporters and followers are invited to take immediate action, through, for example, liking the campaign on social media, signing an online petition, donating to the cause or making phone calls (Gauja 2017).

The digital technologies employed by the British political parties have also facilitated and have developed in parallel with a greater flexibility in membership and options for partisan affiliation (see e.g., Scarrow 2015; Gauja 2015a) with the website templates provided by NationBuilder focused on activities (donations and social-media interaction) that can be performed by supporters and interested citizens. For example, the Labour Party argued that its digital campaigning

> Provides so many opportunities for supporters to get involved. Whether that's donating online, signing up for emails or liking a Facebook status. These actions all make a difference *and they all make you a supporter of the Labour Party* (UK Labour Party 2013, 32) [emphasis added].

Despite the normative democratic promise that is often associated with the use of new technologies for political participation (see, for example, Vaccari 2013, 14–16; Smith 2009, 142–61) Kreiss (2012, 26) has argued that the use of personalized new media in partisan campaigning has 'seemingly not brought about fundamental changes in the levers of accountability, forms of political representation, quality of democratic conversation, or distribution of power in the American polity'. In the US context (the focus of Kreiss's analysis), this may reflect some of the shortcomings of new technologies. However it might also be due to the fact that US politics was already highly personalized before new media were invented (see Bartels 1992), limiting their ability to shift the 'status quo'. Although these bigger questions need to be addressed in other democracies—returning just to organizational transformations—in the British context it has contributed to creating uniformity across party websites and online participatory experiences, as well as facilitating the permeability of party organizations.

Complementing these online initiatives has been the appropriation of community organizing techniques that add another dimension to party-mediated personalized action and campaigning. Originally copied from advocacy and third-sector organizations, the basic principles of community organizing—asking people what they care about rather than telling them what to think (Schutz and Sandy 2011, 5)—have become fused in the campaign practices of US political parties in the last decade through network-building and the 'creation, cultivation, and maintenance of ties with supporters that staffers could mobilize for collective social and symbolic action' (Kreiss 2012, 10).

In turn, what has been successfully used in US campaigning has also been adopted by party organizations in Canada, Australia and the United Kingdom. For example, the Canadian Liberal Party pointed to the experience of the US Democratic Party in its 2009 Change Commission Report, noting that 'Obama's community development model has demonstrated the success in turning every supporter into a worker, a policy source and then a donor' (Liberal Party of Canada 2009, 1). Over in the United Kingdom, the centrepiece of the 2013 Labour Conference 'Train to Win' program was the community-organizing session run by Chicago-based community organizer Arnie Graf. During the Graf-led session, delegates were coached in the power of storytelling and emotional connection, techniques for canvassing, having conversations, involving and recruiting individuals to local campaigns and creating issue priorities at the local level, demonstrating the way in which this party has attempted to synthesize core functions with more personalized opportunities for participation.

Membership, Affiliation, Primaries and Policy

This repositioning of partisan campaign and communication activities towards more fluid, ad hoc and issues-based engagement online and offline has occurred simultaneously with the gradual expansion of a range of affiliation options for party supporters, beyond traditional financial party membership. Under a 'multispeed membership' model, parties offer partisans a myriad of options for 'joining' the organization, ranging from a news audience, to social-media friends, to 'light' members (Scarrow 2015, 30–34). Each of these affiliation options responds to demands for consumer 'choice', and has culminated, most visibly, in the increasing incidence of registered supporters' networks (Gauja 2015a).

The rationale for introducing this category of affiliation has been to allow the reluctant public to engage with political parties on a more ad-hoc basis, with minimal obligation. How these networks are set up and the extent to which they supplement traditional party membership varies among political parties, ranging from formalized networks inviting nothing more than an expression of support for the party (e.g., New Zealand's National Party), to Canada's Liberal Party, which in 2016 dispensed with the idea of formal, financial party membership altogether and moved to an 'open movement' model.

These more fluid types of party membership/affiliation invite personalized participation in two main ways. The first is through facilitating more issues-based, rather than ideological engagement, particularly through participation in intraparty policy development. For example, in 2013 the UK Labour Party launched the online consultation initiative 'Your Britain', which was described as:

> Labour's online policy hub. Whether you're a Labour Party member, a trade union member, a representative of a voluntary organization or business, or none of the above, *we want to hear your ideas on how the next Labour Government can tackle the challenges that face Britain'* (emphasis added).

'Your Britain' allowed citizens to engage with the party on an individual basis, with the primary focus on communicating information around issues rather than on heavily branded principles or ideologies. The Labour Party logo featured only at the bottom of the web page, with lists of issues (e.g., young people and politics, the NHS and health care and the housing crisis) dominating the layout, along with the call to 'tell us what you think' (Gauja 2015b, 97–98). Australian Labor parliamentarians Clare O'Neil and Tim Watts (2015, 26) have described the utility of these policy-oriented supporters' initiatives as enabling

> fellow travelers to determine the nature of their engagement with Labor, enabling them to pursue a specific cause within the party without having to make the full commitment to party membership. It would also enable people to choose the means by which they engage with the party and other members.

Although the rhetoric of choice looms large over this personalized engagement, my previous research has shown that the reality of much of this online policy participation follows the logic of 'consultation', whereby feedback and ideas from individuals are solicited, received and aggregated by party elites (Gauja 2013, 89–116; 2015b). In this sense, the personalization of policy participation has arguably contributed to the policy autonomy of party leaders as empowering individual members of the party in decision making, or in more recent times, supporters beyond it, has reduced the influence of the activist layer of the party. As Poguntke and Webb (2005, 343, citing Mair 1994, 16) suggest, this will inevitably increase the power of leaders, as 'ordinary members'—or in this case supporters—are 'more docile and more likely to endorse the policies (and candidates) proposed by the party leadership'.

The second basis of supporter engagement is the expansion of leadership and candidate selections via direct, individual ballots. The last two to three decades have seen an increase in more inclusive and direct methods of leadership and candidate selection, which includes primaries (Cross et al. 2016; Cross and Pilet 2015; Sandri, Seddone and Venturino 2015; Indridason and Kristinsson 2015a, 2015b; Kenig et al. 2015; Gauja 2012; Cross and Blais 2012a; Hazan and Rahat 2010). It is now a topic of considerable academic interest as the list of political parties having used open or semi-open primaries for the selection of candidates or party leaders is now quite extensive and includes UK Labour, the French Socialists (Faucher 2015b, 804), almost all of the Spanish political parties (Barbera and Teruel 2015), the Israeli parties (Hazan and Rahat 2010), the Italian Partito Democratico (Vassallo and Passarelli 2016; Sandri, Seddone and Venturino 2014), and the Canadian Liberals (Cross 2014, 176).

Although the links between leadership selection and the personalization of party politics are discussed in much greater detail by Stewart (this volume), in the context of a bottom-up examination of party organization and personalization, the example of the changes to the UK Labour Party leadership selection process and the consequent selection of Jeremy Corbyn is worth mentioning. In the name of creating a 'twenty-first-century' Labour Party, 'where individuals rightly demand a voice' and where 'parties need to reach out far beyond their membership', former leader Ed Miliband set in train a party review that would fundamentally reform Labour's leadership selection to a one-member, one-vote process, including registered supporters and trade union affiliates (Gauja 2017, 2).

Although Labour Party membership had waned in previous years, falling to 190,000 in December 2013, the 2015 leadership contest (the first to be run under the new rules) attracted the participation of more than 420,000 individuals, including 105,000 registered supporters. An analysis of the final poll showed that support for Corbyn was highest among registered supporters (84 percent), followed by trade union supporters (58 percent) and finally party members (50 percent). These voting patterns suggest that the outcome of the contest was influenced in large part by those who joined in the months leading up to the vote, rather than by long-standing party members (Gauja 2017, 185–86). For some, this resurgence in popular participation signalled a 'breath of fresh air' and a 'democratic explosion', while for others it represented the selection of a dangerous and radical democratic socialist, with severe electoral repercussions in sight (Gauja 2017, 185). In the context of personalization, Corbyn's election illustrates an interesting paradox. On the one hand, it demonstrates how a leader elected through the mobilization of a large number of party supporters can become entirely synonymous with the brand and image of the party itself and wield significant power within the organization. On the other, it shows how more individualized party politics can be used to mobilize citizens, to create a space for political protest, with the potential that processes can move beyond the control and influence of party elites. If Miliband and the former Labour leadership's intention was to marginalize activists in a sea of 'moderate' voices by opening up the party, they may have received more than they bargained for.

CONCLUSIONS: THE CONSEQUENCES OF BOTTOM-UP PERSONALIZATION FOR PARTY ORGANIZATIONS

As argued throughout the chapter, personalization—from the perspective of studies of party organization—has been concerned with the transfer of power to individual elites, whether they are leaders, politicians or candidates. Examples of organizational changes that facilitate this process are ubiquitous in the literature (e.g., more inclusive leadership and candidate selection processes), although they typically rely on the assumption that these more individualized decision-making processes benefit elites. The primary aim of this chapter was to draw attention to an alternate perspective that is more prevalent in studies of social movements and new media-communications technologies, suggesting that personalization can also be seen as a citizen-driven or bottom-up process.

I previously suggested three areas of debate where a reconceptualization of personalization to shift the focus to individual participation and a bottom-up rather than elite-centred perspective might give us an insight into the future development of party organizations. I return to those three themes here.

In contrast to elite accounts of personalization that view the future of party organizations quite sceptically, more bottom-up perspectives provide a different take on the future of political parties as organizations. Bottom-up personalization is not necessarily antithetical to the party; it is a new way of organizing. Parties can continue to perform their functions but do so by mediating and facilitating more personalized forms of political action that are spontaneous, flexible and issues-based rather than ideologically oriented. This entails important organizational changes (including the increased importance of digital-media platforms, interactive communications, flexible forms of affiliation, and issues-based policy development and activism) that sit alongside the process of personalization at the top of the organization.

If we think about personalization and the individualization of political participation as creating new organizational forms, are these in turn undermining the traditional role and place of political parties in contemporary societies? In so far as we regard political parties as built primarily on ideology and as institutions based on hierarchy and representative forms of intraparty democracy, then it would appear that the shift to individualized decision-making processes (through plebiscites and consultations), as well as ad-hoc, issue-based participation is challenging, if not eroding, traditional party organizations. Yet it is also an argument that has a clear normative element. As Balmas et al. (2014, 47) suggest, how one views the process and consequences of personalization 'depends on one's view of the starting point':

> If one thinks that political groupings had an appropriate amount of power in the past, personalization will be an issue of grave concern. If one thinks that political groupings were too powerful, one might see this process positively in terms of distribution of power.

For scholars such as Micheletti (2003, 26–28), the shift to 'individualized collective action' creates a shift away from a model of organizational politics where

> membership means agreeing to support organizational agendas and assumes that citizens both understand and will acquiesce to the norms, values and rules of these organizations. Formal hierarchy and order are important to traditional organizations, and while an activist membership may have some say on campaign directions, the majority are passive in their support and primarily have only a financial involvement. Indeed, there are high costs for active participants as they need ample resources such as time and acknowledged seniority within an organization. This maintains a very high threshold for active and sustained engagement by members and often reinforces the existing power structures of paid staff and elected officials (Vromen 2017, 23).

Putting aside the issue of whether some forms of participation are of a higher quality or normative value than others, I suggest that personalization can be equated with a process of organizational transformation and should not necessarily be seen as an indicator of the decline of political parties per se. This, however, raises the second point of contention: the capacity of political parties to adapt to these changing preferences. Micheletti and Stolle (2008, 753) suggest that within advocacy organizations and social movements, there is a strategic space for both individualized and collective forms of participation to be accommodated:

> Old civil society associations with their emphasis on membership strength, hierarchical structures, pressure group politics, collectivist collective action, and boycotts couple up with new looser and non-membership networks that use the communicative skills of spin doctoring, the Internet, and individualized collective action to mobilize consumers into urgent actions.

Yet, as illustrated in the examples given, significant tensions arise when political parties attempt to map new processes onto old structures, which create barriers to effectively mediating personalized political participation. Part of this stems from the need to balance both expression, individual participatory demands and beliefs, with maintaining some degree of control over party identity and issue agendas. This balance can shift both ways; as the example of Jeremy Corbyn suggests, the use of individualized ballots and decision-making processes can create a situation in which the party and its broader project moves out of control of the established elites through mass mobilizations. Other examples, particularly from the area of policy development, point to the ways in which personalized participation can be harnessed by elites to increase their autonomy and control the policy agenda.

We also need to think more critically about the impact of 'borrowing' organizational practices from the United States, as parties in the United Kingdom, Australia, Canada and Western Europe have done, particularly in the realm of campaigning techniques. It is important to remember just how weak US political parties are in organizational terms (see, e.g., Katz and Kolodny 1994). If political parties outside the United States are increasingly adopting these techniques, might we come to a point at which, as Katz suggests in this volume, membership becomes so transient and the boundaries of organization become so loose that there is little room for the party organization at all?

A final consideration is whether 'individualized collective action' is even possible. To what extent can political parties continue to act as collective organizations with a common identity when personalized political participation is causing parties to fragment into individual opinions, preferences, beliefs and actions? This question is particularly acute when ideological cues are becoming less important and initiatives such as multispeed membership continue to blur the boundaries of the party. The answer depends on what has previously been discussed: the ability of political parties to successfully adapt to these changes and balance individual demands with collective solutions. The examples in this chapter highlight the power of technological change and shifting social norms in driving this process of adaptation. Although we are witnessing ongoing organizational transformations, it is a question that will remain a moot point. What is certain, however, is that personalization/personalism, both top down and bottom up, challenges the traditional mediating role of political parties based on representative and hierarchical forms of organizational democracy. Whether this is seen as a decline or a transformation, in large part, depends on the reader.

NOTE

1. But see Passarelli (2015, 9) for a distinction between these two concepts.

Chapter 8

Exploring the Role of Decentralized Personalization for Legislative Behaviour and Constituency Representation[1]

Mihail Chiru

A recent strand of scholarship devoted to electoral campaigns in advanced and young democracies has come to the conclusion that candidates running in parliamentary elections engage, to a substantial extent, in constituency level personalization (Zittel and Gschwend 2008; De Winter and Baudewyns 2015; Cross and Young 2015; Chiru 2015), a strategy mainly 'driven by electoral incentives and impacting the cognitions and behaviours of electorates' (Zittel 2015, 293). This is a remarkable finding in itself which illustrates that personalization is not limited to the increasing role of party leaders in national politics and the presidentialization of parliamentary democracies (Poguntke and Webb 2005; see also their chapter in this volume) and corroborates the significant theoretical distinction between centralized and decentralized personalization as set out in the introductory chapter to this volume (see also Balmas et al. 2014). More importantly, however, this scholarship also opens up another potentially salient research agenda: if decentralized personalization, manifested primarily via candidate campaign personalization, has become prominent as suggested by Pruysers and Cross (this volume), does it also shape the legislative and nonlegislative behaviour (i.e., district activities) of the candidates elected? This chapter provides answers to these questions by drawing on an original data set that combines data on the campaign strategies and actions of Members of Parliament (MPs) in Hungary (2010–2012) and Romania (2012–2013) with their legislative behaviour.

One of the key predictions of the proponents of the concept of decentralized personalization is that it would lead to a dispersion of power towards ordinary MPs. Because they feel they have gained a personal mandate by running a personalized campaign, these MPs would 'increasingly engage in individual activities' (Balmas et al. 2014, 40) and they would also believe that they 'can act independently, less restricted by their political party or its leader' (Balmas et al. 2014, 38). Of these two types of behavioural consequences, the latter is likely to be more problematic from the point of view of party leaders and chief executives because it could damage party cohesion as well as constrain their own personal power and ability to achieve policy objectives.

The evidence in the two cases under consideration here does not seem to support this intuition. Thus, although levels of decentralized personalization in electoral campaigns have been high, no observable drop in party legislative voting unity was registered in the two parliaments in the period analysed. The levels of party discipline at roll-call votes remained similar to those in Western European parliaments, with legislators toeing the party line on average more than 90 percent of the time.[2]

For the Romanian sample, it was also possible to assess directly whether higher campaign personalization is related to more dissent at roll-call votes, while controlling for traditional predictors of voting disloyalty such as government—opposition status, electoral marginality, length of parliamentary socialization and ideological distance from the party. The analysis included all final roll-call votes voted on by the Romanian MPs in 2013, an average of 537 votes per MP. The campaign personalization variables did not make any difference for the level of dissent.[3]

Given these empirical results, this chapter focuses on the first type of behavioural consequences mentioned, by investigating whether decentralized personalization makes legislators more interested in individualized legislative behaviour. One specific area prone to such individual legislative activism is constituency service. Decentralized personalization can trigger more requests for casework, given that it advertises a closer personal connection between the MP and his or her constituents, while also fostering expectations among them that the legislator would work hard to defend local interests. At the same time, this type of personalized legislative behaviour can be completely congruent with the party message and brand: parliamentary questions could promote and highlight success stories achieved by the party locally or on the contrary reflect party-desired policy goals or measures whose implementation is lagging behind at the local level.

This brief introduction is followed by a discussion of the theoretical framework and the main arguments of the chapter. The next section includes the research design: the case selection, a discussion of the data and of the methods used. The analysis presents the results of the multivariate tests (i.e., negative binomial regression models). This is complemented by a section comprising further analyses of the main effects and a number of robustness checks. The conclusion synthesizes the results of the study and points to further directions of research.

THEORETICAL FRAMEWORK

A few studies focusing on the US Congress have illustrated the association between individual campaign behaviour and policy positions taken by legislators through roll-call voting, bill initiation and co-sponsorship (Sulkin and Swigger 2008; Sulkin 2011). Moreover, US scholars have analysed the extent to which legislators keep the policy promises made during campaigns (Sulkin 2011) or take up the main issues their challengers had campaigned on, in what is usually called 'issue uptake' (Sulkin 2005). However, no study has analysed the consequences of personalized campaigning for legislative behaviour.

As discussed throughout this volume, much of the extant personalization literature has concentrated on documenting the increasing importance of top politicians' charisma and personal styles in electoral campaigns and on analysing whether this translates into power concentration in running parties and cabinets. However, backbench MPs and first-time candidates can also run their constituency campaigns in a personalized fashion in a quest for extra votes beyond those attracted by the party label or for other strategic reasons (for a full exploration of such motivations see Pruysers and Cross, this volume).

This chapter argues that even if political parties tolerate or even encourage decentralized personalization for its possible electoral gains, it is reasonable to expect that party leaders would want to limit the extent to which such personalism translates into acts of independence and rebellion against the party line. Instead, party leaders would actively look to channel the MPs' ideas of a personalized mandate into individualized legislative or nonlegislative activities that are favoured by voters and do not affect the party policy messages and overall brand. Constituency service work is one such type of activity.

The literature focusing on constituency service has ignored the role of personalized campaigns in fostering engagement in casework and constituency responsiveness. Sulkin (2005, 4) argued convincingly that studies analysing the linkages between the electoral and legislative arenas have been absent for a long time because of the division of labour in contemporary political science between scholars studying voting behaviour and campaign effects and those focusing on legislative behaviour. Moreover, when such a linkage was integrated in legislative theory it happened only through a conception of forward looking, reelection-oriented behaviour: legislators cultivate a personal vote, accumulating locally relevant achievements that they will exploit in the next campaign (Mayhew 1974). Thus, until recently retrospective theories of how campaign experiences shape legislative behaviour after election have been totally absent (Sulkin 2005, 4–5).

Adapting the traditional instrumentalist, rational choice perspective to include formative campaign experiences, one could argue for the need to close the circle and take into account a complete campaign–legislative behaviour–campaign sequence. Thus, MPs should follow up on the constituency related promises they made in the previous campaign by engaging in service, which in turn will help them consolidate their reputation and increase reelection chances. On a different dimension, it should be easier for them to do this than to achieve policy responsiveness. For the latter, an MP would have to mobilize colleagues or convince party leaders to support the implementation of policy promises, a much more complex game of collective bargaining and collective action (Shepsle and Weingast 1994).

This chapter argues that the amount of time and energy put into personalized campaigning via an individualized campaign, a personal constituency agenda and an intense collaboration with local party activists will lead to a similar level of engagement in constituency service. One reason for this is that MPs who put a lot of effort into this type of campaigning would most likely perceive their electoral victory as a mandate for local interest representation. And having invested time in creating a personal reputation, distinct from the party, these MPs will want to maintain and develop it as a valuable asset in the quest for future votes and offices. Therefore, their parliamentary work agenda will include contacts with, and work on behalf of, party activists and constituents. Beyond such rational calculations, a successful campaign focused on a local agenda and local party networks can also play a socialization role, especially for newly elected MPs. For them, acting on the demands and needs of constituents and local party activists will be seen as the appropriate thing to do, the dimension that gives meaning to the job of representative beyond being a cog in the machine of party (collective) representation. In the following paragraphs I discuss in detail the modes and mechanisms through which personalized campaign strategies and activities can influence engagement in constituency service.

Promising to increase the welfare of the district and following up on these promises through constituency questions can be considered a normatively positive scenario, falling into the category of what Mansbridge labelled 'promissory representation' (2003, 515), or traditional accountability (2003, 525). Beyond the reelection drive that most probably motivates a constant transformation of issues from the local campaign agenda into legislative initiatives, parliamentary questions and speeches, localized campaigning should also foster constituency questions because it is a proxy for the MP's awareness of local problems.

In both Hungary and Romania, promises related to the welfare of the district have become more and more common in candidates' campaigns for parliamentary seats (Tudor 2008, 180; Chiru 2015). The frequency and precise character of candidate pledges referring to the constituency are likely to foster a particular type of legislative behaviour. Thus, we would expect a large number of MPs who had run such localized campaigns to ask locally oriented parliamentary questions. Conversely, the minority of MPs who did not personalize their campaign with any district- or county-related promises are certainly less likely to need, from a reelection perspective, to engage in constituency service. Thus, I hypothesize that candidates who had promoted a local agenda during the campaign will ask a higher number of constituency service questions as MPs.

Most scholars understand campaign personalization first and foremost as a strategy of focusing the campaign on the candidate and his or her qualities as opposed to the party's policies and record (Zittel and Gschwend 2008).[4] In terms of personalization content, one of the usual suspects, along with leadership skills and other political or personal qualities, is the candidate's ability to cater for the constituency (Hennl and Zittel 2011). Another type of quality that candidates want to emphasize when they choose to personalize their campaigns is local ties with the constituency, such as residence or a local political career (De Winter and Baudewyns 2015; Shugart, Valdini and Suominen 2005; Evans 2014), particularly because voters prefer local candidates (Campbell and Cowley 2014).

The second part of the argument is that candidates who personalized their campaigns in this manner might feel that their election amounts to a direct mandate for casework and will be more likely to maintain and foster the personal vote they received by engaging in constituency service. Vice versa, a campaign focused on the party can go hand in hand with policy specialization and interest in national political issues. In this case, it would be more reasonable to expect the MP to ask more parliamentary questions and interpellations dealing with nationally relevant issues and policies and less with local matters.

On the other hand, campaign personalization might not include references to local credentials, but emphasize instead the candidate's personal success in business or other national political office. Moreover, it could be that candidates individualize their campaigns as part of the overall party strategy of winning votes (Karlsen and Skogerbø 2015). If such situations are more frequent than the scenarios described previously, the probability that campaign personalization fosters constituency service is rather dim. Thus, I hypothesize that the more individualized his or her campaign, the higher the number of constituency service questions raised by the MP.

Time is generally a scarce resource for politicians, but this should be even more the case during electoral campaigns. Decisions to organize certain events and not others and to meet certain people and not others speak simultaneously about two crucial aspects. First, they reveal the candidate's ideas about how he or she will win the necessary votes to get elected and where these votes are most likely to come from. Second, these decisions speak about which issues the future MP will consider as priorities in his or her representation work. When a candidate chooses to spend considerable time meeting local party members and activists, it can be assumed that both sides can turn to each other later on during the parliamentary term. The party members and activists can ask the MP whom they helped elect to advance their interests in various ways, from putting local problems on the national agenda to mediating interactions with central authorities. At the same time, these activists can be an invaluable source of information about policies or political processes that go wrong at the local level and have the potential to embarrass the government. Moreover, candidates that need to invest a lot of time in meeting party activists might also be in a rather weak position in relation to the local party organization. Promoting local issues in parliament and running other errands could be used in this case by the MPs as a means of consolidating this relationship. Beyond these rational calculations, the time spent with local party activists is also an intense socialization experience, that can create bonds and make MPs more responsive to local issues and requests. Therefore, I expect that the more time devoted to meeting local party activists during the campaign, the higher the number of constituency service questions raised by the MP.

Beyond these three hypotheses, the theoretical model takes into account seven other factors that the relevant scholarship considers influential for engagement in constituency service: the type of election, the type of candidacy, incumbency, parliamentary seniority, experience in local politics, ideological distance from the party and party affiliation. The type of seat the candidate wins in electoral systems with multiple tiers of election[5] has attached to it a series of normative expectations from voters, party leaders and fellow parliamentarians about the appropriate legislative and nonlegislative behaviour associated with that mandate. On the one hand, MPs who won a single member district (SMD) are expected to look after their voters and try to maintain and increase their support, particularly through constituency service. On the other hand, the overriding expectation towards list parliamentarians is that they specialize in particular policy areas, while being allowed the privilege of not engaging in casework.

In the Hungarian case, scholars have been successful in documenting the link between MPs' channels of election and attitudinal differences with respect to representational roles (Judge and Ilonszki 1995; Enyedi 2011; Chiru and Enyedi 2015) but evidence about differences in actual behaviour remains scarce (for the exception see, Montgomery 1999). I expect directly elected MPs to ask a higher number of constituency service questions than list parliamentarians.

A second electoral aspect that needs to be controlled for is the type of candidacy. In electoral systems that allow for multiple candidacies, like

Hungary, there is great potential for role contamination: the logic of candidacy could trump the 'seat logic' and the aforementioned expectations vis-à-vis the mandate. The legislative studies literature has theorized and illustrated empirically instances of 'shadowing behaviour': list MPs who engage in constituency service in the single-member electoral district they lost (Lundberg 2006; Norris 2004). Shadowing was already documented for Hungarian list MPs in the first postcommunist decade, precisely with respect to interpellations on local issues (Montgomery 1999, 514). Therefore, I expect that list MPs in Hungary who have lost SMD battles will raise more constituency-related questions than the rest of their colleagues.

The original mixed member proportional system used in Romania at the 2008 and 2012 elections did not include a list component; all MPs were elected from SMDs, but only those who won the absolute majority of votes received the seat directly, the others being dependent on the aggregation of party votes at the county and national levels (Giugal et al. 2017). In practice, however, the mass-media and the politicians themselves tended to distinguish between MPs who won the plurality of votes in their districts and those who were elected after finishing second, third or even fourth in their districts, and this distinction also fostered different representational roles for the MPs (Chiru and Enyedi 2015). Similar to the shadowing argument, MPs who did not win the most votes in their SMD are expected to invest more time in constituency service, in an attempt to surpass their electoral marginality.

Another seat-related factor that needs to be controlled for in the Romanian case is the number of MPs elected from the same county. A study of the effects of the Romanian electoral reform on constituency service (Chiru 2014) has emphasized that after 2008 this factor has virtually the same effect as district magnitude in the proportional representation (PR) era: the higher the number of MPs elected from the same county, the lower the engagement in constituency service.

The theoretical model also includes three career-related control variables. Incumbency and parliamentary seniority are likely to decrease the engagement in constituency service because these veteran MPs might be able to rely on a record of service and pork directed in the past to the constituency (Heitshusen et al. 2005, 37) or on intraparty resources to ensure an advantageous renomination without having to do too much casework. Conversely, a background in local politics should have the reverse effect, fostering engagement in constituency service (Freeman and Richardson 1996; Russo 2011, 296–99).

A final control is ideological distance, the expectation being that MPs who place themselves further away from the median member of the party on the left-right scale would be more likely to devote time to policy issues than to constituency service. Last but not least, I control for the partisan affiliation of the MPs because different party organizational cultures and electoral contexts (e.g., high incumbent party unpopularity) can influence both the degree of campaign personalization (Pruysers and Cross, this volume; see also De Winter and Baudewyns 2015; Eder, Jenny and Müller 2015) and the engagement in constituency service (André, Gallagher and Sandri 2014, 170).

CASE SELECTION

Neither Hungary nor Romania have a strong tradition of constituency service, nothing that would be even marginally similar with that of Ireland (O'Leary 2011) or other Westminster parliaments. However, the selected cases stand out as countries where campaign localization and a personal campaign norm are relatively common in parliamentary elections. Figure 8.1 compares levels of campaign localization using data from twenty-six campaign studies that are part of the Comparative Candidate Survey wave 1 (CCS1). The phrasing of the question is salient because it emphasized localization as a personalized strategy: 'Did you raise any issues during your campaign that were specific to your constituency and that were not raised by the national or regional party?'

The data reveal that the Hungarian study reported the second-highest share, and the Romanian study the fifth-highest share of candidates promoting a personal constituency agenda. Furthermore, the frequency of candidates assuming personalized campaign norms is comparatively high in the two countries. Figure 8.2 plots the mean level of the campaign norm as measured by the CCS1 question 'What was the primary aim of your campaign?', with a 0–10

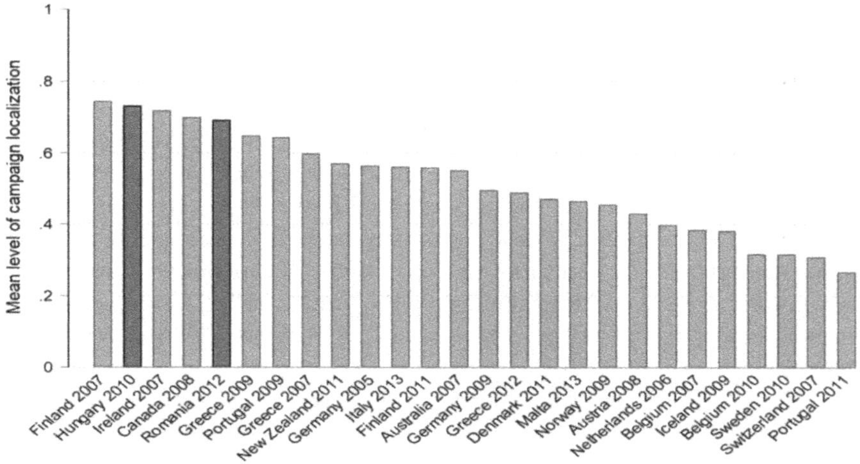

Figure 8.1 Campaign Localization in Twenty-Six Parliamentary Elections (CCS 1).

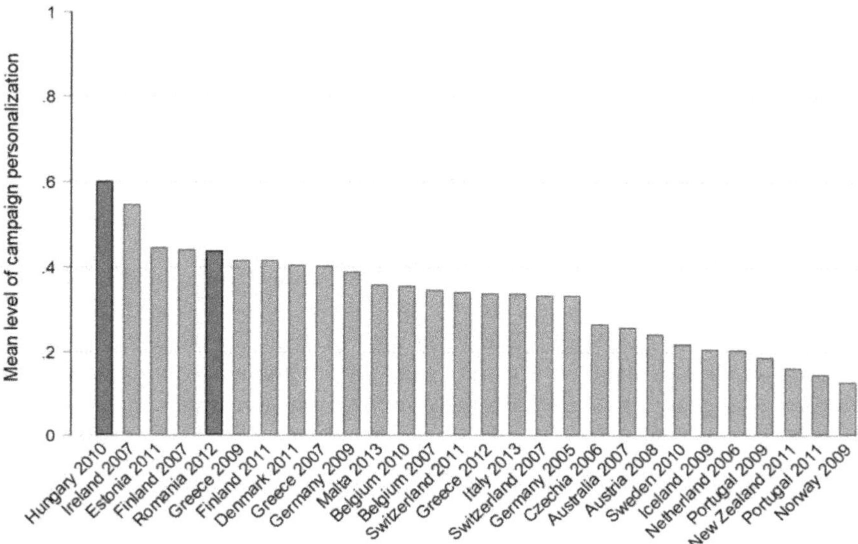

Figure 8.2 Campaign Norms in Twenty-Eight Parliamentary Elections (CCS 1).

scale in which the end points were labelled 'To attract as much attention as possible for my party' and 'To attract as much attention as possible for me as a candidate'. Because some country studies used slightly different scales (e.g., 1–10; 0–11), I rescaled all answers on a 0–1 continuum.

If we compare the full samples, Hungarian candidates seem to have personalized their campaigns the most, whereas the Romanian candidates occupy the fifth place out of twenty-eight country studies. Moreover, given the importance of not selecting cases on (one end of) the dependent variable (Geddes 2003, 89–130), the MPs' engagement in constituency service in the two countries differs substantially. One indicator of this is the fact that there are substantially fewer parliamentary questions on constituency issues in Hungary compared to Romania.

Last but not least, an important difference between the two countries is the extent to which parties control legislative behaviour. Whereas party discipline at roll-call votes is remarkably high in both cases and comparable with Western European levels, the Romanian Parliament is plagued by party switching, with more than 20 percent and up to one-third of the MPs changing their affiliation in each of the last three terms. In Hungary, legislative parties are more cohesive and their grip on legislators is much tighter. Thus, the initiation of private member bills is controlled to some extent by the parliamentary party group leadership and even the usage of parliamentary questions and interpellations has been partially orchestrated for party objectives.

This refers mainly to the practice of majority MPs tabling questions and interpellations that do not attempt to scrutinize but to advertise governmental policies (Ilonszki 2007, 54).

DATA

For the campaigning data, I rely on the two national studies conducted within the framework of the Comparative Candidate Survey, the Hungarian Candidate Study (Enyedi 2010) and the Romanian Candidate Study (Popescu and Chiru 2013). The responses of the 173 elected Romanian candidates and of the 234 elected Hungarian candidates[6] who responded to the surveys are matched with data on their parliamentary questions and interpellations. The operationalization of the independent and control variables is relatively straightforward and is presented in table 8.3 at the end of this chapter.

I conducted a content analysis on two samples of parliamentary questions and interpellations asked by these MPs to establish how many of them referred to issues concerning their constituencies. In doing so I applied the framework for coding localism developed by the Comparative Policy Agendas Project (Baumgartner et al. 2006) and adapted by Martin (2011a). A question was considered local if it dealt with a case concerning individuals living in the MP's county, with problems of local authorities and institutions (e.g., city halls, hospitals, etc.) or issues concerning local nongovernmental organizations. The same applied to questions referring to public works in the MP's county or to local businesses and local events. All these categories were coded separately, but for the purpose of this chapter, only the overall local orientation of the question is of interest.

The 173 Romanian MPs in the sample raised 2736 parliamentary questions and interpellations during the first year of their mandate in 2012–2013. One-third (34 percent) of the MPs never raised a constituency related issue, whereas one of five did not table any question or interpellation whatsoever. The content analysis showed that 1275 questions (47 percent of the total) referred to constituency issues. The 234 Hungarian MPs in the sample asked 871 parliamentary questions and made 414 interpellations during the first two and a half years of their mandate (May 2010–December 2012). In total, 58.1 percent of these MPs never raised a constituency-related issue, whereas almost one-third (31.6 percent) did not table any question or interpellation whatsoever. Content analysis of all of the 1285 questions and interpellations revealed that only 235 of them (18.3 percent) can be considered acts of constituency service. The difference in temporal coverage in the two countries is due to the fact that at the time of the collection and coding of the parliamentary question data, the Romanian MPs who had participated in the Candidate Study were just entering the second year of their term.

Comparing the extent to which parliamentary questions are used as a tool for local interest representation, the Romanian Parliament appears more similar to the Irish legislature, where Martin (2011b) found that 45 percent of the written parliamentary questions submitted between 1997 and 2002 addressed constituency issues and the Italian Parliament, where Russo (2011) found that 39.3 percent of all parliamentary questions asked in the 15th Legislature (2006–2008) could be considered 'constituency oriented questions'. Conversely, the rate of local parliamentary questions in Hungary is more similar to that of three other western European parliaments: a comparative study found that the share of oral parliamentary questions on local issues is 15 percent in the Netherlands, 13 percent in France and 12 percent in Germany (Van Santen et al. 2015).

In the Romanian sample there is a relatively high correlation between the number of policy questions and interpellations and the number of constituency questions, whereas in Hungary the correlation is only moderate. This implies that there is little to no division of work in terms of asking parliamentary questions and that the most active members engage in both policy-making activities and constituency service. A positive interpretation of this finding would be that in both countries a constituency orientation does not mean a parochial profile of politicians interested solely in advancing local interests. Moreover, it remains an empirical question whether the candidates who personalize their campaigns also ask more nationally focused questions, and I will return to this issue later on.

The analysis is carried out in two steps. In the first stage, I use multivariate tests (i.e., negative binomial regression models) to answer the main research questions of the chapter.[7] The second stage includes further analyses of the effects of the main independent variables that keep constant all other factors and a discriminant validity test: a replication of the multivariate models with policy questions as the dependent variable.

CONSTITUENCY SERVICE ENHANCED BY CAMPAIGN PERSONALIZATION

We start by examining the relationship in the Hungarian sample. The results of the negative binomial regressions are reported in table 8.1. The baseline model emphasizes the importance of campaign activities and strategies while also presenting a counterintuitive finding: list MPs seem to ask more constituency questions than MPs elected in the nominal tier. First, a 1-point increase

Table 8.1 Determinants of the Number of Constituency Questions in Hungary (Negative Binomial Regressions)

	Model 1	*Model 2*	*Model 3*
Constituency agenda	1.631*	1.103	1.179
Campaign norm	1.148***	1.029	1.055
Meeting local activists	1.475***	1.367***	1.362***
County list MP	3.837***	0.885	0.783
National list MP	3.925***	0.717	0.617
Years in Parliament	1.038	1.045*	1.039
Incumbent	0.470**	0.386***	0.561*
Shadowing MP		7.888***	1.804
Local politics experience		1.021**	1.027***
Ideological distance		0.805**	0.744***
KDNP			0.719
MSZP			3.161
JOBBIK			8.157***
LMP			4.657*
Lnalpha	–0.125	–0.698	–0.930
Alpha	0.882***	0.497***	0.395***
Maximum Likelihood R^2	0.242	0.352	0.386
Observations	211	199	199

Significance at $*p < 0.10$, $**p < 0.05$, $***p < 0.01$.
Cell entries are incident rate ratios.
MP, Member of Parliament.

on the scale of campaign individualization brings an increase in the rate of constituency service questions of 15 percent. Second, MPs who personalized their campaigns by promoting local issues not emphasized by their parties seem to ask significantly more constituency questions. The model also corroborates the third hypothesis: a positive effect is associated with meeting local activists during the campaign. These results are analysed in more depth in the next section.

Introducing three additional controls in the second model: a dummy for shadowing and variables measuring experience in local politics and the ideological distance from the party turns the campaign norm and the degree of campaign localization insignificant, although both still point in the hypothesized direction. This is not surprising given that the type of candidacy (especially the lowest tier in case of multiple candidacies) and experience in local politics are among the main predictors of campaign styles and contents in Hungary (Chiru 2015). On the contrary, meeting local activists during the campaign remains an important predictor of asking constituency questions, the magnitude of the effect being similar to that resulting from the first model. This is evidence that intense campaign socialization episodes can have lasting effects for legislative behaviour, irrespective of candidates' backgrounds and electoral tiers of candidacy.

The second model also reveals the considerable effect of 'shadowing'. Thus, parliamentarians who ran in SMDs and lost initiate eight times more parliamentary questions and interpellations having a local dimension than the rest of their colleagues. This effect was actually driving the unusual finding in model 1; after controlling for 'shadowing' both categories of county and national list MPs appear less active with respect to territorial representation than SMD representatives. Moreover, it seems the candidacy logic trumps the seat logic in fostering a constituency orientation, as the effect of the former (the shadow MP dummy) is several times larger than the effect of the latter.

Socialization into local politics appears to be a significant predictor of constituency service engagement. Thus, if one compares MPs who have never held a local political office with their counterparts who have ten years of such experience, the latter's rate of parliamentary questions regarding local issues is 20 percent higher.

The last control variable included in the second model, ideological distance, entails a negative effect on constituency service. The effect is small but significant: running margins showed that 1-point difference on the left-right scale decreases the number of parliamentary questions and interpellations dealing with local issues by 0.26. The last model accounts for the partisan differences in questioning patterns. The results reveal important interparty differences, with some parties asking as many as eight times more locally oriented questions than others. Just four of the other variables display significant effects when introducing the party dummies: the frequency of meeting party activists during the campaign, incumbency, experience in local politics and ideological distance—all pointing in the expected directions. The shadowing effect disappears when controlling for partisan affiliation. This can be related straightforwardly with the fact that two parties won 173 out of the 176 SMD mandates.

The regression results presented in table 8.2 show that for the Romanian sample a personalized campaign norm and investing time in meeting local activists during the campaign do not make a difference for the engagement in constituency service. On the contrary, the coefficient for campaign localization is significant in all models. More than three-quarters (77 percent) of the elected respondents to the Romanian Candidate Study promoted topics related to the constituency in their campaigns, and the negative binomial regressions suggest this agenda is also reflected in their parliamentary questions. Thus, the second hypothesis is fully corroborated: MPs who have talked about local issues in their campaigns ask more constituency questions than their colleagues who did not focus on local issues at the time of their candidacy. The effect is robust to the three different model specifications. The magnitude of this effect will be analysed in more depth in the next section.

Table 8.2 Determinants of the Number of Constituency Questions in Romania (Negative Binomial Regressions)

	Model 1	*Model 2*	*Model 3*
Constituency agenda	1.645*	1.729*	1.718*
Campaign norm	1.081	1.056	1.048
Meeting local activists	1.032	1.079	1.058
MP won plurality	0.633*	0.74	0.647
N. MPs same county	0.954***	0.963***	0.959***
Years in Parliament	0.937	0.939	0.944
Incumbent	2.950***	3.007***	2.853***
Local politics experience	1.006	1.008	1.018
Ideological distance		0.794*	0.812*
PSD–PC			3.611**
PNL			3.163**
PDL			2.832*
PPDD			2.928*
Lnalpha	0.858	0.839	0.803
Maximum Likelihood R^2	.125	.132	.157
Observations	161	147	147

Significance at *$p < 0.10$, **$p < 0.05$, ***$p < 0.01$.
Cell entries are incident rate ratios.
MP, Member of Parliament.

MPs who failed to win the plurality of votes in their SMD ask 1.6 times more local questions than their more successful colleagues. The effect disappears after introducing party dummies, which is hardly surprising given that the candidates of some parties (the National Liberal Party, PNL) and alliances (the Social Democratic Party–Conservative Party alliance, PSD–PC) won their seats directly in the vast majority of districts.

Moreover, MPs who have fewer colleagues from the same county tend to engage more in constituency service. Another interesting finding is that incumbents seem better able than newcomers to recognize the electoral advantage brought by constituency service. On average, incumbents asked almost three times more constituency questions than the rest.

Although a larger ideological distance does not necessarily equate to being more ideological and less constituency oriented, this variable does decrease the likelihood of engagement in constituency service through parliamentary questions. The magnitude of the effect is not very large: 1-point difference on the left-right scale decreases the number of parliamentary questions and interpellations dealing with local issues by a factor of 1.3, whereas a 2-point difference translates into a decrease of constituency questions by a factor of 1.5.

Parliamentary seniority and local politics experience both point in the expected direction; senior MPs exhibit lower service engagement and local politicians higher, but the effects did not reach conventional levels of statistical significance. Last but not least, MPs of the parties forming the government at the time tend to ask more local questions than the opposition MPs. This rather unusual finding, given that opposition MPs tend to ask more parliamentary questions in general (Vliegenthart and Walgrave 2011), has in the Romanian context two explanations. First, the UDMR (Democratic Alliance of Hungarians in Romania) MPs are traditionally more interested in representing the interests of the Hungarian community as a whole, including the so-called internal Diaspora ('szorvany'), than particular local interests from the county where they received the seat. Moreover, the UDMR parliamentary party group (PPG) includes a number of veteran MPs who have developed significant policy expertise and are highly active in parliamentary policy debates.

The second explanation has to do with the characteristics of the PPDD (People's Party–Dan Diaconescu) MPs. After the 2012 elections PPDD was the second-largest opposition party, and the first new party to gain parliamentary representation since 1992. More than half of the sixty-eight MPs of this populist, anti-establishment party were active in other parties, some of them being 'professional' party hoppers, and the rest of the PPG is composed of journalists, local businessmen, lawyers and other professionals who had no previous political involvement. Given this heterogeneous collection and opportunistic habits, the PPDD MPs were less likely to be interested in developing a strong local connection with voters. By June 2014, 71 percent of their MPs had switched to other parties, the party group in the Senate disappearing because less than seven senators (the membership threshold for a PPG) remained affiliated with the party.

To assess properly the magnitude of the main effects related to personalized campaigning I ran simulations with the STATA program Clarify (King, Tomz and Wittenberg 2000) based on the full models in tables 8.1 and 8.2. Figure 8.3 plots the expected number of Hungarian MPs' constituency questions with 95 percent confidence intervals against the frequency of meeting local activists during the campaign. It turns out that MPs who spent no time meeting local party activists during the campaign asked zero constituency questions, all other things being equal. At the other end of the scale, MPs who got involved the most in this activity raised on average around 1.2 constituency questions.

Figure 8.4 illustrates the Romanian MPs' expected number of constituency questions with confidence intervals for campaign localization. MPs who did not raise local issues in their campaign are expected to ask around four constituency questions, whereas their colleagues who engaged in localized campaigning will ask on average around seven constituency questions a year, all other things being equal.

It might be argued that the connection between personalized campaign activities and asking constituency service questions is simply spurious, being

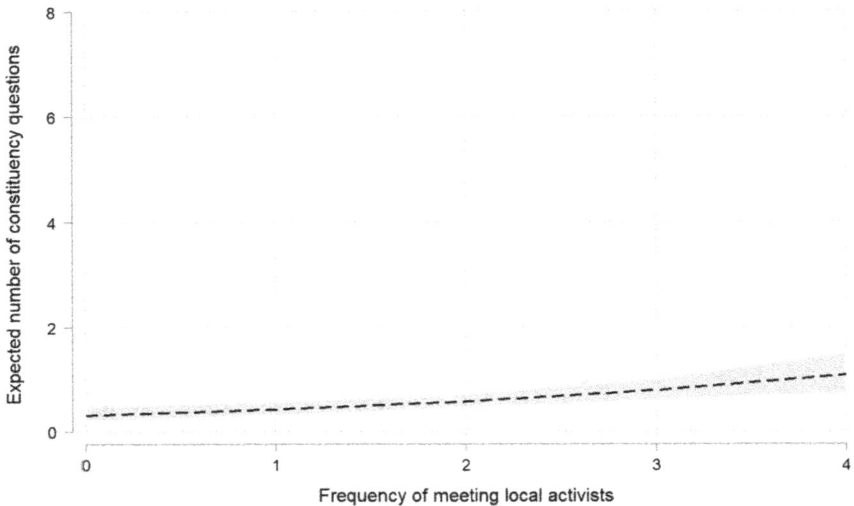

Figure 8.3 Changes in the Number of Constituency Questions Based on Frequency of Meeting Local Activists during Campaign (Hungary).

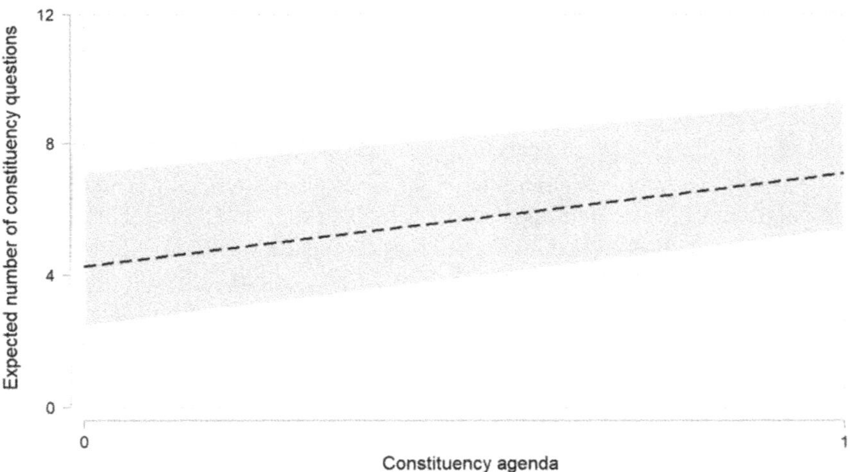

Figure 8.4 Changes in the Number of Constituency Questions Based on Campaign Localization (Romania).

in fact a simple reflection of political ambition in two different arenas. Thus, ambitious MPs who try to build a reputation could simply put more effort into their campaigns and then also maintain a very high level of engagement in various parliamentary activities. If this is the case, then the three campaign-related variables should also be strong predictors of the number of policy questions asked by Hungarian and Romanian MPs. However, re-running the regressions in tables 8.1 and 8.2 with the number of policy questions as dependent variable showed that in both samples campaign decisions and campaign activities do not influence at all the MPs' frequency of asking policy questions.

CONCLUSIONS

This chapter contributes to the literature on decentralized personalization, it goes beyond illustrating its existence to show that it indeed has behavioural consequences for legislators. The latter seem to happen mostly with respect to the MPs' type of work focus, rather than with respect to the dispersion of power or clashes with party leaders over discipline. Thus, decentralized personalism seems to be more a vehicle for nonprogrammatic links than for changes in power structure in parties. Although different aspects of campaigning mattered for subsequent engagement in constituency service in the two samples, the preliminary evidence presented here does indicate that there is a link between the two arenas and that the choice of a personalized campaign results in a reinforced commitment for constituency representation on the part of the MPs.

From a normative point of view the fact that large numbers of MPs in the two countries seem to act on their individual campaign promises at least on local issues is rather refreshing, especially when considering the usually problematic functioning of parliamentary delegation and accountability chains in young democracies. This kind of responsiveness, which remains largely unobserved by national media, could help increase the trust of ordinary citizens in their representatives and in the legitimacy of the political system. Moreover, it could also contribute to a more positive perspective regarding personalism and personalization, which are usually considered harmful for the functioning of political parties and the overall quality of democracy.

Future studies could monitor actual, instead of self-reported campaign behaviour to make a stronger case for the link between personalized campaigning and constituency service. Furthermore, content analysing the campaign pledges of the candidates and of their main challengers and comparing their topics with the issues addressed by constituency questions could be an additionally fruitful direction of research.

Last but not least, the perspective adopted in this chapter is largely cross-sectional, mostly because of data availability (table 8.2). Nevertheless, it can be speculated that the likely increase in decentralized personalization over

Table 8.3 Variable Codebook

Variable	*Operationalization*
Campaign norm	0, The goal of my campaign was to attract the most attention to my party . . . 10, The goal of my campaign was to attract the most attention to my candidacy.
Constituency agenda	1, The campaign promoted constituency specific issues; 0, No issues related to the electoral district were raised.
Meeting local activists	0, I did not meet any; 1, I spent between 1 to 5 hours per week meeting local party members; 2, 5 to 10 hours per week . . . ; 3, 10 to 20 hours per week . . . ; 4, more than 20 hours per week . . .
MP won plurality	1, MP won the plurality of votes in the SMD; 0, MP finished second, third or fourth.
Shadowing MP	1, MP ran in a SMD and lost; 0, MP won the SMD.
N. MPs same county	Number of MPs (Deputies and Senators) elected from the same county.
Years in Parliament	Years of Parliamentary mandate before the 2012 elections.
Incumbent	1, the MP was a member of the previous Parliament; 0, the MP was not a member of the previous Parliament.
Local politics experience	Years in local office.
Ideological distance	0, perfect congruence between the MPs and the party ideological position . . . 10, maximum ideological distance

MP, Member of Parliament; SMD, single-member district.

time (Pruysers and Cross, this volume)[8], propelled by the decline of partisan identification (Bittner, this volume), the adoption of candidate-centred electoral systems (Pilet and Renwick, this volume), and inclusive personnel selection procedures (Stewart, this volume), could also trigger more individualized legislative behaviour in the future. Such a longitudinal analysis certainly represents another avenue worth pursuing by researchers interested in the consequences of decentralized personalization.

NOTES

1. Parts of the chapter related to the analysis of the Hungarian case were previously published in Chiru, M. 2017, 'Cheap Talk or Proper Signaling? Styles of Campaigning and Engagement in Constituency Service', *Social Science Quarterly*, DOI: 10.1111/ssqu.12404
2. Author's own calculation.
3. Normatively this is a positive finding, but it does not rule out the possibility that party leaders might still have to make greater effort and more compromises to extract loyalty from legislators than in a less-personalized environment.

4. This is measured with the question: 'What was the primary aim of your campaign?' The candidates had to respond using a 0–10 scale in which the end points were labelled 'To attract as much attention as possible for my party' and 'To attract as much attention as possible for me as a candidate'.

5. The Hungarian Parliament was elected until the 2012 electoral reform through a mixed-member majoritarian (MMM) electoral formula. According to this formula 176 MPs were elected in SMDs, a maximum of 152 were elected in multimember districts (county lists) and at least 58 through a national, 'compensatory list', that aggregated the surplus votes and distributed any seats not allocated in the county tier (Benoit 2001).

6. This figure represents 30.3 percent of all Romanian MPs and 60.6 percent of all Hungarian parliamentarians. Both samples are highly representative with respect to party affiliation.

7. Because of the nature of the dependent variable (count data and because of its over-dispersion), the appropriate method for modelling was negative binomial regression (Cameron and Trivedi 2013). Moreover, I use incidence rate ratios (exponentiated coefficients), run margins and make simulations with Clarify (King et al. 2000) to make the interpretation of the main results straightforward.

8. In Hungary, the opposite trend seems to have taken place, despite the 2011 electoral reforms that strengthen the SMD tier. Thus, scholars observed lower average levels of decentralized personalization at the 2014 elections compared to the 2010 campaign (Papp and Zorigt 2017). This seems to have happened mostly because of the party endogenous factors related to organizational resources and preelectoral coalition politics.

Chapter 9

Personalization, Personal Authority and Governance[1]

Jonathan Malloy

This chapter focuses on the relationship among personalism, personalization and governance. Similar to the presidentialization thesis (Poguntke and Webb 2005; Poguntke and Webb, this volume), it focuses on the institutional power of modern leaders/chief executives. However, it differs somewhat from the presidentialization thesis by looking more at variations in this personalization between individuals. Although all modern leaders enjoy considerable and seemingly increasing personal power through their institutional offices, the modern state is so complex and multifaceted that institutional power is not always sufficient. Some leaders are able to cultivate a larger ascribed sense of *personal authority* that gives them legitimacy beyond institutional rules and typically greater effectiveness and success. This chapter explores this more intangible concept of personal authority, illustrating it through a brief examination of recent prime ministers in four Westminster systems of government. Although an introductory exploration rather than conclusive study, this chapter contrasts with the presidentialization approach by suggesting that personal authority, at least in these recent Westminster cases, is often rooted *in*, rather than *apart from*, the party. This chapter also finds mixed evidence of personalization—change over time—as while centralized and personalized power has generally grown, personal authority is not necessarily rising.

The general relationship between the centralization of state power and the overall personalization of politics is well established from both directions. Cooper suggests that 'a central cause for the centralisation of power towards the core executive is alleged to be the personalisation of politics, and especially the increased responsibility party leaders now shoulder for the electoral performance of their party' (2017, 4), whereas Poguntke and Webb suggest 'a cyclical (or reciprocal) relationship: The increased power and autonomy of chief executives flowing from the growth of the state and the internationalization of politics drives presidentialization, and as the power and autonomy of chief executives grows, they become even more dominant in the media coverage (i.e., the media coverage becomes more personalized)' (this volume). Although all leaders rely heavily on the instruments and structures of institutional state power to govern and to reinforce their own media presence and electoral popularity, there can be a disconnect between the image of centralized, personalized leadership and the reality of power. Electoral and personal popularity in particular does not automatically translate into omnipotence within cabinets and party backrooms. Some leaders cultivate a more personalized authority over their governments than others, despite similar electoral and institutional circumstances; others may enjoy considerable electoral popularity, yet struggle to establish their authority within the halls of power. And although Poguntke and Webb argue in this volume that '[t]he personalization of the electoral process has made leaders more independent from their parties (including their parliamentary parties)', and McAllister suggests that 'leaders now hold their positions by virtue of a personalized mandate, rather than because of a support base within the party' (2007: 583), this chapter suggests a fusion rather than disconnection between leaders' success and relationships with their parties. The presidentialization thesis focuses more on how leaders go around their parties and operate independently of them, resembling 'the logic that flows from ideal-typical presidential systems in that chief executives increasingly act independently of their parties and attempt to govern through more plebiscitary mechanisms' (Poguntke and Webb, this volume). In contrast, this chapter reflects primarily on how leaders, at least in the Westminster systems that are the focus of this chapter, draw personal authority from their standing and preeminence *within the party* to exert power and influence.

The importance of leaders' relationships with their parties can be immediately illustrated by comparing two Canadian prime ministers: Brian Mulroney (1984–1993) and Jean Chrétien (1993–2003). Both leaders are identified with presidentialization and personalization trends such as the centralization of state power through long-term growth of the prime ministerial office and other central agencies and, as leaders of Canada's two 'brokerage' parties, serving as the media and electoral face of disparate collections of broad regional and ideological interests (Carty and Cross 2010). Yet although Chrétien enjoyed much better overall political popularity than Mulroney, the latter enjoyed greater *personal* authority and loyalty within his party. Indeed, Mulroney was the most unpopular Canadian prime minister ever, with two regional parties splitting from his Progressive Conservative party (see Carty, Cross and Young 2000). Yet he kept the core party intact, and his parliamentary caucus remained intensely loyal with few defections. He maintained close personal and individual contact with Members of Parliament (MPs) and the grassroots party, and this cultivation of favours and loyalty allowed Mulroney to accumulate and maintain remarkable personal loyalty despite terrible political conditions, allowing him to pursue bold policy initiatives and execute his retirement on his own terms.

In contrast, Chrétien led his party to three majority victories, enjoyed continually strong poll standings, and more than Mulroney, is particularly identified with the centralization of personal institutional power in the prime minister's office (Savoie 1999; Simpson 2001). Yet he was overthrown from within, after appearing aloof and distant to many in his party and failing to manage expectations among his MPs amid a major rivalry with his long time finance minister, Paul Martin. Despite a lack of institutional mechanisms to challenge the party leader, Martin managed to force out Chrétien over an extended period of insurrection. In short, despite similar or even greater institutional power, similar party-leadership selection and deselection rules and more consistent political popularity, Chrétien was not able to enjoy the extent of personal loyalty and authority within his party' and government enjoyed by Mulroney. Similar examples can be found in other countries, demonstrating that centralized power and personalization over time are not the whole story. They are shaped by more intangible variables, the most important of which may be leaders' relationships with their political parties.

The 'black box' of parliamentary government makes it difficult to construct empirical tests to assess and measure the precise and complex relationship between institutional power and personal authority. However, through thematic discussion and case studies, we can unpack the relationship and variation in it. This chapter focuses on four Westminster systems: Australia, Canada, New Zealand and the United Kingdom. This provides a well-recognized set of 'most similar' cases (Rhodes, Wanna and Weller 2009) that allows us to illustrate and explore the concept of personal authority given relatively similar institutional contexts. Furthermore, the heavy reliance on evolutionary tradition in the Westminster system, with partly unwritten conventions and an erratic codification of practices recognizing the reality of party government, provides a useful context for understanding the relationship between institutionally personalized power and individual personal authority. With considerable room for interpretation in the powers of prime minister and cabinet, and a sometimes-elusive relationship between parliamentary institutions and political parties, the flexibility of the system gives a great deal of allowance to the *ascription* of power. Much of Westminster leaders' power and authority is because others ascribe and give it to them—or do not—whether or not the institutional rules say so. They thus serve as the best context for exploring the link between institutional personalization of power and personalized authority.

Before turning to specific cases, the chapter begins by exploring elements of the 'core executive' literature on the centralization of power. It then turns to the leadership literature to understand how leaders use or do not use this power, and the crucial concepts of hard (institutionalized) power versus soft (persuasive) power to develop the idea of 'personal authority'. These concepts help bridge the gap between general institutional personalization and variable individual power. They also help us to focus directly on the key link between leaders and party followers and how variations in this link explain how some leaders are able to build and maintain a more truly individual and unique sense of personalism in government compared to others. I then explore and illustrate these themes through the brief Westminster case studies and conclude with reflections on what underlies personal authority and its impact on the long-term health of political parties.

THE CORE EXECUTIVE

Scholars of parliamentary systems are in general agreement that governing institutions have become more centralized over time. One such approach is the 'presidentialization' thesis, already mentioned and presented elsewhere in this volume and thus not elaborated here. Another approach, more dominant in the public administration literature, is the 'core executive'. The core executive approach also emphasizes a centralization of power, but in a less institutionalized and more chaotic form that does not necessarily include personalization—growth of power around individuals—at all. In its original formulation, this approach attempted, among other purposes, to curtail 'the tired debate about the power of the prime minister' (Rhodes 2006, 323) in favour of a more sophisticated and networked model that downplayed personalization and the role of individuals while explaining the centralization of power within larger changes in the nature of the state. By 'emphasizing the collection of institutions that coordinate policy in central government, rather than privileging particular institutions such as the prime minister or the cabinet' (Elgie 2011, 64), the core executive ideas 'reflect the idea that the state, moving beyond formal powers, only steers and regulates self-organizing networks and markets. Such networks and markets encompass state and non-state actors, so state hierarchies are deemed to lack the privileged position granted them under the Westminster model' (Heffernan 2005, 607).

Thus, the core executive approach, at least in its original form, was not necessarily about the *personalization* of power at all, nor even an organized sense of centralized institutional power. Rather, it emphasized the simultaneous centralization *and* fragmentation of power within the centre as well and the notion of a 'hollow crown' (Bakvis, Rhodes and Weller 1997) rather than an omnipotent centralized state with a dominant person at the centre. Examining the Tony Blair UK government, Bevir and Rhodes (2006, 676) argue a 'governance paradox' in which prime-ministerial power may seem supreme but is in fact tempered by complex networks and patterns of dependence that produce 'ubiquitous' implementation gaps and undermine the idea of personalized, prime-ministerial omnipotence. It is this gap that this chapter focuses on: between institutional power ascribed to an individual office and the actual ability to exercise that power in the shifting vortex of the core executive.

Personalization and the core executive approach are not incompatible, and indeed, Elgie (2011) notes that the bulk of core executive studies since have returned to a belief that power has become particularly concentrated in the office of the prime minister. One such approach is by Donald Savoie, who provides a strong link between centralization and personalization by arguing that the complexity of the modern state means the elevation and predominance of individuals and especially prime ministers, but less by structural power or design and more by accident and default as the one figure that can stand out amid chaos. Thus, 'only when the prime minister is directly involved or in moments of crisis is the government capable of bold action and decision' (1999, 317), and 'when the prime minister does focus on an issue and provides clear political direction, the system responds and decisions are made and things do happen. As for the rest, the system will manage the process and the issues, but bold action will hardly be forthcoming' (1999, 8). For Savoie (2008, 230), institutional structures and rules are largely irrelevant for leaders who wield a more personalized form of authority:

> Individuals now rule, starting with the prime minister and his most trusted courtiers, carefully selected ministers, and senior civil servants, and they have more power in a court-style government than they do when formal policy and decision-making processes tied to cabinet decision making are respected. It explains why the most powerful individuals in government, starting with the prime minister, have in recent years put aside formal decision-making processes on things that matter to them. They can roam virtually anywhere within government, focusing on issues that are of direct interest to those that threaten the government's political interest, much as they would in a cafeteria picking up items at will, without regard to formal processes.

Savoie's notion of a prime-ministerial 'court' of close advisors whose authority stems from their relationship to their principal mirrors Bevir and Rhodes's (2006) notion of a 'departmental court', as does the larger image of a government run by individual political and policy entrepreneurs rather than structured and collective entities. It thus also points us to a secondary aspect of the personalization argument explored in this volume: its multilevel nature and the power of individual ministers, public servants and advisors.

Although their power may depend ultimately on the leader, these figures may operate with a high degree of independence with little or no statutory or institutional backing.

But a missing concept in much of the core executive literature is *political parties*. Although the presidentialization thesis pays attention to the party and electoral 'faces' and strongly links leaders' institutionalized power within parties to the personalization of governing power, the core executive literature (including Savoie) tends to leave the question of where prime ministers come from, and the political basis of their power, largely unanswered. Introducing political parties to this literature is not a new idea; Strangio, t'Hart and Walter (2013, 13) provide a partial antidote with their attempt to 'revitalize the study of prime ministerial leadership', and consistent with the above, place parties at the centre:

> Curiously, much of the debate about the contemporary prime ministership concentrates upon their performance in parliament; their relations with cabinet, individual ministers and the civil service; their centrality (or otherwise) in the 'core executive' and their ability to personify the 'story' of their government. Yet their tenure depends not only upon electoral success, but also upon their ability to maintain the confidence and support of their party.

This suggests the continuing validity of George Jones's (1964, 181) assertion that 'the prime minister is only as strong as his party, and particularly his chief colleagues, lets him be'. Although the core executive literature suggests a general centralization and in most cases increasing personalization of state institutional power, party remains key to understanding the true personal role of leaders.

LEADERSHIP

To explore the link among leaders, the core executive and political parties, we move from institutional approaches to the scholarly literature on *leadership*, which by design focuses mostly on individuals and personal agency. Political leadership was long a weakly developed concept (Hartley and Benington 2011), drifting at times into unsystematic biography and focus on the [inevitably gendered] 'great man'. But it at least highlights the individualized and varying nature of power that may be downplayed in the institutionalist approaches to the centralization of power that can overlook the reality of 'living and scheming politicians' (Heffernan 2005, 616). The most established work focuses on the political psychology of leadership, primarily in the United States, with a focus on leaders' 'cognitive, personality, motivational and other psychological attributes as individuals' (Hartley and Benington 2011, 203). But newer work emphasizes the interplay between leaders and their surrounding environment, including institutions, supporters and timing and contexts.

A key concept in leadership literature is the power of *persuasion* and leaders' ability, or inability, to get others to agree and follow, not simply obey. Nye's distinction between 'hard' and 'soft' power (Nye 1990) is often used here to distinguish between leaders' formal rules and powers and their more informal ability to cajole, persuade and exercise influence without formal coercion, with the two not necessarily going hand in hand. Similarly, electoral momentum, public popularity and even a dominating and omnipotent public and media image are not necessarily effective guides to leaders' true power and persuasive ability: 'seemingly all-powerful prime ministers can come unstuck relatively quickly, suggesting that we should not make the mistake of confusing the appearance of dominance with the underlying conditional, contextual and thus potentially ephemeral nature of prime ministerial preponderance' (Strangio, t'Hart and Walter 2013, 8). Soft power emphasizes the idea of an authorizing environment or zone of discretion around leaders that gives them an ability to lead and command without necessarily needing to resort openly to their actual hard legal and constitutional powers. This is similar to Poguntke and Webb's (2005, 7) core concept of *autonomy*: 'a larger sphere of action in which [leaders] are protected from outside interference'. In each case, the emphasis is on the authority freely ascribed to leaders by their followers, though the leadership literature focuses much more on how this authority varies for different leaders rather than a steady increase over time in personalization.

These ideas of soft power and maintaining the confidence of followers, especially when the going gets tough, are developed by Bennister, Worthy and t'Hart (2017) in their work on leadership capital and a 'leadership capital index' (LCI). The LCI emphasizes how leaders respond to their given institutional and contextual circumstances and the 'leadership capital' that is then generated. Defining leadership capital as 'a form of political credit that can be accumulated in office and serve to sustain leadership through good and bad times' (2017, 4), they distinguish it from both general popularity and statutory/institutional powers. Instead, it is determined by a mix of skills, relationships and reputations that give some leaders with high capital the large zones to pursue priorities and goals, whereas others with low capital struggle to do more than stay afloat. By definition the LCI is about personalism, though it does not explore whether this has grown over time. Instead it emphasizes variances in personal power, and the difference between mere 'office-holding' of institutionalized power in a position and the true exercise of power through personally held authority.

Personal authority is admittedly an elusive concept to measure because it focuses on the gap between de jure and de facto power—not what the law says leaders can do, but what they can actually do. Personal authority embodies both specific powers, such as the ability to set and time policies, priorities and decisions; to appoint and move around people; and to structure or restructure institutions and processes but also the broader sphere of the authorizing environment and powers of persuasion that allows them to exercise power with little or no resistance or perhaps even seeming notice. It is perhaps useful to think of this in terms of a continuum from institutionalized/coercive power toward ascribed/voluntary power, including *rules* (statutes and written guidelines that specifically give leaders power or constrain their power); *norms* (assumptions that certain things can only be done by leaders despite no specific statutory or written basis); and *trust/loyalty* (belief in leaders who should be followed and obeyed even when doubts and concerns arise). Personal authority allows leaders to rely less on rules and formal 'hard' power, and predominantly on the 'soft' power of trust and loyalty, often turning this trust into norms that followers simply accept as the way things are.

Leadership in general and personal authority in particular are not always easily tied to distinctive individual personal qualities of a leader or 'privatization' of their lives and inner personalities. Although some leaders have an obvious aura of public appeal and charisma, others operate more subtly and may not project overwhelming personal charm or authority. And personal authority is not interchangeable with personal popularity in electoral campaigns. As Bittner shows (this volume), party leaders clearly 'matter' as important factors in vote choice, though she finds little evidence that this is a new phenomenon or that it is increasing over time. A popular leader may win elections based on his or her personal appeal, and the party may embrace this to the point of downplaying its own identity; for example, in the 2004 Canadian election, the perceived popularity of its leader Paul Martin led the Liberal Party to reduce the party name in much of its advertising in favour of 'The Martin Team' (Cross et al. 2015, 118). But governance is more day to day over the long term. An externally popular leader must work within the fractured core executive and contend with internal cultures, opponents and other obstacles that may be impervious to the leader's personal popularity, as Martin found in his short-lived prime ministership. Some leaders utterly fail to translate electoral enthusiasm into long-term personalized authority; Kevin Rudd was enormously personally popular in the 2007 Australian election but within three years was overthrown by his parliamentary colleagues. Others never hit the giddy heights of popularity but are unquestionably personally dominant inside the black box with overwhelming internal legitimacy and authority. Canada's Stephen Harper is an example. Each of these cases are discussed further in the next section.

PERSONAL AUTHORITY IN THE WESTMINSTER MODEL

To explore and illustrate this concept of personal authority and its relationship to political parties, this next section looks at leaders in the four Westminster systems of Australia, Canada, New Zealand and the United Kingdom. Personalism in governing institutions seems almost a given in the Westminster parliamentary system, which remains nominally organized around individuals forming a ministry and can trace a continuous heritage back to an era predating modern parties and mass politics entirely. The notion of vesting government leadership in a single individual nominally able to organize a sufficient number of MPs to form a stable government is not unique to Westminster systems. But as noted previously, these four 'most similar' Westminster systems with their common institutional baseline provide a useful context for understanding the relationship between institutionally personalized power and individual personal authority. Furthermore, Westminster systems are generally considered among the most centralized parliamentary systems, with typically single-party governments and executives (though I also consider examples of coalitions). They thus serve as the best context for exploring the link between institutional personalization of power and personalized authority. I focus on leaders since the 1980s, given that this is the period most closely associated with the rise of the core executive as part of a 'new public management' paradigm in all four countries (Aucoin 1995), distinct from the 'overloaded' and seemingly diminished executives of the 1960s and 1970s (Campbell 1983; Campbell and Wyszomirski 1991). This gives us a healthy range of broadly comparable cases over more than three decades, though as we will see, there is little evidence of temporal trends when it comes to personal authority; it is neither rising nor falling but unique to each individual.

I will contrast three broad categories of Westminster leaders. The first is leaders who sought authority *above and beyond* the party, in the way typically posited by the presidentialization thesis. However, these are exceptions. The second category thus looks at leaders who cultivated personal authority *within* the party and were able to translate this into long-term political and policy success, often independent of electoral and popular conditions. The third category considers cases of leaders whose power was *limited* by their party; although they may have governed for years and not been complete political failures, they were forced to rely primarily on institutional powers of the office alone and were unable to cultivate a larger sense of personal authority within their parties and governments.

Power beyond Party

As noted, the presidentialization thesis tends to emphasize the idea of leaders who transcend their parties, using their electoral focus, personal popularity and the instruments of state power to cultivate a more independent authority that is less reliant on the parliamentary and extra-parliamentary party. There are examples of such leaders in the Westminster systems, former British Prime Minister Tony Blair being the most prominent. As Foley (2000) argues, Blair used a form of 'spatial leadership' and the constant theme of 'New Labour' to separate himself from the traditional structures, values and factions of his party. Blair constantly sought to transform his image away from party leader accountable to his partisan supporters, to statesman leading the nation, driving the party in directions it did not necessarily want to go, such as participation in the Iraq War. In this sense, Blair is clearly a 'presidential' figure and achieved longevity and success (Foley 2000; Theakston 2013). Another possible example is Bob Hawke of Australia, who enjoyed great personal popularity and appeal and used this image of a direct connection to the Australian people to drive his party and ministers in new and sometimes uncomfortable policy directions (Ryan and Bramston 2003; Laing and McCaffrie 2013).

Yet these may be exceptional cases, and we can identify corresponding recent examples of failure by leaders who sought to rise above the ordinary bonds of party. Paul Martin (Canada) and Malcolm Turnbull (Australia) provide a strikingly similar pair of cases. Both rose to power by overthrowing sitting prime ministers, although through different mechanisms, with Turnbull triggering a spill within the parliamentary caucus against Tony Abbott (as Abbott had done against Turnbull as opposition leader in 2009), whereas Martin spent years organizing and mobilizing against Chrétien within the party at the grassroots level (Jeffrey 2010). Yet both came to power riding waves of extraordinary personal popularity and enthusiasm, enabled by their images of successful businesspeople open to new ideas and with seemingly enormous personal energy. These would seem ideal conditions for presidentialization, and indeed both believed their great general personal appeal and their appealing private stories would allow them to heal internal party wounds and lead to long-term electoral victory and personal success. But both were quickly dragged back into intraparty conflicts and squabbles that distracted and sapped their energy, along with their own excessively ambitious but mercurial agendas that led to disappointment and dashed expectations. Each leader enjoyed the institutional powers of office, but in the swirling vortex of the core executive where power is dependent on relationships and authority, party factions and rivals posed obstacles and distractions they could not easily overcome. Although examples of personalism in both their parties and governing offices, neither were able to cultivate individual *personalized authority* to govern successfully (though Turnbull remains in office at the time of writing). In short, while there are certainly examples of leaders whose authority emanated from their personal standing apart from the party, these may be exceptional. More often, the leader is tied to their party, and the next sections explore examples of both success and failure in this regard.

Power from Party

Although some leaders do rise above their party like Blair and Hawke, the more common pattern of successful personal authority within a Westminster party is found among leaders who invested heavily within their parties. Recent examples of such leaders are John Howard of Australia, Stephen Harper of Canada and Helen Clark and John Key of New Zealand.

Like their national counterparts Martin and Turnbull, Harper and Howard provide a striking pair of similarities. Both were career politicians with long histories in their parties, and despite career setbacks within the party (particularly Howard), had deep reservoirs of experience and contacts that gave them a strong sense of the party at all levels from parliamentary members to grassroots. In contrast to arguments suggesting a link between personalization and privatization (see Thomas, this volume), both had bland personal images, were competent but unexciting communicators and provoked minimal popular excitement, much less buzz or sex appeal. Yet this lack of personal charisma, combined with their great familiarity with every corner of their parties, may have reinforced their deep standing and appreciation within their parties, giving a sense of 'one of us' rather than a distant celebrity. Neither attempted to please all the people all of the time, instead following a disciplined strategy of focusing on marginal voters in lower-middle-class suburbs (Errington and Van Onselen 2007; Ibbitson 2015). This ideologically disciplined strategy meant some more moderate members left the party entirely, yet in both cases the core remained united, and the party as a whole remained a relatively heterogeneous catch-all mix. The result for each leader was not only electoral success (four successive victories and eleven years in power for Howard; three victories and nine years for Harper) but also huge governing authority. Although not omnipotent, both dominated their cabinets and parliamentary caucuses, with no serious personal or factional rivals and challenges, and steered their governments and parties according to the disciplined strategies they had set out. Harper in particular managed to both neutralize and yet retain loyalty among religious and social conservatives in the party whose goals did not fit in his vision (Malloy 2013). And in both cases, their parties remained firmly loyal to the end, when the electorates finally dismissed them with clear though not landslide defeats. While both leaders, and especially Harper, were widely accused of excessive centralization of power in the prime minister's office, the true centralization was the degree of authority given to them by their parties, in the parliamentary ranks but especially in the general membership, which gave them not just presidentialized status but true *personal authority*.

Another set of examples of personal authority rooted in party loyalty are provided by successive New Zealand leaders Helen Clark and John Key. Although of different parties, with Key defeating Clark in 2008, and with somewhat different personal styles both from each other and from Howard and Harper, they each provide further examples of centralized authority rooted *in* rather than *above* political parties. New Zealand political leadership in the mixed member proportional (MMP) era puts particular value on *transactional* leaders who can navigate coalition and minority governments with other parties (Hayward 2010). While this might seem to advantage leaders who can rise beyond their own party and act in a more presidentialized manner, New Zealand leaders can only engage in the necessary negotiations and trade-offs if they enjoy firm authority within their own party—as Jim Bolger learned on being overthrown by his party colleagues in 1997 after being seen as giving away too much to other parties (McLeay 2006; Cross and Blais 2012a).

Clark presented herself as a 'servant leader' who was not authoritarian or visionary, but rather a good listener with sure-footed judgment (Hayward 2010. 235). She had long service in the party beginning with student activism and including eighteen years as an MP when she became prime minister, and several cabinet posts including deputy prime minister, making her an insider in all possible ways (Johansson 2013). Yet she was not a prisoner of party consensus nor caught up in factional politics; instead, like the other leaders, she enjoyed deep legitimacy and standing in the party that gave her the crucial *personal authority* to govern in her preferred incremental and transactional style. Key provides a partial contrast; a relative latecomer to party politics, he had an outsider image of business success similar to Paul Martin and Malcolm Turnbull and a telegenic appeal that leads Jon Johannsen to label him 'our first celebrity leader' (2015, 96). Yet Key was more disciplined than Martin or Turnbull and did not take his popularity for granted, successfully portrayed himself as 'an ordinary bloke' (Vowles, Coffé and Curtin 2017, 32), and also had the advantage of taking over a relatively united party near the end of Clark's aging Labour government. Like Clark, Key stuck close to his party and gave a strong sense of listening to it from MPs to the grassroots and was generally able to avoid splits and factional disputes. Again, we see a clear case of personal authority in Key.

In all these cases, the leaders enjoyed the growing centralized institutional power characteristic of the Westminster system, subject to national variations, along with the preeminence of electoral authority as the electoral face of their party. Yet it was their relationship with the party—comprising often deep roots, broad knowledge and familiarity with all its corners, and an overall sense of mutual comfort between leader and followers—that produced the personalized authority that truly underlay their power, governing effectiveness and electoral longevity. Brian Mulroney, described previously, is a similar case, though his party did see two splinter parties as well as remarkably low popularity that places him in a lower category of success than the others. The UK's Margaret Thatcher can also be placed in this category, though her strong vision remained divisive in the party, and she was ultimately overthrown from within.

Power Limited by Party

A mirror category to the preceding discussion comprises leaders who for various reasons struggled to assert their authority within their parties and this limited their overall effectiveness. This can include short-term Canadian leaders Joe Clark and John Turner (Kim Campbell being a somewhat different story), but also more 'successful' leaders like the UK's John Major and New Zealand's Jim Bolger, both of whom served seven years in office (coincidentally both from 1990 to 1997). Major struggled throughout his prime ministership to keep his party united and supportive of his agenda; he enjoyed the institutional powers of 'office-holding' but less of the more intangible trust and loyalty ascribed through personal authority. Bolger was not as chronically weak and 'bask[ed] in his role as the "Great Helmsman"' (Boston et al. 1996, 56; Hayward 2010, 234) but as noted, was overthrown from within because he was seen as giving away too much of the party's power.

However, one of the strongest examples of how personal authority is not easily detached from party is the UK's David Cameron. Despite two victories and six years in office, Cameron struggled to assert his authority in his party, particularly against rivals like Boris Johnson, leading eventually to the Brexit referendum whose result ended his political career. Cameron's first term was in coalition with the Liberal Democrats, an arrangement that he successfully navigated to overall political advantage for his party, similarly to the transactional style of New Zealand leaders under MMP. However, the limits of his authority were also evident, particularly in his second term. Like Howard, Harper and Clark, Cameron had spent his career within his political party, serving as a political staffer before being elected to Parliament at the age of thirty-four. But unlike those leaders, who enjoyed a deep sense of 'one of us' among both the party elite and grassroots, Cameron struggled to surmount internal party divisions and discontent even while bringing the party to two election victories. Cameron's youthful and optimistic image were key to

Conservative campaigning, a clear example of personalism, and he enjoyed the normal structures and centralized powers of the modern prime ministership, which suggest presidentialization. But in governing he struggled to assert a broader personal authority as the legitimate and unquestioned leader, in a broader as opposed to statutory and institutional sense.

Cameron relied on an instrument unusual for a UK leader, referendums, which have been identified as key vehicles of presidentialization (Poguntke and Webb, this volume). The first two referendums on electoral reform and Scottish independence can be seen primarily as attempts to address and silence critics *outside* his party, namely, Liberal Democrats and Scottish Nationalists, on difficult public issues on which the Conservatives were relatively or entirely united. They are thus less significant for our discussion here. However, the Brexit referendum of 2016 was much more clearly in response to significant critics and anti-EU feeling within Cameron's party. If the result had been pro-EU, as Cameron hoped, this could be seen as an excellent example of presidentialization, a party leader rising above and outmaneuvering dissenting elements of his own party to assert his agenda and authority. Instead the result favoured his critics, leading to Cameron's demise and further splitting the party and nation. The similar difficulties of Cameron's successor Theresa May suggest that Cameron's task of uniting the Conservatives to accept his personal authority may have been insurmountable.

DISCUSSION

This brings us to some overall reflections on what actually determines a leader's ability to cultivate personal authority. Although some leaders seem to have particular skills at cultivating loyalty and trust, and in other cases, we can identify obvious errors of arrogance, complacency or poor judgment, some factors are simply out of a leader's control and depend ultimately on *context* and *timing*. Indeed, looking back at the successful leaders discussed reveals a certain degree of lucky timing with parties that were open and even eager for restoration and strong leadership. For example, Harper took over a newly unified Canadian Conservative Party that was determined to win power after a decade of estranged and divided parties, and Clark assisted in restoring New Zealand Labour to familiar ground after the right-wing detours of the Lange Government. Cameron's Conservatives were not willing to defer for a common good in the same way. Economic conditions, crises and unforeseen developments and the weakness or strength of opposition parties may also be important determinants in a leader's ability to assert his or her personal authority within the party.

But two factors in particular demand attention here: leadership-selection methods and gender. Does the method of leadership selection affect a leader's personal authority? Stewart (this volume) finds mixed evidence for the overall link between changing selection methods and increasing personalization. The evidence is even more unclear for personal authority; indeed, Stewart (this volume) notes that although primaries may encourage more personalized candidacies unconnected to the party base, 'bringing in new people with a limited background and commitment to the party may help a candidate win the leadership, but such support does not provide day to day support or provide the same kind of base in times of trouble that a loyal coterie of parliamentary supporters will bring' (96)—that is, the loyalty connected to personal authority. Australia provides a unique perspective here with its four deposed prime ministers since 1991 (compared to one each in New Zealand and the United Kingdom and a single mixed case in Canada). The saga of Kevin Rudd and Julia Gilliard is particularly interesting here, as both in turn took advantage of the quick-trigger spill mechanism to overthrow each other, meaning enormous distractions and suspicions within their cabinets and caucuses that undermined their personal authority. Yet selection method here must be seen as a mediating variable and instrument, rather than a major independent contributor to levels of personal authority. Rudd in particular failed to translate his initial popularity into personal authority, gaining a reputation for poor internal relationships that encouraged Gilliard to challenge him; Gilliard's mixed public popularity then encouraged Rudd to pursue retribution through his own challenge. Similarly, Abbott's image of ideological inflexibility combined with mixed popularity encouraged Turnbull's 2015 challenge. Caucus selection/deselection mechanisms must therefore be seen more as an instrument available to challenge already weak leaders (or leaders seen as overstaying their welcome, such as Thatcher and Hawke), rather than a major factor in itself. Similarly, we cannot draw a clear link between other methods and personal authority; Canada's Chrétien was highly insulated from leadership challenge, yet Martin managed to push him out through an extended insurrection campaign.

What about gender? Is it more difficult for women to establish personal authority within their party and hence in their prime ministership? Women may face more obstacles in presenting themselves as 'one of us', though the limited number of cases (seven female prime ministers in the four countries at time of writing) provides mixed evidence. We have seen Clark as an example of successful personal authority, with Thatcher another possible case. Gilliard certainly experienced sexism and resistance to her authority (Wright and Holland 2014), but it is difficult to disaggregate from her overall civil war with Kevin Rudd; similarly, Jenny Shipley's challenge of Jim Bolger was successful because she presented herself as more true to party ideals and interests, but she was soon defeated in election, again making a case difficult to assess. Two cases of female leaders can be seen as particularly determined by context and timing as each inherited a poisoned chalice; we have noted May's inheritance of a divided party in which her predecessor was unable to establish his authority, whereas Kim Campbell succeeded a leader who was the most unpopular prime minister in Canadian history and had little time to build her own profile. Jacinda Ardern, however, presents a more optimistic case of a woman assuming leadership of a weak opposition party and managing to turn its fortunes around to win government, at least in part due to her own personal appeal and charisma. We can thus draw few conclusions about gender patterns, though the discussed cases all reinforce the importance of context in determining personal authority.

A final note is whether personal authority has grown over time, that is, whether it is an example not just of personalized politics but personalization, just as state institutions have generally grown more centralized and personalized over time. The cases discussed from the past three decades do not show any particular pattern. It is possible that a greater historical scope may reveal some clearer trends, but that would also introduce more variables and contextual differences that complicate the analysis. Ultimately, personal authority appears to be determined more by individual leaders' attributes and the circumstances they face, and these will always vary.

CONCLUSIONS: PERSONAL AUTHORITY AND PARTIES

This chapter has argued that personalized politics takes both systematic and varying forms when it comes to governance, with mixed evidence of true personalization over time. There is ample evidence of the general importance of individual actors for elections, parties and government, including presidentialization. But less studied is how this importance varies between individuals, regardless of common institutional structures and norms. This chapter has explored this variance by introducing the separate concept of personal authority. To be clear, institutional power remains an essential foundation for the building and exercising of personal authority, but personal authority allows some leaders to make better use of this institutional foundation than others. Furthermore, I have argued that although presidentialization suggests leaders cultivate personalized power beyond their parties, evidence from the Westminster cases suggest that leaders with true personal authority have it rooted in their parties, rather than beyond, and furthermore that there is no obvious pattern over time. An obvious next research step is to expand this analysis to parliamentary leaders beyond the Westminster model, and to see if we can identify a similar phenomenon of party-linked personal authority in a greater variety of party, electoral and governing systems, and if so, whether it is increasing.

A final question is that even if personal authority is not a case of actual growing personalization, what is its ultimate effect on parties? Although I have argued that parties are fundamentally linked to personal authority, the relationship is not always good in the end for the party. Leaders with personal authority may manage the party well but ultimately for their own convenience, leaving it spent, hollow or divided when they exit because they have dominated so long. Indeed, few leaders with personal authority manage to pass the baton to their successor; more likely is an electoral defeat before or soon after their departure followed by years of retooling. Still, the ultimate effect here surely is to reiterate the central importance of political parties to politics and governance—again, a point that is not well recognized in the core executive literature on the centralization and personalization of power in government. The examples in this chapter have repeatedly shown that party matters crucially in determining the success of Westminster party leaders. The most effective leaders are ones whose personal authority is firmly rooted in their parties, while attempts to slip the party's bonds and govern as personalities beyond party usually end unhappily.

NOTE

1. Research for this chapter was completed while the author was a Visiting Fellow at the School of Politics and International Relations at the Australian National University. The author gratefully acknowledges the School's support.

Chapter 10

Presidentialization, Personalization and Populism

The Hollowing out of Party Government

Thomas Poguntke and Paul D. Webb

THE CONTEXT: POLITICS IN AN AGE OF CRISIS AND POPULIST CHALLENGES

We live in an age of populism. The US and Austrian presidential elections of 2016 are the most conspicuous but certainly not the only prominent examples. The success of Syriza in Greece, the French presidential elections, the Five Star Movement which came from nowhere to be the largest party in Italy, the rise of Podemos in Spain and the success of the national-conservative PIS in Poland; this list is by no means exhaustive. Germany, until recently one of the few modern democracies fairly untainted by major populist challenges has seen notable progress for the right-wing populist Alternative for Germany (AfD) in both *Länder* elections (e.g., in Saxony-Anhalt and Baden-Württemberg, where the AfD finished well ahead of the Social Democratic Party [SPD]), and national parliamentary elections (with the AfD emerging as the third-largest party in the Bundestag in 2017). Despite the relatively late breakthrough of populism in Germany, arguably, the writing has been on the wall, as the structural stability of the party system there has been eroding for some time (Poguntke 2014). Meanwhile in Britain, only the constraints imposed by the electoral system prevented the Eurosceptic nationalist populist UK Independence Party (UKIP) from gaining substantial representation in the parliamentary election of 2015, when it took 12.5 percent of the vote.

These examples demonstrate that populism, though mainly associated with the prefix 'right', is by no means exclusively found on the right of the political spectrum. Furthermore, and this can be learned from the German example, there are good reasons to argue that a necessary condition is a previous erosion of the hold of the established party system. It is the contention of this chapter that the trend towards the presidentialization of politics feeds into this process. More precisely, although presidentialization is in many ways a result of the erosion of party anchorage, it also accelerates and exacerbates it.

Clearly, the consecutive sovereign debt, euro and refugee crises have accelerated trends towards populism, but we need to remember that populist parties had been successful in many countries even before this relatively recent sequence of crises began. Furthermore, not all countries have been equally affected by them. Hence, the focus of this chapter is on the effect of long-term shifts in the way modern democracies work and possible effects on the viability of party government.

More precisely, this chapter will explore the way in which trends towards presidentialization and personalization are interrelated. Although these terms are often used interchangeably in the literature, we contend that presidentialization is a clearly defined concept aimed at the explanation of changes in the working mode of modern political systems, whereas personalization is a social and political trend that extends to different facets of political life and all layers of the political system. In effect, presidentialization is a specific development that feeds into personalization but is, at the same time, fed by it.

We will begin with a restatement of the original thesis of presidentialization and a discussion of necessary refinements before we turn to discussion of the relationship between presidentialization and personalization. The chapter will conclude with a discussion of the repercussions of presidentialization for the functioning of party government, including its connection with populism.

THE PRESIDENTIALIZATION THESIS

In a nutshell, the presidentialization thesis argues that power in modern democracies has shifted from collective bodies to individual leaders (or very small inner circles of leaders in coalition governments). These power shifts have been accompanied by growing zones of autonomy at the disposal of these decision makers. In other words, their power resources have grown while they have also enjoyed a growth of the space where they do not need to use them to overcome resistance (Weber 1980, 28).

We have argued that this will happen in three major political arenas, which we have called the executive, the party and the electoral faces of politics. Although these changes are obviously interconnected, they do not necessarily need to happen at the same time and the same pace. Most importantly, these shifts in the working mode of political systems normally occur without formal legal or constitutional changes. In other words, they happen within the boundaries set by the constitutional order. Figure 10.1 illustrates this in that it depicts the possibility of political systems to move to the northern, presidentialized pole and back again towards a more partified mode of politics. However, we do not envisage a horizontal movement. Political systems remain formally what they are, presidential, semi-presidential or parliamentary, and we have never argued that prime ministers turn into something similar to presidents (Poguntke and Webb 2005; Dowding 2013; Webb and Poguntke 2013). The different constitutional settings define the upper and lower limits of such movements. Thus, a truly 'presidentialized' executive in a presidential system with separation of powers will always enjoy greater power resources and autonomy from party than a 'presidentialized' counterpart in a parliamentary system. Conversely, he or she will never be as vulnerable to his or her own party as a leader would be under parliamentarism. An executive leader under a separation of powers system cannot be removed by his or her party in the way that a party leader can be in a parliamentary system.

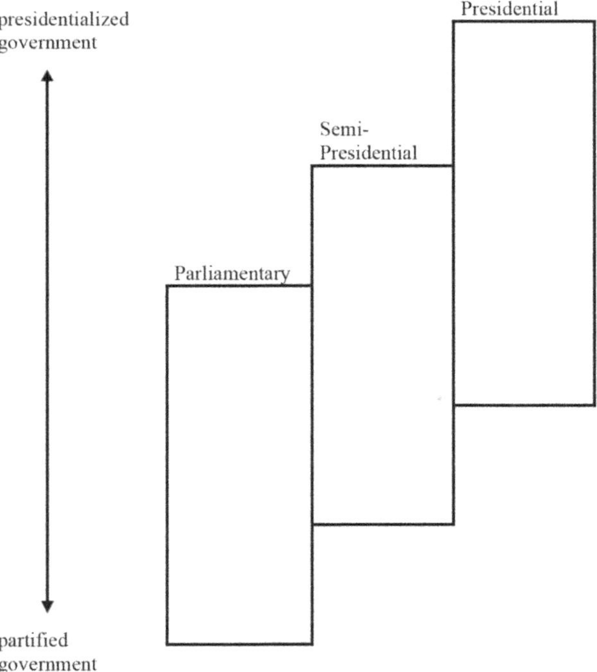

Figure 10.1 Presidentialization and Regime Type. *Source*: 'The Presidentialization of Politics in Democratic Societies: A Framework for Analysis' by Thomas Poguntke and Paul Webb from *Presidentialization of Politics: A Comparative Study of Modern Democracies*, edited by Poguntke, Thomas and Webb (2005). By permission of Oxford University Press.

These shifts are caused by structural and contextual factors. The latter are fairly obvious: It simply needs a strong and capable political leader to use the structural opportunities fully, and political context matters. Executive leaders regularly benefit in times of crisis and in periods that are dominated by foreign policy because these relegate parties and parliaments to secondary importance.

The structural causes are only briefly outlined here as they have been discussed in detail elsewhere (Poguntke and Webb 2005; see also figure 10.2). Trends towards presidentialization are related to the long-term growth of the state, which has induced the attempt to accumulate ever more steering capacity at the centre. These attempts may not always have been successful, but they have, in any case, enormously strengthened the resources at the centre of government. Politics has become a lot more supranational in recent decades, and this has injected a structural executive bias into domestic politics. No doubt, the European Union (EU) member states have experienced this in a particularly pronounced fashion (Hix and Goetz 2000, 11; Tallberg and Johansson 2010) as became evident in the wake of the Greek crisis. Peter Mair's account of the impact of the EU on national democracy (especially in those countries which required European Central Bank [ECB] and EU support to deal with the consequences of the banking crisis) is a clear and trenchant critique of the bypassing of party politics, which privileges national leaders and EU officials (Mair 2013).

A particularly powerful factor behind the presidentialization of politics has been the change of the media landscape with the advent of TV and later private

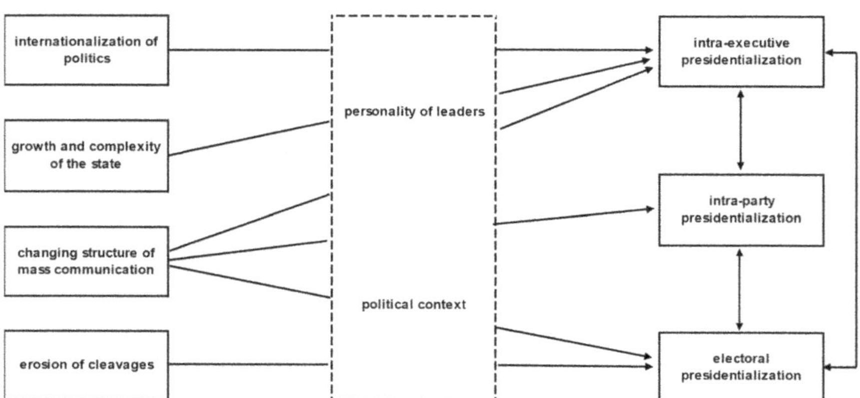

Figure 10.2 The Major Causal Flows Involved in Explaining the Presidentialization of Politics. *Source*: 'The Presidentialization of Politics in Democratic Societies: A Framework for Analysis' by Thomas Poguntke and Paul Webb from *Presidentialization of Politics: A Comparative Study of Modern Democracies*, edited by Poguntke, Thomas and Webb (2005). By permission of Oxford University Press.

TV, which has fundamentally transformed government communication, campaigning and intraparty politics. There is an in-built tendency for the electronic media and particularly TV to work in favour of media-savvy politicians, be they candidates, party leaders or chief executives, and this empowers leaders to the detriment of collective bodies such as party assemblies, parliamentary parties and cabinets. The jury is still out, though, when it comes to the impact of modern forms of online communication. They facilitate the creation of parallel realities which could serve as echo chambers for those who no longer believe the established media. In particular, the rise of social media may promote personalization at all levels of the political process because it facilitates personalized campaigns of local candidates (Zittel and Gschwend 2008; also see Rahat and Zamir and Pruysers and Cross, this volume). In addition, since 2016 we have witnessed the extraordinary example of highly personalized and direct communication between the national leader and the citizenry at large on a daily basis via the medium of Twitter. Donald Trump entirely bypasses party (and frequently, one suspects, his own advisors) in this way.

Finally, the decline of cleavages has freed voters from strong loyalties and hence made them more available to the lures of personalized politics (see, e.g., Franklin 1992). Party leaders can therefore claim to have a personal mandate when they win an election and use this as justification for strong leadership vis-à-vis (or even past) their parties.

Challenges and Evidence

In the following section, we will revisit the three faces of presidentialization. Rather than providing more evidence for our original argument, which we have done elsewhere on the German and British cases (Poguntke and Webb 2015), we will concentrate on relevant aspects that have not yet been spelled out in detail. Although we mainly refer to chief executives, it is important to remember that changes in the nature of the party and electoral faces also apply to non-governing parties. They are subject to the same structural causes. Furthermore, presidentialization is also a competitive phenomenon: A strongly presidentialized governing party is likely to induce similar changes within opposition parties.

Chief Executives and Their Parties

The Politics of U-turns and Lone Decisions

Chief executives have increasingly used their personal mandates to implement sudden policy U-turns or lone decisions. A few examples may suffice here: German Chancellor Gerhard Schröder's neoliberal reforms, almost single-handedly imposed on the SPD, are a classic example of chief executives governing past their parties (Egle and Zohlnhöfer 2007). Similarly, Angela Merkel's incumbency is characterized by some spectacular U-turns such as the decision to phase out nuclear energy or open the borders for refugees. Equally important are many less spectacular yet important policy changes which have repositioned the Christian Democratic Union (CDU) as an essentially centrist party with strong pro-welfare and 'greenish' elements (Poguntke 2015). Similarly, David Cameron decided to introduce a bill legalizing 'gay marriage' in 2012 in the face of the clear opposition of a majority of his own party's grass roots (Webb and Bale 2014). More recently, Theresa May suffered the embarrassment of performing a 2017 mid-election campaign U-turn on an unpopular social care policy that had been inserted into the party manifesto by her with no consultation of cabinet or party colleagues (Bale and Webb 2017).

Matteo Renzi's style of governing was entirely characterized by governing past his party and against a considerable portion of the party's activists. His ascent to power was orchestrated as a plebiscitary way of bypassing the die-hard party activists, and his constitutional reform package was again based on a cross-party coalition; ultimately, it failed to gain the consent of the Italian electorate (Bull 2015).

Probably the two most conspicuous examples of U-turns come from southern Europe and they also demonstrate the relevance of the 'supra-nationalization' of politics. In May 2010, the Spanish Prime Minister Zapatero of the governing Socialist Party announced the largest ever cut back in social security spending to combat the growing deficit in the wake of the euro crisis. Greek Prime Minister Alexis Tsipras fought tooth and nail to avoid the cuts and reforms requested by the EU and even held a referendum in July 2015—only to force through exactly these cuts shortly afterwards, even though a majority of the population had voted 'yes' in the referendum (meaning 'no' to EU-imposed cuts).

To be sure, these examples vary regarding the exact political context, the power resources of the respective chief executive and the degree of international pressure. While Tsipras, for example, had little room for manoeuvre vis-à-vis his European partners, Merkel's decision to phase out nuclear energy production took everyone by surprise. Yet, the common denominator of all these decisions is that they clearly go against the line of the party of the leader of government. In other words, they all enjoy considerable autonomy vis-a-vis their parties even though this autonomy may be severely limited through other forces such as supranational constraints emanating from membership in a currency union.

Nonparty Experts

So far we have only focused on examples of pronounced policy independence of chief executives from their parties. If we push this perspective further, government by 'non-party experts' is the logical next step. To be sure, there are not enough examples to identify any trend here. Yet, there are three recent examples which deserve mentioning. The appointment of Mario Monti as Italian prime minister at the height of the euro crisis is significant because it involves one of the large EU countries with a tradition of strong party government. Furthermore, it was evident that the resignation of Prime Minister Berlusconi followed strong pressure by the EU. The appointment of Lucas Papademos as prime minister of a caretaker government in November 2011 following the resignation of George Papandreou (PASOK) at the height of the Greek debt crisis is another example of the direct impact of the EU constraints on domestic politics. The relevant point from the perspective of the presidentialization thesis is that the crisis resulted in a situation in which someone was suddenly elevated to executive leadership without having a base in the party; this autonomy from the party is central to the idea of presidentialization.

Austria is another country with a very pronounced tradition of strong party government. It was one of the original examples of a consociational democracy (Lehmbruch 1976; Lijphart 1968). Following the resignation of Chancellor Faymann (SPÖ) in May 2016, the governing Grand Coalition agreed to support the managing director of Austrian Railways to take over as chief executive. This was the direct consequence of the disastrous result in the first round of the Austrian presidential elections, in which both candidates of the governing Grand Coalition finished nowhere, and the run-off election was held between the FPÖ candidate Norbert Hofer and the former Green leader Alexander Van der Bellen who ran (allegedly) as an independent. Strictly speaking, the new Austrian Chancellor Christian Kern did not qualify as a nonparty chief executive because he was a member of the SPÖ and had previously worked for the government. Yet, he had worked in the economic sector (presumably mainly publicly controlled) for almost twenty years—hardly the background of a typical party politician.

Under certain (admittedly, unusual) circumstances, then, these examples indicate that a strong anchorage within a political party may no longer be the precondition of prime ministerial office. Of course, political parties do not abrogate their gate-keeping function for senior political office, but they may be becoming less demanding when it comes to a traditional party career because other exigencies have become of overriding importance, such as pressures from supranational institutions or electoral considerations.

Chief Executives in Government: The Erosion of Parliamentary Constraint

The main focus of the executive face of presidentialization is on the resources available to the chief executive and factors that strengthen his or her role vis-à-vis cabinet such as the ability to appoint outsiders to cabinet or the outsourcing of policy formulation to nonparty commissions.

This focus on the role of chief executives within their government in our initial thesis may have somewhat underemphasized the relationship between leaders and parliamentary followers. But the presidentialization thesis should not neglect the role of chief executives vis-à-vis parliament. Under conditions of the (prevalent) model of parliamentary government, this means that we need to focus more on the relationship of chief executives to their parliamentary majorities (in most cases coalitions). By and large, governmental parties and chief executives have moved apart in the process of presidentialization, which may manifest itself in a growing number of dissenting votes in the government camp. At the same time, this may not matter as much as in the past because parliament as a whole is increasingly less able to constrain the actions of the chief executive as a result of the increasing internationalization of politics (see below).

The rationale behind this is that the domination of cabinet and the core executive depends on the ability of chief executives to act (fairly) independently of their parliamentary base (frequently a coalition). After all, a chief executive can only hope to dominate his or her cabinet if other cabinet members are limited in their ability to mobilize parliamentary support against the chief executive. There are a number of scenarios under which this may be the case:

1. The domination of the (parliamentary) party by the chief executive.
2. The chief executive invokes a personal mandate and attempts to govern past his or her party. This usually involves either reference to the personal electoral appeal of the leader or the use of referenda.
3. Oversized coalitions allow the chief executives to ignore dissenting parts of the coalitions.
4. The internationalization of politics (e.g. EU) delegitimizes dissent.

Although the first is the classic case of an oligarchic party as was famously depicted by Robert Michels, this has rarely, if ever, been empirical reality in the era of modern party government. The stratarchical nature of modern political parties has meant that party leaders tended to be leaders of dominant coalitions rather than dominators of their parties (Panebianco 1988; Eldersveld 1964). The presidentialization thesis maintains that this has changed in that the remaining three scenarios have become more prevalent. The presidentialization of the electoral process (see below) has made leaders more independent from their parties (including their parliamentary parties). Furthermore, the increasing promiscuity of political parties in coalition formation (Mair 2008, 216) gives leaders more policy discretion because coalitions are becoming ideologically less coherent. This tends to generate additional opportunities to bypass dissent among their own ranks, where the loyalty to programmatic positions may be higher than among party elites. This has been demonstrated by analyses showing that parties which give their rank and file more say in programmatic decisions tend to be programmatically less flexible (Bolin et al. 2017; Hennl and Franzmann 2017). Finally, the internationalization of politics increasingly creates situations where a national parliamentary majority can only ratify agreements between governments.

Inevitably, many examples of this aspect of the executive face of presidentialization will echo what has been said above about chief executives and their parties. After all, the party in parliament is one crucial party arena. Hence, we will be brief here.

A telling example is Italian Prime Minister Renzi's attempt to reform the Italian constitution. It could only pass parliament because Renzi managed to build alliances beyond his own majority. Eventually, the reform needed approval by a popular referendum which was lost, arguably, because Renzi tied his own political survival to it and hence provoked a negative coalition against himself. Even more significant for our argument is the unprecedented number of Italian MPs who switched their party allegiance during the 17th legislative period, which entirely undermines the idea that a chief executive governs with his or her majority (Der Standard 28 September 2017).

The German chancellor is another conspicuous example of the disregard of parliament. Angela Merkel's decision to suspend the Dublin regulations in late August 2015 and to open the borders for refugees coming via the so-called 'Balkan route' was never subject to a parliamentary debate. To be sure, there were many debates about administrative details of social security, tightening the rules, etc., but there was not a single debate in parliament where the general purpose and direction of German refugee policy was debated (Deutscher Bundestag). Instead, the Chancellor went twice to the country to explain her policy via a TV interview.

The role of national parliaments in the decision-making processes during the handling of the euro crisis and, particularly, the financial rescue packages is probably an even more significant example of the side-lining of parliament. Frequently, the required response time was so short that MPs had no realistic chance to even read the relevant documents. Characteristically, Chancellor Merkel did not even address parliament in the debate about the third rescue package for Greece on 19 August 2015. For a comparable example see Peter Mair's talk to the Central European University (CEU) on the Irish bailout (Mair 2011).

Party Leaders and Elections

The electoral face of the presidentialization thesis encompasses three aspects, namely an increasingly leadership-centred conduct of election campaigns; an increasing media attention to what leaders say and do; and, finally, an increasing leadership effect on actual voting behaviour. Again, we will not review the relevant literatures in detail here, although much research has been conducted on these themes since we published the thesis (see for recent overviews Aarts, Blais and Schmitt 2011; Karvonen 2010; Kriesi 2012; Lobo 2014). However, there is growing evidence that leaders are important for individual voting decisions, and that this may indeed be on the rise (Bittner 2011; Lobo and Curtice 2015; Costa and Ferreira Da Silva 2015; Garzia 2014; McAllister 2015; Mughan 2015; Schmitt-Beck et al. 2014, 359).

Certainly, this is plausible from several perspectives. We have already mentioned the growing number of unattached voters who are, in principle, available for personalized voting (Lobo 2015). Furthermore, the ongoing supranationalization of politics means that it is also rational for voters to base their voting decisions on who will actually be sitting at the conference table of supranational negotiations instead of mainly looking at party positions. This, for instance, was an explicit part of the UK general election of 2017: Prime Minister May campaigned strongly on the question 'who do you want representing the country in Brexit negotiations (Labour leader)—Jeremy Corbyn or me?' (Bale and Webb 2017) Finally, the increasing uncertainty of political contexts in an age of growing economic and international insecurity has a similar effect: If it is simply not likely that manifesto pledges can be put into practice as a result of changing circumstances, why not rely on personality instead of pledges in the first instance? The personal qualities and attributes of the principal contenders for high office become the most important criteria for deciding in the minds of voters.

There is every reason to expect that the results of research on the aspects mentioned will remain somewhat inconclusive. The reasons for this are fairly obvious: Every election campaign is different, every set of candidates is different, national political cultures and communications cultures vary, and not least, operationalizations are often not really comparable (Lobo 2014, 366). This is again demonstrated by Bittner's contribution to this volume that shows that leaders clearly have an effect in Canadian and British elections, while there is no clear upward trend.

Yet, the personalization of voting is just one element of the presidentialization of the electoral process. Arguably, what matters most is the fact that parties and leaders behave *as if* their leaders matter more than party programmes (see Pruysers and Cross, this volume). This is why parties focus their campaigns increasingly on their leaders and media coverage tends to reflect and reinforce this. The tendency to hold televised leadership debates testifies to this (LeDuc, Niemi and Norris 1996). Likewise, leadership selection is often driven by electoral considerations. If successful, these leaders have a legitimate claim to a personal mandate, but if they fail, they will quickly be relegated to secondary importance. Again, it is difficult to demonstrate a clear trend here, but it is easy to find conspicuous examples such as the selection of Tony Blair (Labour), David Cameron (Conservative), Matteo Renzi (Democratici), Gerhard Schröder, or more recently, Peer Steinbrück and Martin Schulz (all SPD) as electoral leaders even though they were not really the leaders of the dominant coalition within their respective political parties. Peer Steinbrück's unsuccessful candidacy exemplifies the claim that such leaders will be left with little or no intraparty power after an unsuccessful election campaign. After Peer Steinbrück lost in 2013 against Angela Merkel, he disappeared from front stage politics. More recently, May, who emerged as Conservative leader and prime minister in the United Kingdom after David Cameron's shock defeat in the Brexit referendum of 2016, called an early general election in 2017, and tried to run a highly personalized campaign based on the polling evidence that she was far more highly regarded than leader of the Labour opposition, Jeremy Corbyn; but her lacklustre campaign performance resulted in an unexpected loss of the Conservatives' parliamentary majority. This hugely undermined her authority within the party but did not lead to her direct removal, given the lack of an obvious alternative (Bale and Webb 2017). This illustrates the precariousness of the presidentialized leader's position in the face of electoral setbacks.

It should perhaps be said that, if we wanted to take the growing prominence of electoral personalization to its logical conclusion, we should expect open primaries to have become more frequent. Yet, the Political Parties Database (PPDB) project, which gathered relevant data between 2011 and 2014, found only four cases of open plebiscites on personnel or policy. Clearly, this confirms findings by the leadership project that parties are very reluctant to change their rules concerning leadership selection (Cross and Pilet 2015, 172). Furthermore, as the recent example of the election of Jeremy Corbyn as British Labour leader reminds us, open (or semi-open) primaries are particularly vulnerable to a backlash by party activists who want to reinstate the party's old principles.

PRESIDENTIALIZATION AND PERSONALIZATION

The preceding restatement of the presidentialization thesis demonstrates that there are several connections between personalization and presidentialization.

However, as has been indicated in the introduction of this chapter, the exact relationship between both concepts needs further exploration.

In line with the discussion in the introductory chapter, we conceptualize personalization as a 'process in which the political weight of the individual actor in the political process increases over time, while the centrality of the political group (i.e., political party) declines' (Rahat and Sheafer 2007, 65). This conceptualization of personalization encompasses all possible aspects of the political process and different levels (e.g., the national level as well as the personalization of local candidate campaigns in national or local elections), whereas presidentialization focuses on the concentration of power at the apex of political systems and the shifting position of leaders vis-à-vis collective bodies such as cabinets, parties and parliaments.

Broadly speaking, personalization shares some of the causal factors with presidentialization, but it has its roots also in institutional changes such as changing electoral laws, which may drive the personalization of constituency or local campaigns (see Pilet and Renwick, this volume). Yet, there are common causal factors such as the individualization of *voting behaviour* and changes in the structure of *political communication* (McAllister 2007). As the chapter by Rahat and Zamir in this volume shows, the new social media are becoming powerful new tools that drive personalization. These factors are drivers of the personalization of political campaigning at national and local levels. Arguably, this allows national or subnational political leaders to claim a personalized mandate which permits them to govern (or lead) past their parties to a certain degree. At the same time, it furnishes local candidates such as MPs with a comparable sense of a mandate independent of their party, which they may use to define their role independently of their national (or regional) leadership.

From this perspective, personalization can have contradictory effects on the process of presidentialization, which depend on the nature of specific party organizations and the degree of the nationalization of election campaigns. In cases where the centre controls the nomination of local candidates, they may comply with the political directives of their leader despite having run a personalized campaign because they need to secure renomination. The opposite mechanism applies if nomination is strongly decentralized. This reduces the leverage of the national leader over the career of individual candidates and may create an incentive to behave more independently from the national leadership.

However, renomination is not the only concern of local candidates. The overriding goal of politicians is election or reelection, and in parliamentary systems this depends to a considerable degree on the appeal of the national party and its leading candidate. This means that decentralized personalization may actually strengthen the national leader because it atomizes the dominant coalition within the party and makes MPs or candidates followers of their leader. They may be independent followers because they run independent campaigns. However, these campaigns are independent of, or at arm's length from, the party. Yet, the success of their independent campaign increasingly depends on the appeal of the prime ministerial/leading candidate rather than on the attractiveness of the party manifesto and the policy beliefs of the middle-level elites. The currency of allegiance of parliamentary candidates to the leader is the appeal of the leader. If he or she fails to deliver, there is not much loyalty left, simply because this loyalty is no longer firmly rooted in an ideology and a concomitant social milieu. It is simply based on electoral success, and this is, as we all know, increasingly unstable. Hence, the personalization of politics across the board weakens parties as organizations and strengthens leaders, but it also makes them a lot more dependent on electoral success, just as we stated in our original thesis.

In a nutshell, the most important link between personalization and presidentialization can be found in the two lower left-hand boxes of figure 10.2, namely the mediatization of politics and the erosion of cleavages. They make more personalized campaigning technically possible and politically rewarding. Yet, there are other drivers of presidentialization that have little direct bearing on personalization in its general sense. Take the growth of the state and the internationalization of politics, which has equipped chief executives with more resources and leverage to 'force through' their policies. This has little effect on the personalization of local campaigning, but it is not without impact on the personalization of media coverage of national politics. Summitry drives the personalization of reporting, which in turn becomes a power resource for chief executives. From this perspective, presidentialization can be regarded as a driver of personalization at the top. Arguably, it is a reciprocal relationship: The increased power and autonomy of chief executives flowing from the growth of the state and the internationalization of politics drives presidentialization, and as the power and autonomy of chief executives grow, they become even more prominent in media coverage (i.e. the media coverage becomes more personalized). At the same time, the greater prominence of chief executives in media coverage serves in turn to further enhance their power and autonomy.

From the latter perspective, presidentialization seems to be little more than a special case of personalization which applies only to leaders. Yet, this would ignore the *effects* of personalization at the apex of political power. The concept of presidentialization is not just about the increased weight of individuals at the expense of collective bodies. It is, in the first instance, concerned with the *effects* of this increased weight on the working mode of political systems. In other words: The crucial question is how the logic of the political process changes as a result of the increased weight of political leaders.

Importantly, this increased weight is not just the result of a general process of personalization, it is also caused by changes specific to the way political systems function and are embedded in supranational governance networks (see figure 10.3). We argue that the patterns of interaction between the central political actors of modern democracies change as a result of presidentialization, namely the interaction between chief executives, parliaments, parties and the electorate. In essence, these patterns begin to resemble more the logic that flows from ideal-typical presidential systems in that chief executives increasingly act independently of their parties and attempt to govern through more plebiscitary mechanisms; note that this includes not only formal plebiscites as such but also direct appeals to the people via both the traditional media and new social media instead of addressing parliament. In some respects this resembles the trend of 'going public'—that is, making direct presidential appeals to voters to intimidate Congress into passing legislation—identified by Kernell (2006). Kernell argues that a number of causes lay behind this development, including the new communications technologies (especially television), and the growing use of primaries, which favour outsiders who lack a strong base of support in Congress, and thus continue to do what they do best: campaign directly to the people.

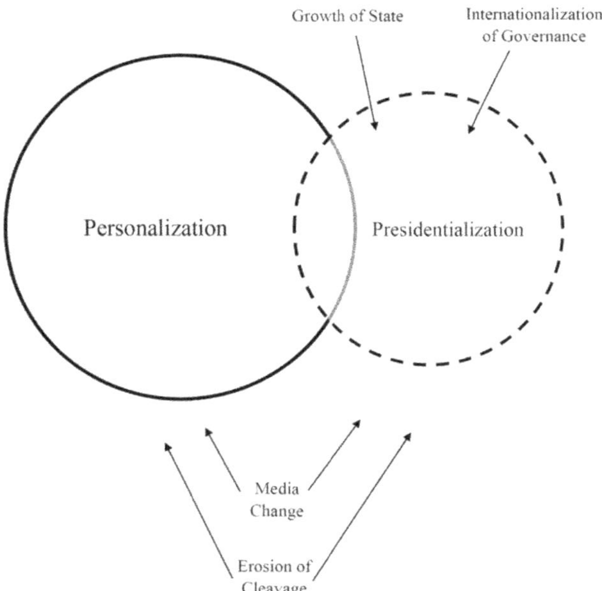

Figure 10.3 The Relationship between Personalization and Presidentialization.

To sum up, presidentialization is an elaborated concept concerned with the changing power relations in and between different arenas of the process of democratic governance. It is a process that manifests itself in a changing logic of interaction between and within these arenas. From this perspective, personalization is just one element of it, alongside structurally changing power resources. Presidentialization needs personalization, but it is not synonymous. Personalization across the board may not lead to presidentialization, but presidentialization cannot occur without personalization. Personalization is a necessary but not a sufficient condition of presidentialization.

THE FUTURE OF PRESIDENTIALIZATION AND PARTY GOVERNMENT

We will conclude our brief revisiting of the presidentialization thesis with some reflections concerning the wider implications of presidentialization for the future of democratic party government.

1. *Presidentialization is essentially a mechanism that feeds itself. One could also say that it is a vicious circle.*

   Parties are getting weaker. Hence they need strong leaders to win elections, which, in turn weakens them further. Often strong leaders do not only govern 'past their parties'; they govern—or are forced to govern—against their parties (because of constraints by EU or globalization). This further erodes the already disintegrating ideological coherence of their parties. Put differently, it undermines a central element of party government, namely the 'partyness of government' (Katz 1986 and this volume).

   The most conspicuous examples have been discussed here and need only brief mention. Merkel has shifted the CDU so far to the centre that the right-wing populists represent, in many respects, a breakaway from the CDU (even though they also draw, like all populists, votes from the left). Schröder had shifted the SPD so far to the centre that the Die Linke is in many respects also a breakaway from the SPD (witness the senior role of former SPD leader Oskar Lafontaine within Die Linke). Blair has done the same to the British Labour Party. However, under the conditions of the UK's electoral system, the foundation of new parties is not a sensible strategy. From this perspective the election of Corbyn can be seen as a de facto take over by the populist left. Meanwhile, Tspiras was compelled to do the exact opposite of his election pledges.
2. *There is no way back to the golden age of party government.*

   This point flows from an understanding of the structural factors feeding into presidentialization; they are unlikely to be reversible in the foreseeable future. In addition, the secular decline of party membership is an important reason why the age of membership-based politics is over (Gauja 2015; Scarrow 2015; van Biezen, Mair, and Poguntke 2012; Biezen and Poguntke 2014). Finally, the growing importance of online media, which facilitates the construction of parallel realities, de-legitimizes the established press and provides fertile ground for populist mobilization.

3. *Presidentialization means that leadership selection mechanisms assume central importance for the viability of democracy*

   If the 'partyness' of government is increasingly replaced by the 'leadershipness' of government, the mechanism of leadership selection becomes a lot more important (see also, Katz and Stewart, this volume). At the same time, the US example reminds us that the popular call for 'more democracy' (i.e., open primaries) may have problematic results (to put it mildly). The ability of modern democracies to produce responsible and capable leaders has become more important for the viability of democracy. The reason is essentially twofold: on the one hand, strong parties, which may serve as correctives for weak leadership have all but ceased to exist. On the other hand, the trend towards populist challenges (which are amplified by presidentialization) makes capable, moderate democratic leadership all the more necessary.

4. *Presidentialization feeds into populism.*

   Strong executive leaders weaken parties and their ideological identity. As a result more voters are 'set free' from the old loyalties and may become available for populists. Furthermore, strong executive leaders are tempted to (and capable of) pushing through sudden policy change which legitimizes the idea often maintained by populists that we need radical, sudden change to address (alleged) crises. Finally, presidentialization increases the ideological similarity of major parties, which legitimizes the argument of populists who claim that established parties 'are all the same'. Although these mechanisms have mainly manifested themselves in right-wing populist electoral advances, the Greek Syriza and the Italian Five Star Movement remind us that populism can be found anywhere across the traditional political spectrum, namely left, centre and right.

Chapter 11

Personalism, Personalization and Gender

Melanee Thomas

As noted in the volume's introduction, defining personalization is both straightforward and complicated. Some of the chapters in this volume address processes over time that increase the emphasis on individual politicians; that is, they examine personalization (see Bittner and Pilet and Renwick, this volume). Others assess personalism: the current importance of individual politicians or the extent to which politics is personalized (see Chiru and Rahat and Zamir, this volume). Some chapters examine these phenomena at a centralized level, focusing on party leaders and elites (see Stewart, Malloy and Poguntke and Webb, this volume), whereas others take a more decentralized approach, assessing how personalization and personalism affect local candidates or even party members (see Pruysers and Cross and Gauja, this volume). This diversity in approaches highlights the many avenues and areas in which personalization and personalism can occur.

This chapter takes a different approach from the others and uses gender to interrogate personalized politics and its consequences for political parties and politicians' careers. Much of the chapter's focus is on personalism, gathering a snapshot of how and why politics are personalized in different ways for women and men. Particular attention is paid to institutional, media and behavioural personalism, as well as their centralized and decentralized variants where applicable. Gendered personalization is also addressed throughout this chapter, as the extent to which women politicians are personalized or the importance of gender to politics has changed considerably over time. This chapter particularly critiques the concept of privatization; previous scholarship on personalization argues that privatization occurs when personal, 'nonpolitical' information is presented about a politician. When seen through a gendered lens, much of the past work on privatization is problematic because women politicians both experience privatization at a considerably higher rate than men and are evaluated differently based on this private content. Yet, because this private information is about them as individuals and draws focus to the politician as an individual, this suggests that women in politics are personalized as much as, if not more than, their male peers. Thus, through a gendered lens, it is difficult to observe much of a conceptual difference between personalism and privatization; empirically, the reality for women in politics, and for some men, is that personalized politics is (still) about their private lives. Instead, privatization could be seen as an example of how personalism manifests itself differently for women and men in politics. There is some reason for optimism, though, as gender equality in politics improves over time, gendered personalism may actually diminish over time.

GENDERING PERSONALISM AND PERSONALIZATION

There are four key things about gender that make it relevant for political personalism and personalization. The first is that it is public. It is commonly understood that gender is a characteristic that is socially produced through interactions with others (Butler 2011). Thus, although gender identity—that is, one's own experience with their gender—is deeply personal, the expression of that gender identity is public. Gender identity expressions include names and pronouns and physical appearance, including clothing, hair, makeup and body language (Ontario Human Rights Commission 2017). This constitutes gender as appearance and performance of a number of acts for a social audience; so gender is, in effect, something that is generated and maintained collectively. Through these interactions, some presentations of gender are clearly valued over others (Butler 1988, 2010, 2011). Because this is inherently public, gender becomes one of the first, and most easily observed and evaluated characteristics of a person.

Second, gender is politically relevant. Gender was, and in some cases continues to be, used legally to bar women from participating in politics. Even in the absence of formal, legal barriers, gender is still grounds for many (regardless of their own genders) to argue women are not well-suited to engage in politics (Streb et al. 2008; Chen et al. 2017). And, although there is a considerable diversity among women and men, consistent gender differences in public opinion (Anderson 2010), political participation (Cross 2004; Blais 2000; Gidengil et al. 2004), vote choice (Gidengil et al. 2012) and voter evaluations (Streb et al. 2008) exist. Thus, political assessments vary across genders, both for those doing the assessing (voters) and those being assessed (politicians).[1] This suggests that most aspects of gender are both public and politically relevant.

The third is particularly relevant for personalization as a longitudinal process. Other processes developing at the same time may have implications for personalization that ought to be taken into account in its conceptualization. Women's descriptive representation, or women's political presence, is one of those processes. The time period most commonly associated with personalization begins in the 1970s and continues to more contemporary politics. One of the seminal studies on political personalization examines Israeli politics between 1949 and 2003, noting that personalization appears in force in the mid- to late 1970s (Rahat and Sheafer 2007). Notably, Golda Meir was prime minister around this time (1969–1974). However, women's presence in the Knesset did not increase appreciably until 1999 (Jewish Women's Archive 2016). In this context, one could argue that personalization predates considerable increases in women's legislative or descriptive representation.

The difficulty is that in many democracies, personalization coincides with nontrivial increases in women's legislative presence (i.e., 1970s to the present). In Canada, for example, no more than five women were elected to the House of Commons in any given election before 1974; women's presence in the House of Commons increased steadily in most of the subsequent elections (Parliament of Canada 2016).[2] A similar pattern is found in the Swedish Rikdsdag (Thomas 2012). Similarly, women's presence in US politics started to increase in the early 1980s in the House of Representatives and from the early 1990s in the Senate (Manning and Brudnick 2015). In the United Kingdom, the proportion of women in the House of Commons began increasing in the mid-1980s, spiking in 1997, and has continued to increase since (Keen 2015). This suggests that processes that increase women's presence in legislative politics in many democracies occur around the same time as the processes associated with political personalization. Theories of personalization as a longitudinal process do not appear to take gender into account; as a result, this literature may be missing important gendered facets to personalization.

It is certainly possible that these processes are linked. In the United States, the Presidential Commission on the Status of Women was established in 1961, leading to the creation of seminal legislation on equal pay and the creation of key advocacy organizations such as the National Organization for Women. In Canada, the Report of the Royal Commission on the Status of Women was tabled in Parliament in 1970, leading to the creation of a cabinet ministry for the Status of Women in 1971. Internationally, the United Nations adopted the Convention on the Elimination of All Forms of Discrimination Against Women (CEDAW) in 1979. What is notable about these institutional reactions to the status of women is that they explicitly bring issues previously relegated exclusively to the private sphere into politics.[3] Stated differently, these early developments related to women in politics quite literally bring the personal into the political sphere.

Early research on gender and political behaviour reflects this, too. Research on women's political behaviour from the 1970s and early 1980s suggests that women are less engaged and participatory than are men because women's access to the public sphere (e.g., education) is restricted and because of role socialization and expectations that explicitly tie women to the private sphere. For example, Sapiro argues, 'motherhood and homemaking appear to be particular inhibitors' of women's political development (1983, 101), and Carroll (1988) argues that autonomy in the private sphere has considerable political consequences for women. Thus, a fair (though literal) interpretation of women's integration into politics in the 1970s and 1980s is that through their presence in politics, they are making the private and the personal political.

Finally, gendered analyses highlight how personalism and personalization can be perceived differently for women and for men. The literature suggests that although personalization and privatization both highlight the individual politician, personalization is more 'political' than is privatization in that it focuses on a politician's ideas, competencies and policy positions. Privatization, by contrast, still examines the individual, but in a 'nonpolitical way' on 'nonpolitical' grounds, such as a politician's personal life, marital status, parental status, appearance or any other personal characteristic (Van Aelst, Sheafer and Stanyer 2012; Rahat and Sheafer 2007; Balmas and Sheafer 2016). Phrased differently, one interpretation of the literature is that the 'political information used for personalization is appropriate in politics, but private information and privatization as a phenomenon is less 'political' and therefore, less relevant in general and to the study of personalism and personalization in particular.

It may be true that for some political actors, mainly men, private information may be deemed 'non-political'. For others though, this same content is deeply political and commonly used by voters and the media in their evaluations of women in politics. As a result, women politicians both experience privatization at a considerably higher rate than men and are evaluated differently based on this private content. Yet, because this private information is about them as individuals and draws focus to the politician as an individual, this suggests that women in politics are personalized as much as, if not more than, their male peers. Thus, through a gendered lens, it is difficult to observe much of a conceptual difference between personalization and privatization; empirically, the reality for women in politics, and for some men, is that personalism and personalization is (still) privatization. This will be explored in greater detail in this chapter.

Taken together, the public, political, and longitudinal features of gender and its effects on politics make it potentially foundational for political personalism and personalization. The question is not, then, if personalism and personalization are gendered, but how. Though fulsome longitudinal studies are beyond the scope of this particular chapter, it is possible to explore how gender shapes personalism and personalization in an institutional, media and behavioural context. The gendered dynamics of each of these types of personalized politics, at both centralized and decentralized levels, are discussed in turn.

INSTITUTIONAL PERSONALISM, PERSONALIZATION AND GENDER

Institutional personalism occurs when formal rules and institutions place (more) emphasis on individuals (Rahat and Sheafer 2007). This suggests that any rule changes that decentralize candidate or leadership selection processes may result in personalization (see Stewart, this volume). More open leadership-selection processes, such as primaries or universal member votes, are associated with personalized politics, although it is unclear whether these selection processes are a cause or a consequence of personalization. Here, the leader defines the party, as do her main policy initiatives (Rahat and Sheafer 2007), creating an individualistic definition of the party and its performance. Although this is certainly not a new process (Seigfried 1966 [1907]), the widespread use of these more open forms of leadership and candidate selection is, as more parties have adopted them in recent years (Cross and Blais 2012a).

Given that women are less likely than men to be party leaders and more likely to lead small, left-leaning, electorally uncompetitive parties than are men (Cross and Blais 2012a; O'Neill and Stewart 2009), it follows that leadership selection processes may be gendered (but see also Wauters and Pilet 2015). There is some evidence to suggest that the more open the leadership-selection process, the more poorly women fare in the contest (Bashevkin 2009). Indeed, before 2011, no woman had been selected to lead a Canadian political party with a universal member vote (UMV). Since then, three women have been selected leader using a UMV, and another using a hybrid primary/convention (Thomas, 2018).[4]

These differences could simply reflect existing bias in politics against women, particularly as political elites and leaders, rather than an effect of personalized politics. To assert that leadership-selection mechanisms change or increase the kind of personalism women encounter as leadership candidates, a more detailed, longitudinal study of multiple leadership-selection contests is required than is possible here. Existing research, though, is suggestive. Both Hillary Clinton and Elizabeth Dole's personalities and private lives received more attention, and more negative evaluation, during their primary campaigns than did those of their male competitors (Miller, Peake and Boulton 2008; Heldman, Carroll and Olson 2005). Similarly, since the 1990s, women's candidacies for Canada's federal conservative parties have generated more interest in their issue positions than some of their competitors and more coverage of their backgrounds and private lives than all of the men in the race (Trimble 2007, see also Trimble and Wagner 2012). Notably, though, this was not the case in the 1970s (Trimble 2007); whether this reflects how gendered personalization increases over time or simply the increased viability of women candidates is unclear. Indeed, because more open, personalized leadership selection processes and the rise of women as competitive leadership candidates appear to happen at roughly the same time, it is not clear whether the higher levels of personalism women leadership candidates encounter is a consequence of personalization or if there is a common process at work that produces both more open leadership-selection processes (and thus, increased personalization in general), as well as the stronger focus on women's personal lives and issue positions when they are leadership candidates.

The personalized effects of electoral systems may also be gendered. As Bittner (this volume) observes, candidates and leaders are evaluated based on voter perceptions of their character and their competence. When the occupants of these positions are directly elected—that is, when voters cast their ballots for an individual rather than a party, such as is the case in a single-member plurality electoral system—these perceptions of character and competence may have gendered consequences. Although there is some research to suggest that voters, in some systems, are more likely to apply partisan rather than gender stereotypes (Dolan 2014), other evidence suggests that when campaigns activate stereotypes about women in politics—they are caring, honest and family-oriented—this may reduce support for women candidates (Bauer 2014). Other research shows that evaluations of women's ability to handle stereotypically masculine issues, such as terrorism, has a profound effect on a voter's willingness to support women candidates in some contexts (Dolan 2010). Similarly, sexist perceptions of women in politics also factor in these processes because voters who explicitly state they prefer male leaders are considerably less likely to vote for women, even if those women are clearly more qualified than their male competitors (Mo 2014). Thus, when institutions personalize politics, either by requiring that voters cast ballots for individual candidates, or when party leader evaluations are especially important for vote choice, it is possible that this personalism is strongly structured by gender.

Evidence further suggests that parties are aware of this and may engage in bias against women candidates, potentially through decentralizing candidate-selection processes. Research from already decentralized candidate selection contexts suggests that decentralized party selectorates exhibit considerable gender bias in candidate selection (Thomas and Bodet 2013). In this sense, decentralized institutional personalism may make it more difficult for women to be nominated as candidates. Other reactions could include eliminating intraparty groups, such as women's caucuses or auxiliaries (see Gauja, this volume). Other parties may observe these gendered effects of personalism and try instead to normalize women's presence in politics by instituting gender quotas and initiatives such as parity cabinets. Both could use institutional personalization to neutralize negative stereotypes about women in politics, or normalize their presence. In so doing, these institutional features may contribute to personalization through their focus on gender.

Quotas may seem like an odd fit for personalization; however, if quotas are viewed as a mechanism that takes a characteristic of an individual into account in their political recruitment, then quotas' connection to personalism becomes clearer. All types of quotas—voluntary, legal and constitutional—help focus political recruitment onto gender as a personal characteristic of a candidate; reactions to the applications of these quotas also highlight their connection to personalism. For example, parity cabinets can be seen as a particular form of quota, where women are appointed to 50 percent of the cabinet seats. As expected, given the research outlined, a common reaction to quotas in general and parity cabinets in particular is to question the credentials and skills of the women who enter a particular political role through this mechanism and suggest that they are somehow unqualified for the job (i.e., Coyne 2015; Walker 2016). Evidence routinely suggests, however, that despite fraught and unclear definitions of candidate 'merit' or 'qualifications', the women selected using quotas are as, if not more, experienced and meritorious than their male peers, as well as representatives selected using other mechanisms (Nugent and Krook 2016; Franceschet, Krook and Piscopo 2012; Franceschet, Annesley and Beckwith 2015). In some cases where women do appear less experienced than their male peers on selection, investigations of their effectiveness as representatives shows that quota women are as effective as men and nonquota women (Murray 2010). Research further shows that despite parity cabinets, women are less likely to be appointed as cabinet ministers for portfolios that are traditionally seen as masculine, such as defence. However, when women's presence in politics increases considerably, especially in executive positions, or when countries transform their view of the military and defence towards peacekeeping, women are considerably more likely to be appointed as ministers of defence (Barnes and O'Brien 2018).

This debate creates an interesting tension for personalism. Institutional personalization through directly electing candidates or leaders, gender quotas or parity cabinets can spark debates about politicians' individual characteristics, yet these debates often ignore or downplay these women's credentials.

Thus, for women selected using a quota or appointed to a parity cabinet, the focus can be more on their gender—a personal but public characteristic, as noted— rather than personal information that the literature has identified as being more 'relevant' or 'political', such as their ideas, qualifications and skills and policy positions. This suggests that institutional measures to increase parity and equity in representation may produce personalized reactions that load stereotypes about credentials or competence onto women politicians that do not comport with reality (c.f., Kanter 1977). This form of personalism appears to be blunter, and less individualistic as the literature would suggest is typically the case.[5]

MEDIA PERSONALISM, PERSONALIZATION, AND GENDER

Personalized politics occur through the media when news coverage of politics places emphasis on visibility of individual actors, such as candidates or party leaders, over more collective identities such as parties, cabinets and governments (Rahat and Sheafer 2007). There is considerable evidence to suggest that this phenomenon is heavily gendered because the volume, content, and tone of political news varies consistently by politician gender (c.f., Tuchman 1978; see also Goodyear-Grant 2013). For women politicians, this news coverage is also more likely to be focused on them as individuals than it is for their male peers. Thus, one area where these personalized politics are likely to change over time—that is, where we are most likely to see gendered personalization—is through changes in women politicians' media coverage.

Volume is one area where women in politics have seen changes typically described in the literature as positive; they are more likely to be covered as often and as prominently as men now than was the case in the past, particularly if they are government leaders or competitive candidates (Miller, Peake and Boulton 2010; Thomas, Harell and Gosselin forthcoming; Goodyear-Grant 2013; Trimble 2007). Because women in politics used to receive fewer mentions, less in-depth coverage, fewer first mentions and less front-page coverage than their male competitors (Heldman, Carroll and Olson 2005), this increase in coverage could mean that more opportunities now exist for women politicians to be personalized in the media than was the case in the past.

A good example of this change in volume of media coverage over time comes from comparing Elizabeth Dole to Hillary Clinton (Heldman, Carroll and Olson 2005; Miller, Peake and Boulton 2010). Both women actively sought the presidential nominations for their parties: Dole for the Republicans in 1999, and Clinton for the Democrats in 2008 and again in 2016.

Though Dole polled a strong second throughout the campaign, media coverage did not reflect this. Instead, she received considerably less coverage than candidates with far less support than her. Because she was not covered in a manner proportionate to her popularity, Dole was not *perceived* as viable or competitive, struggled with fund-raising and withdrew from the primary (Heldman, Carroll and Olson 2005). By contrast, Clinton was perceived to be the front-running candidate in the 2008 Democratic primary, and unlike Dole, Clinton received the most media coverage of the candidates in the campaign. This is in keeping with Clinton's frontrunner status (Miller, Peake and Boulton 2010).

Another example comes from the Canadian provinces. Since 2010, a number of women have become provincial premiers, leading subnational governments in Canada. There is no good reason to expect that, as heads of government, women should receive less coverage than men. Yet, significantly fewer stories are published online about women premiers in their first year of office than is the case for men (Thomas, Harell and Gosselin forthcoming). However, despite fewer stories overall, women premiers are not disadvantaged with respect to two other indicators of volume: total word count and prominence. Instead, women leading provincial governments have as many words written about them and are as likely to be mentioned first in news stories as are men. Despite the gender gap in total number of news stories, women Premiers are covered like the heads of government they are, at least with respect to volume (Thomas, Harell and Gosselin, forthcoming).

Gendered media personalism is found now through the content and tone of media coverage. The first way this can occur is through a novelty frame where women seeking political office are highlighted as being new or anomalous because of their gender. This is typically found when women represent 'firsts': the first woman candidate to be nominated by a major party for a high-profile post, the first woman to lead her party to an electoral victory and so on (Heldman, Carroll and Olson 2005; Miller, Peake and Boulton 2010; Trimble 2007). This particular form of coverage highlights gender above other qualities and characteristics; in so doing, it by definition draws attention to the person of the politician in question.

Even if women are not the 'first' and thus not covered using the novelty frame, media still cover women candidates and politicians using considerably more gender identifiers than they do when covering their male peers (Meeks 2012). For example, women Canadian premiers are substantially more likely to be gendered than are their male peers. Feminine gender labels, such as *woman*, *female* or *feminine*, are exclusively linked to women premiers, whereas the same is not true for masculine gender labels and male premiers (Thomas et al. 2017). This suggests that women in politics are explicitly gendered in ways that men are not.

Women in other executive positions, such as cabinet ministers, are sometimes presented in explicitly physical terms by the media; comparable coverage is not found for men (Verge and Pastor 2017). Explicit reference is made to women's appearance, marital and parental status and relationships to (powerful) men; again, evidence shows that media do not employ the same coverage for men (Sourd 2005; Miller, Peake and Boulton 2010; Burke and Mazzarella 2008; Heldman, Carroll and Olson 2005). For example, both Hillary Clinton and Sarah Palin were disproportionately covered as mothers on the campaign trail during the 2008 US presidential election (Miller 2017). Spanish media covering then-Defence Minister Carme Chacón made reference to her 'eight-centimeter heels and flowery maternity blouse', ensuring her clothes, shoes and fertility were included in a media report ostensibly about her carrying out her cabinet duties (quoted in Verge and Pastor 2017, 17). Women running as candidates for parliamentary elections are not immune because the media presents their appearance, private lives and parental status as important for their seriousness and viability as candidates in ways that are not found for men (Goodyear-Grant 2013). This means that gendered personalism through the media appears to operate in both a centralized and decentralized way.

Gender also structures the tone of political media coverage. Women candidates for presidential nomination in the United States receive considerably more negative media coverage than their male peers. Much of this negative coverage is further disproportionately directed at women's character and personality traits; men's negative coverage appears to be more about their credentials (Miller, Peake and Boulton 2010; Heldman, Carroll and Olson 2005). Media coverage further uses different verbs to cover women compared to men; women's coverage includes verbs that emphasize their combativeness. In some cases, verbs are exclusively used to discuss women's aggressive behaviour (Gidengil and Everitt 2003a, 2003b). Similarly, negative tone is used to highlight women politician's emotions in ways not experienced by men (Wright and Holland 2014; Verge and Pastor 2017). For example, when then-Prime Minister Julia Gillard delivered a speech against sexism in Australian politics, some media coverage characterized her as 'blistering', 'quivering with rage', or otherwise suffering from 'uncontrolled emotion' (Wright and Holland 2014, 463). Even in contexts where women and men appear to generate about the same volume of coverage about their appearance, marital status and parental status, the coverage of women's appearance and private lives is significantly more negative than is coverage for men's (Thomas et al. 2017). Notably, research suggests this type of negative coverage can factor more into evaluations of women in politics than it does for men (Ditonto 2017). In short, media coverage of women in politics is mediated to present those women as anomalous outsiders.

This carries four clear implications for personalism and personalization. The first is that the media present the public with information that personalizes candidates and politicians differently based on their gender. The public is more likely to receive information about women politicians' private lives and appearance, in addition to, or sometimes instead of, information about their credentials and policies. Importantly, this is often *not* a deliberate act on the part of women politicians. Second, in addition to presenting different information about women in politics than it does about men, the media also present personalizing information about women in a more negative manner. When this negative tone is applied to women's character, this carries considerable implications for elections because voters' character evaluations have a considerable effect on vote choice (Bittner this volume; 2010). Third, because the media are now covering women in politics at the same rate as they do men, the potential for media personalism for women in politics is increasing over time. The implication is that media personalization has potential to be a stronger, more negative phenomenon for women politicians than it is for men.

The fourth implication is that gendered media personalism may affect both the supply and the demand for women politicians. With respect to demand for women, parties are arguably aware of these patterns in gendered media personalism, as well as their potential effects on vote choice. This might help explain, at least in part, why some party selectorates are more reluctant to nominate women as candidates in districts the party is likely to win (Thomas and Bodet 2013). Similarly, the harmful effects of negative media presentations of women's personal information may be one reason why, in some contexts, women politicians routinely need to be more qualified than men to enjoy the same electoral success (Fulton 2012). Thus, some parties may only be willing to field women as candidates when they are exceptionally well qualified, holding female aspirants to higher standards than their male peers. Other parties might attempt to minimize media personalization by using template biographies that are deliberately silent on all candidate or Member of Parliament (MP) personal information (Thomas and Lambert 2017), thus minimizing the content media could use for this form of personalized politics.

On the supply side, qualified, ambitious women may choose not to volunteer for these levels of negative scrutiny, even if they otherwise would like a career in politics (Pruysers and Blais 2017). Those who do opt for a political career modify their behaviour, strategies and campaigns to address media personalization. This creates considerable, gendered differences in behavioural personalism.

BEHAVIOURAL PERSONALISM, PERSONALIZATION AND GENDER

Political behaviour as personalized politics is somewhat different than its institutional and media counterparts in that it potentially occurs in two places: with voters and with politicians. Voters engage in personalized politics when they evaluate candidates and leaders on personal or private characteristics. Politicians, by contrast, may deliberately work to emphasize particular issues or strategically disclose private information in an attempt to make themselves more desirable or relatable to voters (Rahat and Sheafer 2007). These strategic behaviours may be in direct response to other forms of personalization or personalized politics, including through the institutions and media, as outlined previously.

Voters clearly evaluate leaders on their personalities. Voters compare leaders to one another, assessing their character and their competence, and then use this information to help determine their vote choice (Bittner this volume; 2010, 2011). Furthermore, although both character and competence matter for vote choice, it appears as though character may matter more for vote choice than competence does (Johnston 2002). The gendered link to this personalism is clear; as noted, there is some evidence to suggest that the media present the character and competence of women in politics differently than they do for their male peers. In the 2008 primary, Hillary Clinton's character comprised the bulk of her negative coverage, whereas Barack Obama's negative coverage was mostly about his credentials (Miller, Peake and Boulton 2010). Although persuasive arguments can be made that serious questions ought to have been asked about each candidate's character and competence, this is also clearly an area ripe for future research as more women seek executive office. Evidence of the effects of this negative coverage are mixed; if voters are undecided or unaware of women politicians, this information has the potential to negatively affect their ratings of and willingness to vote for that candidate (Miller 2017).

It may be tempting to suggest that voters ought to use more political or concrete information to evaluate leaders and candidates than perceptions of those politicians' characters. Evidence appears to suggest that voters who are equipped (i.e., are knowledgeable enough) to use policy and issue positions to inform their vote choice do so; however, all voters, regardless of their levels of policy or issue knowledge, still use sociodemographic information to evaluate candidates and leaders. Importantly, those with higher levels of information rely on these sociodemographic cues as much as do their more poorly informed counterparts (Cutler 2002; Roy 2009). This carries two implications for personalized politics. First, it suggests that levels of behavioural personalism can vary considerably by levels of voter knowledge, with more-knowledgeable voters being more likely to personalize candidates and leaders than their less-knowledgeable counterparts. Second, the most common forms of voter-based behavioural personalism appear to be more private in nature, in that voters regardless of knowledge levels are using a candidate or leader's sociodemographic characteristics (i.e., their gender) to evaluate them. Given how gendered media personalism is, this second implication is not necessarily surprising. It is, however, important to integrate into the personalization literature.

Less is known, though, about how gender affects voters' behavioural personalism. Though research shows that personality clearly matters for vote choice, there is little research that investigates if these patterns are different for women than they are for men. Bittner's work (this volume) is suggestive and leads to the hypothesis that that effect of personality on women's vote choice is slightly weaker than it is for men. This is an area that is certainly ripe for future research.

Behavioural personalism is also a useful lens through which to view politicians' strategic actions. Even in party-dominated systems, candidates and elected representatives supplement their own brands and communications with traits or issues they wish to emphasize (Parker 2012; Cross and Young 2015; Pruysers and Cross, this volume). Provided it fits with a politician's personality and communication strategies, their personal life can be politicized deliberately and strategically. Doing so demonstrates they have the 'capacity to offer a "human" persona' (Langer 2010, 61; Stalsburg 2012). This 'politicization of the private persona' is then used to build the political brand and to underwrite political values and legitimize policy (Langer 2010, 61; Stalsburg 2012). For party leaders, this means that they must 'embody the party brand, [because] their personal lives can personify the party's values and policies . . . and function as the unifying narrative' that links policies and platforms (Langer 2010, 61–62). This holds for candidates as well, through an expectation that they all strictly adhere to, and communicate, their party's brand. Overall, the party brand framework facilitates an understanding of why displays of various aspects of politicians' private lives, including their parental status, might vary across genders, across and within political parties, and across and within regions.

Britain offers paradigmatic cases of the political personalism and the use of a politicians' own family as part of the political brand. Tony Blair strategically displayed interactions with his children, both during election campaigns and in the lead up to the invasion of Iraq (Langer 2010). David Cameron employed similar strategies by using his family to authenticate policy positions and decontaminate his party's brand (Langer 2010, 67). By contrast, Gordon Brown opted to keep much of his private life private. Thus, parental status can be a cue for a politician's brand or how to interpret a politician under the umbrella or rubric of their party's brand.

THE PROBLEM OF PRIVATIZATION

Politicians' behavioural personalism helps identify the problems with seeing privatization and privatized politics as a subset or subcategory of personalization. Key to the distinction is that although both processes draw emphasis to the individual politician, personalization is more 'political' than is privatization. For example, when personalization occurs, the argument is that the emphasis is placed on the individual because they are the occupant of a particular institutional role, such as party leader or political executive. The literature on personalization argues that it generally places emphasis on that politician's ideas, capacities and policies. Privatization, by contrast, draws attention to the same individual, but in a distinctly 'nonpolitical' way on 'nonpolitical' grounds. Thus, attention paid to a politician's personal life, marital status, parental status, appearance or any other personal characteristic is argued to be a form of nonpolitical personalization (Van Aelst, Sheafer and Stanyer 2012, 207; Rahat and Sheafer 2007; Balmas and Sheafer 2016).

It is perhaps not surprising that a gendered lens critiques this division between political and nonpolitical personalism as a false dichotomy. This critique can be effectively made on two grounds. First, what exactly counts as political, nonprivate information about a politician? What counts as private, nonpolitical information? Second, as noted, politicians engage in behavioural personalization and use their private lives as explicit grounds for political strategy. As expected, the options for politicians to do this are gendered. Thus, if politicians use their private lives for political gains, it is not convincing to suggest the information they use is non-political.

Similarly, even a cursory look at character-related traits used to describe candidates and leaders in the media, or those supplied in public opinion surveys designed to probe how voters evaluate leaders, shows that a neat characterization of these traits as political or non-political is difficult. For example, is honesty a political or nonpolitical trait? Intelligence? Trustworthiness? Ambition? Good judgement? Is competence political, whereas character is not? Although arguments could be made to suggest each of these characteristics is political or not, it is perhaps most convincing to suggest that even if one thinks it best to conclude these traits are non-political, they remain *politicized.* Voters use these traits to assess candidates and determine their vote choice, candidates campaign on these traits and leaders use these traits in government to help persuade the public to support them and their policy initiatives. Given this, the utility of drawing a strong distinction between personalization and privatization becomes questionable.

Even if this were not the case, evidence shows that the private lives of women in politics receive a different kind of scrutiny than those of their male colleagues. This is where women's political ambitions may collide with gender stereotypes about politics. Women politicians have to ask themselves, 'how do I best present myself to voters?' just as male candidates do, but women in politics face a double bind: do they politicize their personal lives and open themselves up to critique for being 'bad mothers', or do they downplay or refuse to disclose aspects of their personal lives and potentially miss out on an effective political brand?

Some women in politics, such as Angela Merkel and Tarja Halonen, have deliberately chosen to rigidly conceal their private lives while holding executive office (Van Zoonen 2006). In both cases, this decision was treated as newsworthy and potentially problematic for their reelection. Similarly, Thomas and Lambert (2017, 147) find that male politicians are more likely than their female peers to use family photos to give themselves greater credibility on some issues. Though most of the politicians Thomas and Lambert study suggest that strategically politicizing their private lives was a positive, effective strategy, they also confirm that this is gendered. They report:

> Several MPs noted that if a woman politician displayed photos of young children, 'somebody's going to say, "who's looking after the children?!" [pause] which they don't if you put up the husband with young children.' Another MP, upon recollecting the experiences of his caucus colleagues, noted hearing 'especially with regard to cabinet ministers both provincial and federal, especially when they have younger children, "well, I suppose the taxpayers are paying for a babysitter in their office," because you see a picture of the mother with the young child. [pause] It is usually snarly.'

Interestingly, one finding Thomas and Lambert report is that safety concerns can stop women in politics from politicizing their private personae in ways that do not necessarily appear for men. For some women politicians, this safety consideration is considerable enough to trump the advantage they feel they would have with voters if they used a more personalized strategy. Women politicians and political staff alike agreed that 'it's always *safer* to keep younger children out of the spotlight' because it 'protects them and their safety', even if doing so means that MPs 'believe that I am at a distinct disadvantage by not using pictures of my family' (Thomas and Lambert 2017, 148). Thomas and Lambert report, 'This theme was entirely absent in our interviews with male MPs and staffers' (Thomas and Lambert 2017, 148).

Some tentative conclusions can be drawn from this. First, women and men in politics both use their private lives for their political gain. Though this is a gendered process and often very different for women and men, the reality is that politicians will use personalism, or the politicization of the private persona, as an effective political tool. Second, because of this, it is problematic to draw an analytical distinction between personalization in a 'political' compared with a 'private' sense because it reflects the traditional view of women, gender and politics where women occupy the private but not public sphere. Politics remains a masculine domain where the feminine and women are seen as anomalous. In a sense, until it fully integrates gender, the concept of personalization and personalism is masculine, just as is politics itself.

CONCLUSIONS

This chapter argues that personalism and personalization are gendered, and that in ignoring gender, past research has omitted what appears to be a key facet of the concept. Notably, this omission has created a false dichotomy in the literature; through a gendered lens, it is difficult to see much of a difference between personalization and privatization, both conceptually and empirically. Similarly, the gendered consequences for personalism and personalization appear to be ubiquitous because they can be centralized or decentralized and found across institutional, media and behavioural forms of personalism. It is clear that the process and consequences of personalism and personalization are different for women than they are for men.

This suggests that fully integrating gender into personalism and personalization theory may provide interesting insights into how the processes of personalization begin in some contexts. For example, in contexts where women's legislative presence is sparked by institutional change (i.e., the introduction of gender quotas in the 1970s, as was the case in Sweden), longitudinal analyses could be used to ascertain how a gendered institutional change affects processes of political personalization. In general, because broad social processes are at least theoretically associated with both personalization and increases in women's political representation, it may be worth exploring how these sets of processes are linked.

The gendered analysis also shows how the forms of personalism are connected. For women in politics, media personalism feeds clearly into behavioural personalism, both for voter evaluation and for women's own strategic actions. Similarly, institutional personalization feeds directly into media personalization. By examining women's experiences with personalization, new theoretical insights about how personalization operates across contexts and actors may be generated.

Finally, women are moving into politics in greater numbers, and they occupy political executive positions more consistently. Given that personalism is clearly a gendered phenomenon, women's changing presence in politics, particularly in the most powerful political offices offers a prime opportunity to study how personalization evolves over time. Parity cabinets are becoming more common just as cabinets are becoming less powerful relative to chief political executives (Annesley, Beckwith and Franceschet 2016; see also Poguntke and Webb 2005 and this volume). Similarly, as more women lead governments, it will be important to determine if the contours of personalism and personalization change. Clearly, integrating gender fully into the study of personalism and personalization provides a fruitful opportunity for future scholarship.

NOTES

1. Very little is known about how gender outside the binary affects political phenomena. What is known, though, is that genders are diverse and that it is reasonable to hypothesize that this has political consequences, particularly given that exploratory measurements suggest that sizeable portions of the population are not captured by traditional measures of gender used in political science research (Bittner and Goodyear-Grant 2017). This is a fruitful area for future research.

2. That said, women's presence in the Canadian House of Commons was stalled between sixty-two and sixty-nine members of Parliament (MPs) between 1997 and the 2011 election. Though eighty-eight women were elected in 2015, the proportion of women candidates elected remains static; the increase is due, in large part, to an additional thirty seats added to the House of Commons as part of a redistricting process.

3. Some issues remained too controversial to be political or public for these commissions' reports. For example, the report of the Royal Commission on the Status of Women in Canada is silent on domestic violence.

4. Christy Clark (British Columbia) and Alison Redford (Alberta) were selected using UMV in 2011; Rachel Notley (Alberta) was also selected using UMV in 2014. Kathleen Wynne (Ontario) was selected using a hybrid primary/convention model in 2013.

5. The other aspect of this type of gendered institutional personalization is that it can be both decentralized, when it is focused on a candidate accessing office through a quota, or centralized, when it is focused on a member of the political executive in a parity cabinet.

Chapter 12

Personalization, Party Government and Democracy

Richard S. Katz

As Rudolf Wildenmann observed more than thirty years ago, at least since World War II the idea of democratic party government has been the 'dominant legitimating myth' in Western Europe—and one might add in the established parliamentary democracies outside of Europe as well. Indeed, it is not stretching the literature unreasonably to assert a broad consensus among scholars and members of 'the democracy promoting industry'[1] that democracy can in large measure be defined as that which results from free and fair electoral competition among political parties.[2] Even in the countries such as Switzerland and the United States, in which the party government model does not apply to the same degree (Lehner and Homann 1987; Fiorina 1987), it is sometimes held up as the standard for legitimate and effective democratic government (APSA 1969). Moreover, the twin articles of faith that 'democratic government means party government' and that 'democratic government is good government' have sometimes led to suggestions that poor performance of ostensibly democratic governments must indicate insufficient 'partyness of government' (see discussion herein for an elaboration of this term).

As many of the preceding chapters have suggested, there is a strong current in the literature that suggests that growing personalization of politics necessarily undermines parties, and therefore also undermines the legitimating capacity of the party government myth. This chapter addresses the questions of whether personalism and partyness are necessarily incompatible, and whether or not incompatible, what the potential impact of personalization on parliamentary party government might be.

Parliamentary government effectively is defined by having an executive that is responsible to parliament in the sense that he or she can be turned out of office at any time by a vote of no confidence.[3] Although that does not mean that the cabinet must be supported by a cohesive and stable majority (particularly the Scandinavian countries, and also Canada,[4] have a record of minority cabinets that survive on the basis of shifting majorities or strategic abstentions by opposition parties), it does mean that there should never be a majority that is so strongly opposed to the cabinet that it prefers to turn the cabinet out rather than letting it continue in office. Indeed, parties developed in the predemocratic era in part to make the problem of building and maintaining majorities tractable, first so as to wrest the power to decide who would become ministers away from the monarch—precisely because no minister appointed by the monarch could long survive in office if confronted with 'reliable' majority opposition, and second to serve as effective 'nominating committees' to select ministers whom the monarch would be obliged to accept.

In Britain, for example, there were elements of parliamentary party government well before the process of democratization, which arguably began only with the Reform Act of 1832, or perhaps more realistically with the Reform Act of 1867. This system was democratized by the broad expansion of suffrage. But although suffrage expansion might produce a Parliament whose members were democratically responsible to their constituents (so that Members of Parliament [MPs] might plausibly be characterized as the agents of their constituents rather than as the agents of 'the duke or lord or baronet', or borough corporation, that effectively appointed them or sold them their seats (see Beer 1969, 23), it also had the potential to undermine party government by empowering local electorates and thus limiting the capacity of parliamentary leaders to maintain stable majorities.[5] The transition to what we would now recognize as democratic party government required, in addition, coordination across constituencies so that people's choices could be aggregated into an overall selection of government, either directly through the election of a single majority party or indirectly through the building of a majority coalition once the Parliament had been elected.

In these terms, conformity to the party government model can be seen to be an important element of the procedural legitimation of contemporary parliamentary democracies—and one of the reasons why party switching by MPs, especially if it occurs in large numbers, often is regarded as democratically problematic. Of course, as Margaret Levi among others would argue (Levi, Sacks and Tyler 2009), this is only one of the contributors to legitimacy writ large (trustworthiness, for example, being at least as important). And, as is true of all ideal types, the party government model will only be approximated, not realized, in actual cases.

At the same time, it must be recognized that party government in this strong sense is not without challenges, nor, as the US and Swiss examples indicate, is it the only model of government that might support a sense of democratic legitimacy. In the Swiss case, the system is legitimized in democratic terms by easy access to the instruments of direct democracy. The US exception is facilitated by presidentialism, which means that the executive does not need the support of a reliable legislative majority to remain in office. Of particular relevance to the question of personalization in politics, and also contributing to the US exception, is the fact that the party government ideal runs counter to the idea that the mandates of members of legislatures should be understood to be personal rather than partisan, and that it also runs counter to the idea that an MP's primary loyalty should be to his or her conscience or to his or her own local constituents rather than to a national party or its leadership.[6] This contradiction is mirrored in Germany, for example, when the Constitutional Court attributes constitutional status (as *verfassungsrechtliche Institutionen* in their words) to political parties, while at the same time, the German Basic Law also says that Members of the Bundestag 'shall be representatives of the whole people, not bound by orders and instructions, and shall be subject only to their conscience'.[7]

That said, to assess the likely impact of personalization on the capacity of the party government ideal to continue to undergird the democratic legitimacy of contemporary parliamentary systems, it is necessary first to clarify what precisely the ideal type of party government, and within that the ideal type of party, are. There are, of course, an almost unlimited number of definitions of 'party' and 'party government' (for a very partial list of definitions of 'party', see Katz 2017, 209), but primarily as categories with internal variation rather than as ideal types that can be more or less closely approximated. This is important because it is unlikely that personalization, at least as experienced to date in the established parliamentary systems, will have brought about changes of sufficient magnitude as to constitute categoric change, notwithstanding that the changes may be quite significant with regard to the way the systems operate within the same category.

The definitions that I articulated in the context of the 'Future of Party Government' project in the 1980s, however, are an exception.[8] In that project, I defined 'partyness of government' as a continuous variable that would indicate the degree to which any particular system approximates the party government ideal type, which I suggested consists of three (later subdivided into five) elements (Katz 1987, 7):

1. Decisions are made by elected party officials or by those under their control.
2a. Policy is decided within parties which
2b. then act cohesively to enact it.
3a. Officials are recruited and
3b. held accountable through party.

In turn, the 'party' of the party government ideal is also an ideal type, thus suggesting a continuous concept of the 'partyness' of an organization, defined by three characteristics:

1. Exhibiting team-like behaviour
2. in attempting to win control over all political power
3. and basing claims of legitimacy on electoral success.

In considering the relevance of personalism for party government, these definitions are significant both for what they say and do not say. With regard to the former, the crucial elements are team-like behaviour and a focus on the party as a singular entity rather than as a collection of loosely affiliated independent actors. On the one hand, for the votes cast for individual candidates, or for regionally diverse lists of candidates, to be translated into a democratic mandate for a government requires that the candidates of a party all stand for the same thing, regardless of where they are located, and that those of them who are elected then act together to implement that popular verdict. On the other hand, it is only if parties act as a team that governments and individual office-holders can be held accountable through party.[9] With the necessary changes to allow for multiparty systems and coalition governments, the centrality of this kind of behaviour to democratic parliamentary party government was well expressed by Clement Attlee (1957):

> The candidate of one of the major Parties stands for a connected policy and for a certain body of men who, if a majority can be obtained, will form a Government. This is well understood by the electors. If the Member fails to support the Government or fails to act with the Opposition in their efforts to turn the Government out, he is acting contrary to the expectation of those who have put their trust in him.

In other words, and notwithstanding constitutional provisions to the contrary, full realization of the party government model must assume that the popular mandate resulting from an election belongs to the party and not to its individual representatives.

Equally important, however, is what these definitions do not say. First, they say nothing about the internal organization of the parties. Any particular party may conform to the ideal type of the mass party with policy programs and leadership chosen through internally democratic processes, it may be governed by its parliamentary Fraktion (or the like) or it may be, as John Ramsden metaphorically described the pre-Margaret Thatcher constitution of the British Conservative Party (analogizing to Czarist Russia), a system of 'autocracy tempered by assassination' (see Hennessy 2002, 295). All that is required is that once decisions are made, the party unite behind them, although, of course, these differences among party organizations may have a substantial impact on the degree to which that unity is actually achieved.

Second, these definitions say nothing about the basis for the unity or for popular choice of party. A party may be based on social or geographic segmentation (the Bloc Québécois or the Israeli Arab Democratic Party), on ideology (liberal, social democratic or Christian democratic parties) or on loyalty to a particular leader (for example, Silvio Berlusconi's *Forza Italia*). Again, all that is required is team-like behaviour by politicians and that electors perceive themselves to be choosing among parties or among candidates whose political personae are defined by their parties.

Third, the definitions say nothing directly about cross-level coherence or autonomy in systems of multilevel governance. On the one hand, the overall partyness of government would be maximized by complete coherence within each party spanning all levels of government. On the other hand, however, as Eldersveld's (1964, 9) idea of stratarchy suggests, and the experience of Canada—where national and provincial parties of the same name may have little or no connection, so that it was plausible for federal Progressive Conservative leader Jean Charest to become leader of the Quebec Liberal Party, and in which voters may have different and nominally inconsistent party identifications at national and provincial levels—illustrates, it is possible to have high partyness of government at each level without cross-level team-like behaviour,[10] provided there is sufficient territorial division of powers that governments at each level can operate autonomously from each other.[11]

Taken together, these observations suggest two criteria according to which the impact of personalization on party government might be assessed. The first is the possibility that personalization might affect the degree to which parties behave as cohesive teams, and therefore the degree of 'partyness of party', and ultimately the possibility of high partyness of government. Given the variety of specific forms that high partyness of government might take, there is unlikely to be a monotonic relationship between personalization and partyness, however. At one extreme, for example, high personalism might take the form of a cult of personality, with the result that all dissidents either leave the party or are expelled from it, leaving a totally cohesive party of sycophants, in effect turning very high partyness of government (at least in the single-party majority case) into an elective, albeit time-limited, dictatorship. Alternatively, personalization might turn every politician into an independent operator, undermining the notion of party as a team, and therefore destroying party government. Naturally, the expectation is that the real consequences of real changes in the level of personalism will be less extreme. Conversely, low levels of personalism might mean that party as a team looms larger in politics, but equally partyness could be undercut by factors other than personalization, such as the increased use of institutions of direct democracy, once described by Samuel Finer (1975, 18) as 'the Pontius Pilate of British politics' because they allow the parties to wash their hands of important decisions.

The second way in which the impact of personalization might be assessed reflects the possible variations in the nature of the parties, and thus in the character and operation of party government even if the degree of approximation of the party government ideal type were to remain the same. In this regard, the central point is that because personalities, and persons more broadly understood, are 'multidimensional', greater personalization in politics may mean increased focus on a variety of personal characteristics. Changes in the degree of personalism may be reflected in the demographic composition of candidate slates or leadership cadres (more or fewer women, for example) or result in greater or lesser value being accorded to certain aspects of the career trajectories of political aspirants (e.g., having an established media presence outside of the explicitly political). Relatedly, personalization may influence the nature of party campaigns and the emphasis placed, for example, on character as opposed to policy, and indeed may have an impact on the substantive definition of 'character'. As Melanee Thomas (this volume) suggests, personalization may take the form of 'privatization', increasing the relevance of things like marital fidelity that at other times or in other contexts might have been regarded as properly in the private sphere and thus irrelevant to political choice. And, as Thomas also suggests, these changes may interact with one another—in her case, with privatization having a differential impact on both the recruitment prospects and the campaign strategies of male and female aspirants to office. In these senses, personalization may change the nature or type of party government without necessarily changing overall partyness.

PERSONALIZATION AT THE TOP

Discussions of personalism in politics frequently focus on the national level and assume that personalization comes at the expense of party. In these terms, the presidentialization of politics necessarily reduces the partyness of politics, and the weight voters give to the persons of party leaders in casting their ballots necessarily reduces the salience of party, at least implicitly equating party with policy or ideology and assuming a clear separation between the message and the messenger. Particularly in the case of highly centralized parties, it is not clear whether party and leader can actually be separated, with the leader being the human face of the party and the party being the support network of the leader. Moreover, even if presidentialization in the full sense introduced by Poguntke and Webb (2005, but see their chapter in this volume) is a relatively recent development, personalism at the top more generally is not. For example, in 1950 (the fiftieth anniversary of his birth) membership applications for the French Communist Party were headed with the statement 'I hereby join the party of Maurice Thorez', not 'I hereby join the Communist Party' (Duverger 1969, 115), but although support for the Communist Party, and leadership within it, may have been highly personalized, it would be hard to deny either the strong ideological flavour or the strong internal cohesion of the party. In the British case, if one were to crudely operationalize the degree of personalism at the top as the proportion of the references to the cabinet in *The Times* (London) that are to 'the [name of Prime Minister] government or cabinet' rather than to 'the [name of party] government or cabinet', there was a marked increase in personalism at the top during the last quarter of the twentieth century (followed by a modest decline in the first decade of the twenty-first century, albeit still at levels much higher than in the earlier postwar period). This late-twentieth-century increase, however, was only to a level that had been quite normal in second half of the nineteenth century. Indeed, two highest values in the entire period from 1850 were recorded for the first Palmerston (1855–1858) and second Derby (1858–1859) governments (see figure 12.1).

More specifically, personalization at the top has been understood to involve three related aspects. The first is increased emphasis on the leader generally, but specifically on the leader as a person: his or her character and personal history as the authoritative voice of the party and as the object of support and basis for choice and loyalty—all at the expense of emphasis on policy or collective identity. The second is increased concentration of authority in the hands of the leader both within the party and within the cabinet, in effect answering Brian Farrell's (1971) question about the role of the Irish Taoiseach ('Chairman or Chief?') with an increasingly definitive 'Chief!'. The third is a resulting shift in the intraparty balance of power in favour of the party in public office at the expense of the party on the ground.

Whether personalization at the top actually has been increasing is still a subject of debate. Looking specifically at the weight of coverage in election reporting given to politicians as persons rather than to parties as organizations, for example, Kriesi (2012) finds little consistent change since the 1970s, although as the data in figure 12.1 (albeit about coverage of a government during its entire term, rather than coverage of all contenders during general election campaigns) suggest, the 1970s may be too late a starting point. But while Kriesi finds little support for a generally applicable hypothesis of personalization, he does find large differences among countries in the levels of personalism. Amanda Bittner (this volume), in looking at the electoral importance of party leaders' traits in Britain and Canada since the 1980s, also finds no long-term trend in personalization, but rather that evaluations of leaders' personalities have always been a factor in electoral choice.

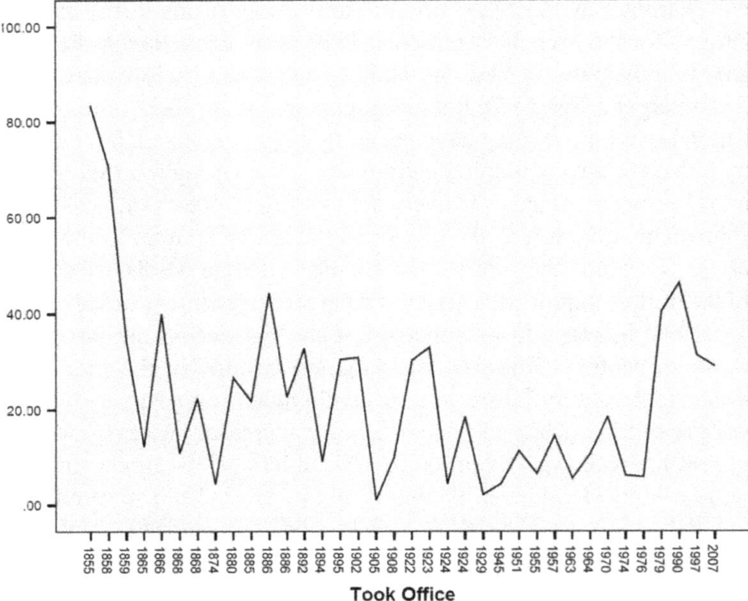

Figure 12.1 Percentage References to [Name of Prime Minister] Government or Cabinet Rather Than [Name of Party] Government or Cabinet by Year in Which the Prime Minister Took Office.

The magnitude of the impact of personalities has varied over time (albeit not reflecting a monotonic trend) and across parties. Moreover, within the general category of 'personalities', the relative importance of competence versus character has also fluctuated. This is a finding echoed in Melanee Thomas's contribution to this volume, in which she argues for the increased relevance (in gender-specific ways) at all levels, not just at the top, of personal characteristics like having young children or marital fidelity that in a previous era might have been regarded as irrelevant. At the other end of the chain that begins with election and ends in governing, Jonathan Malloy (this volume) shows that although the degree of concentration of authority in the hands of the prime minister is in part a consequence of various institutional and societal developments, these interact with the personality and political capabilities of particular incumbents. Again, while the level of personalism may vary over time, there is less support for a hypothesis of secular change.

While these suggest that both the level and character of personalism may strongly influence the nature of party competition and the ways in which party decisions are made and party unity is maintained, they do not necessarily suggest changes in the level of party government or in the clarity of a party government's democratic mandate. Indeed, contrary to the notion that personalism is in competition with partisanship, personalism may increase the partyness of government by focusing attention and control. Consider, for example, Winston Churchill's 1949 speech to the Tory Conference:

> All I will promise to the British electorate in your name, and the only pledge that I will give on behalf of the Conservative party is that if the government of Britain is entrusted to us at this crisis in her fate, we will do our best for all, without fear or favor, without class or party bias, without rancor or spite.[12]

Although Churchill is proposing to be the voice that articulates the pledge to 'do our best', he is also proposing to make that pledge in the name of the party. Moreover, notwithstanding that this speech was made long before the idea that focus on personalities was diminishing concern with policy or ideology, the pledge was only to do 'our best for all' (i.e., asking the voters to 'trust us') in contrast to advancing a clear policy program.

Although the evidence casts doubt on the simple claim that increasing personalism (itself subject to doubt) necessarily undermines the legitimating capacity of party government, it also suggests that the relationship between varieties of personalism and varieties of party government requires far more nuanced study. The Israeli experiment of combining a parliamentary system with direct popular election of the prime minister is illustrative of the problem. Direct election was intended to strengthen the position of the prime minister as a person vis-à-vis the parties (including his own) that constituted his parliamentary majority: an increase in personalism at the expense of partyness. Although the reform may have given the prime minister a personal mandate to form a government, however, it also resulted in dramatic losses of seats by the major parties (again including the party of the prime minister), thus increasing the strength of the smaller parties. The result actually left the prime minister in a weaker position personally, thus increasing the partyness of government formation and maintenance. But although the result may have been higher partyness, it was not greater efficiency, belying the 'syllogism' suggested previously.

One obvious driver of the high personalism of US presidential politics—and the low partyness of US government in general—has been the importance of primary elections (rather than party meetings in 'smoke-filled rooms') to select the candidates, including presidential candidates, who on selection effectively become the leaders of their parties.[13] In recent years, a number of parties in parliamentary systems have adopted primary-like procedures (e.g., choice by all member votes or by votes open even to those who are not party members, coupled with easy entry onto the final ballot) to choose their leaders.[14] These have two potential effects. On the one hand, as discussed by David Stewart in this volume, expanding the final selectorate beyond those who could possibly have personal interactions with or knowledge of the candidates may alter the relative importance of their many personal and political characteristics in determining the outcome. On the other hand, these processes may require candidates to build their own personal, support networks or organizations within the party. A strong group of personal loyalists is almost certain to prove an asset to the winner of these contests, and in that sense to increase the importance of the personal relative to the organizational in defining the party, but this does not necessarily mean weakening the coherence (partyness) of the party. To the extent that the personal networks of defeated candidates survive the contest and to the extent that aspirants to replace the current leader build their own networks in anticipation of a contest, however, leadership selection by primary-like processes has the potential to support personalized factionalism at the expense of partyness.

Whatever the impact of personalization (or not) at the top on the *level* of partyness of government, focus on an individual is likely to be a less stable base for support or continuity of policy than focus on an institution, if only because of both the natural mortality and the political mortality of leaders. It may focus internal policy debates on the personality of the leader—one changes party policy *by* changing the leader. This has always been obviously the case in factionalized parties, but even in parties that are not obviously factionalized, the policy positions of the contenders have usually played a significant role in the choice of a new leader when that has been necessary. Ironically, although personalization at the top may strengthen the position of the leader *while in office*, personalization at the top may also make leaders less secure, as the decreasing capacity of party leaders to survive electoral defeats suggests; simply, the mirror image of being able to claim personal credit for victory is to be assigned personal blame for defeat.

PERSONALIZATION IN PARLIAMENT AND PARLIAMENTARY ELECTIONS

Although presidentialization/personalism of politics at the level of national party leadership may be having a significant impact on the practice of party government, as several of the preceding chapters make clear, personalism is hardly limited to 'the top of the greasy poll'. But while the possible conflation of leader and party may render personalism at the top compatible with high partyness, the same conflation is much less possible at lower levels; an individual member of parliament or subnational office-holder may be *of* his or her party or even *defined by* the party, but precisely because none of them is the top leader of the party, there is no way in which any one of them can be taken individually to be synonymous with the party.

As Pruysers and Cross (this volume) observe, personalism in local election campaigns may increase citizen involvement and put a human face on what might otherwise appear to be a distant and impersonal institution. To the extent that voting for a party is accomplished by voting for an identifiable local candidate or candidates—something that is true even with closed-list PR provided that the candidates on the party lists themselves publicly campaign—the personal attributes of the candidates can be assumed to compete with, or at least to complement, the collective attributes of their parties in influencing nomination and campaign decisions and ultimately electoral choice and behaviour in office in ways analogous to those already discussed with regard to the top party leadership.[15] This has always been the case, but in most systems the effect has been modest. Even in Britain, where single member plurality (SMP) should maximize the visibility of individual candidates, Philip Williams (1966) estimated the advantage of 'familiar' candidates over 'newcomer' challengers in marginal seats (a proxy for 'the MP's personal vote') to be less than 3.5 percent for Labour (and less than 2 percent for Conservatives), and Bruce Cain and colleagues (1984) attribute most of the effect to the familiar candidates' records of constituency service rather than to their personal attributes.

Although SMP in Britain (and Canada) makes the identities of constituency candidates particularly obvious, the acts of voting for the local candidate, the candidate's party and the associated prime-ministerial candidate are still totally conflated. As Pilet and Renwick (this volume, see also Renwick and Pilet 2016) show, however, in a growing number of systems, voters in parliamentary elections are allowed (or required) to express preferences among the multiple candidates of the party they are supporting. On the one hand, this should increase the relevance of the personal attributes of the candidate, although not by itself determining which attributes—personalities, policy preferences, physical appearance (e.g., Rosar, Klein and Beckers 2008) or even the candidate's record of party loyalty—will be relevant. On the other hand, from the perspective of candidates, intraparty choice means that aspirants to office are to a greater or lesser degree (depending on the specifics of the intraparty choice mechanism) *forced* to compete, as individuals, against their copartisans. This competition may be based primarily on constituency service (see Chiru, this volume) or a desire for demographic diversity purely in terms of a politics of presence, either of which may represent an internal 'division of labour' within a party and thus be entirely consistent with party unity and effective party government. Intraparty competition can also be based on policy preferences or loyalties to alternative leadership cadres, however. As Thayer (1969) and Katz (1980) argue, particularly the last two of these can have the effect of promoting factionalism, and thus undermining partyness. Indeed, during the so-called 'first republic' in Italy, with an electoral system in which the particular candidates elected to fill their party's share of the parliamentary seats were determined entirely by the *voto di preferenza* (a personal preference vote for up to three or four candidates on the list of the party for which the elector had already voted), cabinets were more likely to collapse because of the defection of one or more of the factions of the Christian Democratic party than because of the defection of one of its coalition partner parties—in effect suggesting 'factionness of government' rather than partyness.

Because candidates have to mount individual campaigns, they have to amass the necessary resources (money, campaign workers, etc.) and precisely because these resources are required for intraparty competition, they cannot be expected to come from the party itself. The result is likely to be direct electoral dependence of individual candidates (and then MPs) on patrons and subgroups (wealthy or well-connected individuals, organized interests) within the party or the electorate more generally significantly beyond what would be expected from competition contained within a formal party organization, and particularly from competition contained within party conferences or executive bodies. Although these supporters may value party unity in the abstract, it is not a given that they will favour party unity over their own particular interests or that they will reward and not punish loyalty to the overall party line when it goes against those interests. Moreover, the fact that MPs are elected based on votes that were cast for them individually rather than merely as a by-product of votes cast for their party is likely to increase their sense of having a personal rather than a purely partisan mandate. In providing or encouraging an incentive, the capacity and a normative rationale for personal differentiation and independent action by representatives from the same party, personalization in the form of intraparty electoral choice at least has the potential to seriously undermine party government.

That said, two additional points require mention. First, the increasing (see, e.g., Ohmura 2014) use of free or conscience votes in parliaments[16] is incompatible with the model of party government, and thus the outcome of these votes cannot be democratically legitimated with reference to it. Rather, some degree of personalism, and a resulting individual mandate, in the choice of MPs must be assumed if such votes are to have any democratic legitimacy; the parties having effectively 'washed their hands' of the decision, unless the individual MPs can individually claim authorization by the people to decide the issue they have no more legitimacy than would be inherent in any other arbitrarily chosen small group. Second, for MPs to switch parties during the course of a parliament while retaining their seats is also incompatible with the model of party government, although like the acceptance of conscience votes it is a practice reflective of the idea of a personal mandate enshrined in many constitutions (for example, see note 7), and again the substantive (as opposed to the rhetorical) legitimation of the practice is furthered by an element of personalism in the original election of the MP.

PERSONALIZATION WITHIN PARTIES

In theory, the party government model is catholic with respect to the nature of party membership and the role of party members. Nonetheless, personalization within parties understood as the evolution of more individualized, direct and flexible connections between the party and its individual members or supporters—as opposed to connections mediated by party branches and ancillary organizations—like personalization at the top or among members of parliaments can have an impact on the degree of partyness, and thus of party government. The question, raised by Gauja (this volume), is how well parties can find a way to balance apparent demands for more direct and individualized involvement on the part of their base with the kind of unified collective action that is the essence of partyness.

The kinds of changes that Gauja (this volume, but see Katz 2013) identifies as contributing to personalization within parties frequently are advanced as ways to revitalize parties, and especially to stem the widespread decline of party membership numbers. Even if the introduction of forms of 'membership-lite' succeed in numerical terms, however, they have the potential to significantly change the nature of parties in at least two ways. First, they tend to convert party from a well-defined organization with clear boundaries and a stable and committed membership into a far more permeable and transitory 'cloud' of temporary supporters. They may also tend to convert party from a 'body of [wo/]men united, for promoting by their joint endeavours', some 'principle in which they are agreed', into a set of structures through which each individual participates separately in trying to influence politicians to act in accordance with the particular preferences of that individual. Second, in conjunction with increased personalization at the top, and the use of membership ballots to select leaders and order candidate lists, they may alter the substantive nature even, or especially, of this contingent membership and its role in the life of the party: not members who support the party choosing their leaders, but individual would-be leaders recruiting members for the sole purpose of providing them with votes in internal ballots. At the same time, the kind of individualized participation that Gauja describes may actually increase the independence of the party elite, and thus ironically increase partyness as viewed from outside of the party, by short-circuiting the means through which disagreements can be organized even while facilitating their individualized expression. Similarly, personalized connections between members and their party, unmediated by affiliated organizations like trade unions, are likely to reduce the influence of those organizations within the party—and potentially their propensity to work through a particular party rather than attempting to work directly on the government, whatever its partisan complexion.[17]

PERSONALIZATION AND REPRESENTATION

Consideration of representation requires that three questions be addressed: Who is the representative, who is being represented and what does a representative do? At least with respect to the world external to a party, the party government ideal type effectively assumes that the representative is the national party (or subnational party for subnational levels of government); that the represented is the national electorate of the party and what a good representative does is adhere to the promises made and take responsibility for the results produced as a collective entity. For local representatives within a single party to represent local differences would detract from the ability of voters everywhere to hold the party as a totality accountable for its actions in government. In a sense, individual MPs are interchangeable cogs, although to the extent that they are influential in establishing party policy or determining party actions or leadership (see following discussion), they can be quite significant. But to the extent that these differences spill over into party disunity (or even ambiguity) vis-à-vis the external world, they would undermine partyness. Even in the absence of an intraparty electoral choice, this may result from parliamentary campaigns in which candidates emphasize locally specific issues (see Chiru, this volume). Even if these are not included in the national program, and hence cannot contradict it, the result may be a perception of individual, and possibly contradictory, mandates with regard to these local issues and raises questions about the degree to which each MP's mandate really reflects popular endorsement of the national party and its program and leadership.

There are other forms of representation that are also important, however. One falls under the general rubric of constituency service, be it bringing the interests of particular social segments (e.g., local constituencies, interest or ethnic groups and genders) to the attention of decision makers or serving as an ombudsman in addressing the problems of individual constituents. In this case, the representative might be an individual MP or a small group of MPs, possibly even cutting across party lines. An internal division of labour such that this form of representation is parcelled out on the basis of locality (or some other basis) would be compatible with high partyness, as would consideration of differences in effectiveness in performing this function in the selection of candidates or in voters' choices among candidates. Although this kind of representation might be an asset in intraparty contests, and thus contribute to reduced partyness, as Chiru's chapter shows, personalization in this sense does not necessarily undermine party unity.

Another prominent sense of representation is demographic mirroring, that is, the representatives 'looking like' the represented, both as a symbol/embodiment of full and equal citizenship and as the representation of demographically defined interests. By making a party more representative of either its membership or its electorate, demographic diversity (e.g., gender, age or ethnicity) and diversity of policy preferences may make the party more attractive to them.[18] Diversity may also improve party policy formulation and leadership selection. Although the party government model requires that parties behave as unitary actors vis-à-vis the external world, it goes without saying that no party is totally uniform (even the Dutch PVV, a party with only one member, founder Geert Wilders, cannot be totally undifferentiated if its twenty members of the Tweede Kamer are taken into account). A diverse party may be better able to inform itself of evolving societal needs and desires (although increasingly professionalized parties may prefer to rely on polls and focus groups), and meaningful internal testing of ideas is unlikely to occur without some internal diversity of opinion in the first place. The problem in terms of the party government model is to contain these differences within the party, rather than allowing them to undermine external perceptions of party cohesion.

CONCLUSIONS

Some aspects of the phenomenon of personalization clearly are corrosive of party government in the way it was understood in the mass party model of parties as well-defined membership organizations committed to a coherent overarching political program (whether or not one wishes to identify that as an ideology) and encompassing a strong sense of political identity that united leaders and members. This is not the only way in which parties can be understood, however, and hence the mass-party model does not define the only possible sense of party government. Moreover, notwithstanding the deference paid to that model, party government (at least as I defined it in the Future of Party Government Project) is not the only way in which democracy can be embodied or legitimated. Indeed, it is worth remembering that when Schattschneider (1942, 1) penned the often quoted phrase that 'modern democracy is unthinkable save in terms of the parties', he was writing about a political system notorious for the low partyness of its parties and low partyness of its government.

As noted, personalism is hardly new. Despite nostalgia for the mass-party model, both the nineteenth century and the last third of the twentieth century are perhaps better seen as exemplifying a pluralist model, with party leaders working as brokers among interests and builders of coalitions. Although that may involve interaction with supporters in the mode of focus groups, customer service or complaint departments, it necessarily requires freedom of manoeuvre for the brokers, and that the negotiator (whether understood in institutional terms as the party or in personal terms as its leader) has to be a trustee rather than a delegate. It suggests movement in a direction that some have criticized as an elitist model of party in which, on the one hand, the core decisions are made by the party in public office and in particular by the party leader (i.e., more presidentialization), and on the other hand, citizen involvement/power is to be exercised on the parties rather than within them and is more limited, unmediated and contingent (i.e., more personalized).

These developments are not incompatible with democratic legitimation through the model of party government, although they do present serious challenges to it. Party government requires that parties behave as unified teams in competition (or collaboration) with one another, whereas personalization at the top, but especially among parliamentary candidates and within parties, creates incentives for individual entrepreneurship and the development of, or deference to, principals other than the electorate. In particular, while personalization as fostered by the 'democratization' of top leadership selection may simply alter the relative importance of the personal characteristics of aspirants without undermining party unity in the more public sphere, personalization as a consequence of intraparty electoral choice in parliamentary elections almost inevitably creates a dual-principal situation in which lines of accountability are muddied, and thus party government is undermined (see Katz 2014).

As with all developments assessed against an ideal type, the effects of personalization present questions of 'more or less', not 'either–or'. Nonetheless, taken in conjunction with other changes in the nature of party politics (e.g., cartelization, Katz and Mair 1995), the disjuncture growing between legitimizing myth and demonstrable practice already is presenting serious challenges to party democracy. The 2015 Eurobarometer finding that parties were the least trusted political institution in twenty-three of the twenty-eight member states, and the 2014 GfK Verein study of twenty-five countries (including fifteen industrialized democracies) that found politicians to be the least-trusted of thirty-two professions in every one except Sweden (where retail sellers ranked even lower) and Indonesia (in thirty-first place, just above insurance agents), illustrate the magnitude of the problem. More particularly, personalization may be contributing to the rise of populist competitors to the existing parties: to the extent that ties to party are personalized and weakened and to the extent that electoral choice focuses on the personal qualities of individuals rather than enduring connections to established parties, why not vote for the party of a personally charismatic populist?

NOTES

1. For example, International IDEA, OSCE/ODIHR.

2. Indeed, this is true even as they insist on the right of nonparty candidates to stand for election.

3. Provisions such as the German 'constructive vote of no confidence' that allow a government to be dismissed only coincidentally with the election of a successor modify, but do not essentially change this definition.

4. In the Canadian case since 1945, the governments of John Diefenbaker (1957–1958 and 1962–1963); Lester Pearson (1963–1965 and 1965–1968); Pierre Trudeau (1972–1974); Joe Clark (1979–1980); Paul Martin (2004–2006); Stephen Harper (2006–2008, 2008–2011).

5. The same was, of course, true in previous parliaments, in which 'nominated' members might have divided loyalties between their parliamentary group's leadership and their patrons. For an illustration, see Beer's (1969, 29–32) discussion of British eighteenth-century canal politics.

6. Of course the potential conflict between loyalty to constituents and loyalty to party is limited in proportional-representation systems, in which it can be argued that each's MP's 'constituents' are only those voters who supported his or her party's list, but even then it is easy to imagine a conflict between the policy or interests of an MP's national party and the preferences even of that party's voters in a particular district.

7. Similarly, Article 27 of the constitution of the Fifth French Republic bars any imperative mandate: *Tout mandat impératif est nul. Le droit de vote des membres du Parlement est personnel.*

8. Aside from being useful in their own right, the context in which these definitions were proposed illustrates the point that concerns about the continued viability of party government are by no means confined to recent decades.

9. As Mayhew (1974) points out for the US Congress (relevant here because it is *not* a strong case of party government), in the absence of party cohesion (i.e., team-like behaviour) it is impossible for politicians to take or be assigned credit or blame for outcomes, only for individual positions.

10. The separation of federal and provincial parties in Canada should not be exaggerated, however, especially at the local level. Pruysers (2014, 2015, 2016), for example, finds considerable informal linkages at the grassroots level both during election campaigns and between elections: overlapping memberships, joint social events and coordinated campaign efforts.

11. This would be less true with institutions like those in Germany, in which the *Land* governments are themselves represented in the federal *Bundesrat*. In this case, failure of *Land* governments to act in concert with their federal copartisans in the *Bundestag* would reduce partyness of government at the federal level.

12. Quoted in Beer 1969, 99.

13. See for example the characterization by Katz and Kolodny (1994) of the US national party organizations as 'suites of empty offices' waiting to be occupied by the supporters of whatever individual emerges victorious from the party's primaries.

14. Institutionally, these vary along two dimensions. The first concerns eligibility to vote, with 'primary-like' implying a broad franchise not limited to long-standing party members, and certainly not selection by a party committee (e.g., any Italian citizen in the case of the Italian *Partito Democratico* [more than 1.8 million votes in 2017], anyone who had been a member of the Conservative Party of Canada for at least two months before the leadership vote [roughly 141,000 votes in 2017] and any member or person who became a 'registered supporter' at least two months before the vote in the case of the British Labour Party [roughly 400,000 votes in 2016]). The second concerns eligibility for candidacy in the final vote, ranging, for example, from only the two candidates receiving the most votes in the parliamentary party (British Conservative Party) to any party member nominated by at least 300 party members (from at least thirty electoral districts in at least seven provinces and territories—Conservative Party of Canada, thirteen candidates in 2017).

15. Of relevance both for parliamentary nominations and for leadership contests as discussed previously, Cross and Pruysers (2017) find that party members who supported a losing candidate for nomination are less likely to remain as party members and less likely to engage in high intensity activism during the general election, suggesting that their tie to the party is significantly a reflection of their connection to the individual candidate rather than to the party as such.

16. These are votes for which no attempts are made to enforce party unity. Although 'conscience votes' generally concern issues about which MPs may be assumed to have strong moral commitments (e.g., capital punishment and homosexuality), 'free votes' may be allowed on any question on which there is internal disunity and the leadership chooses not to expend the political capital required to impose discipline.

17. On the potential decline of ties between parties and social groups, see Allern and Verge 2017; on the strategies of working through a particular party as part of its 'family' as opposed to establishing relations with the government that 'bypass' parties, see LaPalombara 1964.

18. Although the claim implicit in this phrase, that a more diverse party will automatically be more attractive electorally, is often taken as a truism, it should be noted that it is not self-evidently true. One implication of the phenomenon of 'working-class Tories' (Nordlinger 1967) is that there are some members of the working class who affirmatively prefer to be governed by their 'betters'. For them, the nomination of working-class candidates would not be an attraction. Similarly, in a climate of high Islamophobia, it is quite conceivable that the nomination of a Moslem candidate would alienate more voters than it would attract.

References

Aalberg, Toril, and Anders Todal Jenssen. 2007. 'Gender Stereotyping of Political Candidates: An Experimental Study of Political Communication'. *Nordicom Review* 28(1): 17-32.

Aarts, Kees, André Blais, and Hermann Schmitt, eds. 2011. *Political Leaders and Democratic Elections*. Oxford: Oxford University Press.

Achury, Susan, Susan E. Scarrow, Karina Kosiara-Pedersen and Emilie van Haute. 2017. 'The Consequences of Membership Incentives: Do Greater Political Benefits Attract Different Kinds of Members?' Paper presented at the ECPR Joint Sessions, Nottingham, United Kingdom.

Adam, Silke, and Michaela Maier. 2010. 'Personalization of Politics: A Critical Review and Agenda for Research'. In *Communication Yearbook 34*, edited by Charles Salmon, 213-257. London: Routledge.

Allern, Elin, and Karina Pedersen. 2007. 'The Impact of Party Organisational Changes on Democracy'. *West European Politics* 30(1):68-92.

Allern, Elin, and Tania Verge. 2017. 'Still Connecting with Society? Political Parties' Formal Links with Social Groups in the Twenty-First Century'. In *Organizing Political Parties: Representation, Participation, and Power*, edited by Susan E. Scarrow, Paul D. Webb, and Thomas Poguntke, 106-137. Oxford: Oxford University Press.

American Political Science Association. 1969. *Toward a More Responsible Two-Party System*. New York: Johnson Reprint Corporation.

Anderson, Cameron. 2010. 'Regional Heterogeneity and Policy Preferences in Canada: 1979—2006'. *Regional & Federal Studies* 20(4-5): 447-468.

Anderson, Karrin Vasby. 2011. '"Rhymes with Blunt": Pornification and U.S. Political Culture'. *Rhetoric and Public Affairs* 14(2): 327-68.

Andeweg Rudy, and Joop van Holsteyn. 2011. 'Second Order Personalization: Preference Voting in the Netherlands.' Paper presented at the ECPR General Conference, Reykjavík, Iceland.

André, Audrey, Sam Depauw, and Matthew Soberg Shugart. 2014. 'The Effect of Electoral Institutions on Legislative Behavior'. In *The Oxford Handbook of Legislative Studies*, edited by Shane Martin, Thomas Saalfeld, and Kaare Strøm, 231–250. Oxford: Oxford University Press.

André, Audrey, Michael Gallagher, and Giulia Sandri. 2014. 'Legislators' Constituency Orientation'. In *Representing the People. A Survey among Members of Statewide and Substate Parliaments*, edited by Kris Deschouwer and Sam Depauw, 166–187. Oxford: Oxford University Press.

Annesley, Claire, Karen Beckwith, and Susan Franceschet. 2016. 'Merit in Cabinet Appointments? Informal Rules and Women's Ministerial Recruitment'. Paper presented at the Annual Meetings of the American Political Science Association, Philadelphia.

Attlee, Clement. 1957. 'Party Discipline is Paramount'. *National and English Review* CXLVIII, no. 887, Philadelphia.

Aucoin, Peter. 1995. *The New Public Management: Canada in Comparative Perspective*. Montreal: Institute for Research for Public Policy.

Bailo, Francesco. 2015. 'Mapping Online Political Talks Through Network Analysis: A Case Study of the Website of Italy's Five Star Movement'. *Policy Studies* 36(6): 550–572.

Bakvis, Herman, R. A. W. Rhodes, Rand Patrick Weller, eds. 1997. *The Hollow Crown: Countervailing Trends in Core Executives*. London: Palgrave Macmillan.

Bale, Tim. 2016. 'Corbyn's Labour: Survey of post-2015 Labour Members and Supporters'. *Queen Mary University of London,* June 28. http://www.qmul.ac.uk/media /news/items/178403.html

Bale, Tim and Paul Webb. 2017. 'Honey, I Shrunk the Majority: Theresa May and the Tories'. *Political Insight*, September.

Balmas, Meital, Gideon Rahat, Tamir Sheafer and Shaul R. Shenhav. 2014. 'Two Routes to Personalized Politics: Centralized and Decentralized Personalization'. *Party Politics* 20(1): 37-51.

Balmas, Meital and Tamir Sheafer. 2016. 'Personalization of Politics'. In *The International Encyclopedia of Political Communication* edited by Gianpietro Mazzoleni, Kevin Barnhurst, Ken'ichi Ikeda, Hartmut Wessler, Rousiley Maia, 945–951. London: Wiley.

Bang, Henrik. 2011. 'The Politics of Threats: Late-Modern Politics in the Shadow of Neoliberalism'. *Critical Policy Studies* 5(4): 434–48.

Barbera, Oscar and Juan Rodriguez Teruel. 2015. 'The Internal Consequences of Introducing Party Primaries in Spain'. Paper presented at the Annual Conference of the UK Political Studies Association, Sheffield, United Kingdom.

Barnes, Tiffany D. and Diana Z. O'Brien. 2018. 'Defending the Realm: The Appointment of Female Defense Ministers Worldwide'. *American Journal of Political Science* 62(2): 355-368.

Bartels, Larry. 1992. 'The Impact of Electioneering in the United States'. In *Electioneering: A Comparative Study of Continuity and Change*, edited by David Butler and Austin Ranney, 244-277. Oxford: Clarendon Press.

Bartolini, Stefano, and Peter Mair. 1990. *Identity, Competition and Electoral Availability. The Stability of European Electorates 1885–1985*. Cambridge: Cambridge University Press.

Bashevkin, Sylvia. 2009. *Women, Power, Politics: The Hidden Story of Canada's Unfinished Democracy*. Oxford: Oxford University Press.

Bauer, Nichole M. 2014. 'Emotional, Sensitive, and Unfit for Office? Gender Stereotype Activation and Support for Female Candidates'. *Political Psychology* 36(6): 691–708.

Baumgartner, Frank R., Christoffer Green-Pedersen, and Bryan D. Jones. 2006. 'Comparative Studies of Policy Agendas'. *Journal of European Public Policy* 13(7): 955–970.

BBC News. 2015. 'Jeremy Corbyn Elected Labour Leader: How did he Win?' *BBC News,* September 12. http:''www.bbc.com/news/uk-politics-34126758

Beck, Ulrich and Elisabeth Beck-Gernsheim. 2002. *Individualization: Institutionalized Individualism and Its Social and Political Consequences*. London: Sage.

Beer, Samuel. 1969. *British Politics in the Collectivist Age*. New York: Vintage Books.

Bellefontaine, Michelle. 2016. 'Alberta PC Party Ends One Member, One Vote System to Choose Leaders'. *CBC News,* May 7. http://www.cbc.ca/news/canada/edmonton/alberta-pc-party-ends-one-member-one-vote-system-to-choose-leaders-1.3572040

Bennett, Lance. 2012. 'The Personalization of Politics: Political Identity, Social Media, and Changing Patterns of Participation'. *The Annals of the American Academy of Political and Social Science* 644(1): 20–39.

Bennett, Lance, and Alexandra Segerberg. 2011. 'Digital Media and the Personalization of Collective Action'. *Information, Communication and Society* 14(6): 770–799.

Bennett, Lance, and Alexandra Segerberg. 2013. *The Logic of Connective Action: Digital Media and the Personalization of Contentious Politics*. New York: Cambridge University Press.

Bennister, Mark, Ben Worthy, Paul t'Hart, eds. 2017. *The Leadership Capital Index: A New Perspective on Political Leadership*. London: Oxford University Press.

Benoit, Kenneth. 2001. 'Evaluating Hungary's Mixed-Member Electoral System'. In *Mixed-Member Electoral Systems: The Best of Both Worlds?* edited by Matthew Shugart and Martin P. Wattenberg, 477-193. Oxford: Oxford University Press.

———. 'Models of Electoral System Change'. *Electoral Studies* 23(3): 363–89.

Bevir, Mark, and R. A. W. Rhodes. 2006. 'Prime Ministers, Presidentialism, and Westminster Smokescreens'. *Political Studies* 54(4): 215–39.

Biezen, Ingrid van, and Thomas Poguntke. 2014. 'The Decline of Membership-based Politics'. *Party Politics* 20(2): 205–226.

Biezen, Ingrid van, Peter Mair and Thomas Poguntke. 2012. 'Going, Going, …… Gone? The Decline of Party Membership in Contemporary Europe'. *European Journal of Political Research* 51(1): 24-56.

Bittner, Amanda. 2010. 'Personality Matters: The Evaluation of Party Leaders in Canadian Elections'. In *Canadian Voting Behaviour*, edited by Laura Stephenson and Cameron Anderson, 183-211. Vancouver: University of British Columbia Press.

———. 2011. *Platform or Personality? The Role of Party Leaders in Elections*. Oxford: Oxford University Press.

———. 2014. 'Party Leaders in the NDP'. In *Reviving Social Democracy: The Near Death and Surprising Rise of the Federal NDP*, edited by Lynda Erickson and David Laycock, 197-218. Vancouver: University of British Columbia Press.

———. 2015. 'Leader Evaluations and Partisan Stereotypes, A Comparative Analysis'. In *The Role of Leader Evaluations in Democratic Elections*, edited by Marina Costa Lobo and John Curtice, 17-38. Oxford: Oxford University Press.

———. Forthcoming. 'The Personalization of Canadian Elections?' *Electoral Studies*.

Bittner, Amanda, and Elizabeth Goodyear-Grant. 2017. 'Sex Isn't Gender: Reforming Concepts and Measurements in the Study of Public Opinion'. *Political Behavior* 39(4): 1019–1041.

Blais, André. 2000. *To Vote or Not to Vote? The Merits and Limits of Rational Choice Theory*. Pittsburgh: University of Pittsburgh Press.

Blais, André, Elisabeth Gidengil, Alexandra Dobrzynska, Neil Nevitte, and Richard Nadeau. 2003. 'Does the local candidate matter? Candidate effects in the Canadian Election of 2000'. *Canadian Journal of Political Science* 36(3): 657–667.

Blais, André, Elisabeth Gidengil, Richard Nadeau, and Neil Nevitte. 2001. 'Measuring Party Identification: Britain, Canada, and the United States'. *Political Behavior* 23(1):5–22.

Blais, André, Elisabeth Gidengil, Richard Nadeau and Neil Nevitte. 2002. *Anatomy of a Liberal Victory: Making Sense of the Vote in the 2000 Canadian Election*. Toronto: Broadview Press.

Bolin, Niklas, Nicholas Aylott, Benjamin von dem Berge and Thomas Poguntke. 2017. 'Patterns of Intra-Party Democracy across the World'. In *Organizing Political Parties: Representation, Participation, and Power*, edited by Susan E. Scarrow, Paul D. Webb, and Thomas Poguntke, 158-185. Oxford: Oxford University Press.

Boston, Jonathan, Stephen Levine, Elizabeth McLeay, and Nigel S. Roberts. 1996. *New Zealand Under MMP: A New Politics?* Auckland: Auckland University Press.

Bowler, Shaun, and Todd Donovan. 2013. *The Limits of Electoral Reform*. Oxford: Oxford University Press.

Bowler, Shaun, and David, Farrell. 2011. 'Electoral Institutions and Campaigning in Comparative Perspective: Electioneering in European Parliament Elections'. *European Journal of Political Research* 50(5): 668–88.

Braüninger, Thomas, Martin Brunner, and Thomas Daübler. 2012. 'Personal Vote-seeking in Flexible List Systems: How Electoral Incentives Shape Belgian MPs' Bill Initiation Behaviour'. *European Journal of Political Research* 51(5): 607-45

Brown, Steven D., Ronald D. Lambert, Barry J. Kay and James E. Curtis. 1988. 'In the Eye of the Beholder: Leader Images in Canada'. *Canadian Journal of Political Science* 21(4):729–55.

Buell Emmett, and Lee Sigelman. 2008. *Attack Politics: Negativity in Presidential Campaigns Since 1960*. Lawrence: University of Kansas Press.

Bull, Martin J. 2015. 'Institutional Reform in Italy to Respond to the EU Challenge: Renzi's Constitutional Reform Project'. Paper presented at the Conference, 'The 2014 European Elections: Italian Politics and the European Challenge', European Policies Research Centre, Glasgow, Scotland.

Burke, Cindy, and Sharon R. Mazzarella. 2010. 'A Slightly New Shade of Lipstick: Gendered Mediation in Internet News Stories'. *Women's Studies in Communication* 31(3): 395-418.

Butler, David, and Austin Ranney. 1992. *Electioneering: A Comparative Study of Continuity and Change*. Clarendon Press: Oxford.

Butler, Judith. 1988. 'Performative Acts and Gender Constitution: An Essay in Phenomenology and Feminist Theory'. *Theatre Journal* 40(4): 519-531.

———. 2010. 'Performative Agency'. *Journal of Cultural Economy* 3(2): 147–161.

———. 2011. *Gender Trouble: Feminism and the Subversion of Identity*. New York: Routledge.

Cain, Bruce, John A. Ferejohn, and Morris P. Fiorina. 1984. 'The Constituency Service Basis of the Personal Vote for U.S. Representatives and British Members of Parliament'. *American Political Science Review* 78(1):110-125.

Cain, Bruce, John A. Ferejohn, and Morris P. Fiorina. 1987. *The Personal Vote: Constituency Service and Electoral Independence*. Cambridge: Harvard University Press.

Cain, Bruce, I.A. Lewis, and Douglas Rivers. 1988. 'Strategy and Choice in the 1988 Presidential Primaries'. Social Science Working Paper 686, Division of the Humanities and Social Sciences, California Institute of Technology.

Calise, Mauro. 2011. 'Personalization of Politics'. In *International Encyclopedia of Political Science*, edited by Bertrand Badie, Dirk Berg-Schlosser, and Leonardo Morlino, 1857–1863. London: SAGE.

Cameron, A. Colin, and Pravin K. Trivedi. 2013. *Regression Analysis of Count Data*. Econometric Society Monograph No.53. Cambridge: Cambridge University Press.

Campbell, Angus, Philip E. Converse, Warren E. Miller and Donald E. Stokes. 1960. *The American Voter*. Chicago: John Wiley & Sons, Inc.

Campbell, Colin. 1983. *Governments Under Stress: Political Executives and Key Bureaucrats in Washington, London and Ottawa*. Toronto: University of Toronto Press.

Campbell, Colin, and Margaret Jane Wyszomirski, eds. 1991. *Executive Leadership in Anglo-American Systems*. Pittsburgh: University of Pittsburgh Press.

Campbell, Rosie, and Philip Cowley. 2014. 'What Voters Want: Reactions to Candidate Characteristics in a Survey Experiment'. *Political Studies* 62(4): 745–765.

Caramani, Danielle. 2006. 'Is There a European Electorate and What Does It Look Like? Evidence from Electoral Volatility Measures, 1976-2004'. *West European Politics* 29(1): 1-27.

Carey, John, and Matthew Soberg Shugart. 1995. 'Incentives to Cultivate a Personal Vote: A Rank Ordering of Electoral Formulas'. *Electoral Studies* 14(4): 417–39.

Carroll, Susan J. 1988. 'Women's Autonomy and the Gender Gap: 1980 and 1982'. In *The Politics of the Gender Gap: The Social Construction of Political Influence*, edited by Carol A. Mueller, 236-257. Newbury Park, CA: Sage Publications.

Carty, R. Kenneth. 1988a. 'Campaigning in the Trenches: The Transformation of Constituency Politics'. In *Party Democracy in Canada: The Politics of National Party Conventions*, edited by George Perlin, 84-96. Scarborough: Prentice-Hall.

———. 1988b. 'Choosing New Party Leaders: The PCs in 1983, The Liberals in 1984'. In *Canada at the* Polls, *1984*, edited by Howard Penniman, 55–78. Washington: American Enterprise Institute.

———. 1991. *Canadian Political Parties in the Constituencies*. Dundurn Press.

———. 2002. 'The Politics of Tecumseh Corners: Canadian Political Parties as Franchise Organizations'. *The Canadian Journal of Political Science* 35(4): 723–745.

———. 2004. 'Parties as Franchise Systems: The Stratarchical Organizational Imperative'. *Party Politics* 10(1):15–24.

———. 2013. 'Has Brokerage Politics Ended? Canadian Parties in the New Century'. In *Parties, Elections, and the Future of Canadian Politics*, edited by Royce Koop and Amanda Bittner, 10–24. Vancouver: University of British Columbia Press.

———. 2015. *Big Tent Politics. The Liberal Party's Long Mastery of Canada's Public Life*. Vancouver: University of British Columbia Press.

Carty, R. Kenneth, and Donald E. Blake. 1999. 'The Adoption of Membership Votes for Choosing Party Leaders'. *Party Politics* 5(2): 211–224.

Carty, R. Kenneth, and William P. Cross. 2006. 'Can Stratarchically Organized Parties be Democratic? The Canadian Case'. *Journal of Elections, Public Opinion and Parties* 16(2): 93–114.

———. 2010 'Political Parties and the Practice of Brokerage Politics'. In *The Oxford Handbook of Canadian Politics*, edited by John Courtney and David Smith, 191–207. Toronto: Oxford University Press.

Carty, R. Kenneth, and Munroe Eagles. 2005. *Politics is Local: National Politics at the Grassroots*. Oxford: Oxford University Press.

Carty, R. Kenneth, William P. Cross, and Lisa Young. 2000. *Rebuilding Canadian Party Politics*. Vancouver: University of British Columbia Press.

CBC. 2015. 'Canada election 2105: Where the leaders are Sunday'. *CBC News*, August 16. http://www.cbc.ca/news/politics/canada-election-2015-where-the-leaders-are-aug16-1.3192682

Chen, Philip, Melanee Thomas, Allison Harell, and Tania. Gosselin. 2017. 'Gender Stereotypes, Social Desirability, and the Foundations of Stereotype Threat'. Paper presented at the annual meeting of the Western Political Science Association. Vancouver, British Columbia, 29–31 March 2017.

Chiru, Mihail. 2013. 'Personalized Campaigning and Constituency Service Questions Under Mixed Electoral Rules'. Paper presented at the ECPR Joint Sessions, Mainz, Germany.

———. 2014. 'Improving MPs' Responsiveness through Institutional Engineering? Constituency Questions Under Two Electoral Systems'. Paper presented at the APSA Annual Meeting, Washington, DC.

———. 2015. 'Multiple Candidacies and the Role of the Lowest Electoral Tier for Individualized Campaigning'. *East European Politics and Societies* 29(4): 892–914.

Chiru, Mihail, and Zsolt Enyedi. 2015. 'Choosing Your Own Boss: Variations of Representation Foci in Mixed Electoral Systems'. *Journal of Legislative Studies* 21(4): 495–514.

Clarke, Harold, Jane Jenson, Lawrence LeDuc and Jon Pammett. 1991. *Absent Mandate: Interpreting Change in Canadian Elections*. Agincourt: Gage Publishing.

Coates, Denis. 1995. 'Measuring the 'Personal Vote' of Members of Congress'. *Public Choice* 85(3-4): 227–48.

Coleman, Stephen. 2005. 'Blogs and the new Politics of Listening'. *Political Quarterly* 76(2): 273–280.

Colomer, Josep M. 2004. 'The Strategy and History of Electoral System Choice'. In *Handbook of Electoral System Choice*, edited by Josep M. Colomer, 3–78. Basingstoke: Palgrave Macmillan.

———. 2005. 'It's Parties That Choose Electoral Systems (or, Duverger's Laws Upside Down)'. *Political Studies* 53(1): 1–21.

———, ed. 2011. *Personal Representation: The Neglected Dimension of Electoral Systems*. Colchester: ECPR Press.

Cooper, Christopher A. 2017 'The Rise of Court Government? Testing the Centralisation of Power Thesis with Longitudinal Data from Canada'. *Parliamentary Affairs* 70(3): 589–610.

Costa, Particio, and Federico Ferreira Da Silva. 2015. 'The Impact of Voter Evaluations of Leaders' Traits on Voting Behaviour: Evidence from Seven European Countries'. *West European Politics* 38(6): 1226–1250.

Courtney, John C. 1995. *Do Conventions Matter? Choosing National Party Leaders in Canada*. Montreal: McGill-Queens University Press.

Coyne, Andrew. 2015. 'Trudeau Cabinet Should be Based on Merit, not Gender'. *National Post*, November 2. http://nationalpost.com/opinion/andrew-coyne-trudeau-cabinet-should-be-built-on-merit-not-gender

Cross, William P. 2004. *Political Parties*. Vancouver: University of British Columbia Press.

———. 2014. 'Party Leadership in Canada'. In *The Selection of Political Party Leaders in Contemporary Parliamentary Democracies: A Comparative Study*, edited by Jean-Benoit Pilet and William P. Cross, 171–188. London: Routledge.

———. 2016. 'The Importance of Local Party Activity in Understanding Canadian Politics: Winning from the Ground up in the 2015 Federal Election'. *Canadian Journal of Political Science* 49(4): 601–620.

Cross, William P. and André Blais. 2012a. *Politics at the Centre: The Selection and Removal of Party Leaders in the Anglo Parliamentary Democracies*. Don Mills: Oxford University Press.

———. 2012b. 'Who Selects the Party Leader?' *Party Politics* 18(2): 127–150.

Cross, William P., Ofer Kenig, Scott Pruysers and Gideon Rahat. 2016. *The Promise and Challenge of Party Primary Elections: A Comparative Perspective*. Montreal: McGill-Queen's University Press.

Cross, William P., Jonathan Malloy, Tamara Small, and Laura Stephenson. 2015. *Fighting for Votes: Parties, the Media, and Voters in an Ontario Election*. Vancouver: University of British Columbia Press.

Cross, William P., and Jean-Benoit Pilet, eds. 2015. *The Politics of Party Leadership: A Cross-National Perspective*. Oxford: Oxford University Press.

Cross, William P., and Scott Pruysers. 2017. 'Sore Losers? The Cost of Intra-Party Democracy?' *Party Politics*. On-line First.

Cross, William P., and Lisa Young. 2015. 'Personalization of Campaigns in an SMP System: The Canadian Case'. *Electoral Studies* 39: 306–315.

Curtice, John, and W. Phillips Shively. 2009. 'Who Represents Us Best? One Member or Many?' In *The Comparative Study of Electoral Systems*, edited by Hans-Dieter Klingemann, 171–192. Oxford: Oxford University Press.

Cutler, Fred. 2002. 'The Simplest Shortcut of All: Sociodemographic Characteristics and Electoral Choice'. *The Journal of Politics* 64(2): 466–490.

Dahlgreen, Will. 2014. Britain's Changing Political Spectrum. Yougov poll. https://yougov.co.uk/news/2014/07/23/britains-changing-political-spectrum/

Dalton, Russell. 2000. 'The Decline of Party Identification'. In *Parties without Partisans: Political Change in Advanced Industrial Democracies,* edited by Russell J. Dalton and Martin P. Wattenberg, 19–36. Oxford: Oxford University Press.

———. 2004. *Democratic Challenges, Democratic Choices: The Erosion of Political Support in Advanced Industrial Democracies.* Oxford: Oxford University Press.

Dalton, Russell, David M. Farrell, and Ian McAllister. 2011. *Political Parties and Democratic Linkage: How Parties Organize Democracy.* Oxford: Oxford University Press.

Dalton, Russell, and Mark Gray. 2003. 'Expanding the Electoral Marketplace'. In *Democracy Transformed? Expanding Political Opportunities in Advanced Industrial Democracies*, edited by Bruce E. Cain, Russell J. Dalton, and Susan E. Scarrow, 23–43. Oxford: Oxford University Press.

Dalton, Russell, Ian McAllister, and Martin P. Wattenberg. 2000. 'The Consequences of Partisan Dealignment'. In *Parties Without Partisans: Political Change in Advanced Industrial Democracies*, edited by Russell Dalton and Martin P. Wattenberg, 37–64. Oxford: Oxford University Press.

Dalton, Russell, and Martin. P. Wattenberg. 2000. *Parties Without Partisans: Political Change in Advanced Industrial Democracies*. Oxford: Oxford University Press.

Dalton, Russell, and Stephen A. Weldon. 2005. 'Public Images of Political Parties: A Necessary Evil?' *West European Politics* 28(5): 931–51.

De Winter, Lieven, and Pierre Baudewyns. 2015. 'Candidate Centred Campaigning in a Party Centred Context: The case of Belgium'. *Electoral Studies* 39: 295–305.

Der Standard. Daily Newspaper. September 28, 2017.

Deutscher Bundestag. 'Minutes from 15 January 2015–26 February 2016'. https://www.bundestag.de/protokolle

Dewachter, Wilfried. 2003. 'Elections, partis politiques et représentants. La quête d'une légitimité démocratique. 1919–2002'. In *Histoire de la Chambre des représentants en Belgique*, edited by Eliane Gubin, Jean-Pierre Nandrin, Emmanuel Gerard, and Els Witte, 63–86. Bruxelles: Chambre des Représentants.

DiClerico, Robert E. and Eric M. Uslaner.1984. *Few are Chosen: Problems in Presidential Selection.* New York: McGraw Hill Book Company.

DiStaso, Marcia. 2012. 'The Annual Earnings Press Release's Dual Role: An Examination of Relationships with Local and National Media Coverage and Reputation'. *Journal of Public Relations Research* 24(2): 123–143.

Ditonto, Tessa. 2017. 'A High Bar or a Double Standard? Gender, Competence, and Information in Political Campaigns'. *Political Behavior* 39(2): 301–325.

Dolan, Kathleen. 2010. 'The Impact of Gender Stereotyped Evaluations on Support for Women Candidates'. *Political Behavior* 32(1): 69–88.

———. 2014. 'Gender Stereotypes, Candidate Evaluations, and Voting for Women Candidate: What Really Matters?' *Political Research Quarterly* 67(1): 96–107.

Dolezal, Martin. 2015. 'Online Campaigning by Austrian Political Candidates: Determinants of Using Personal Websites, Facebook, and Twitter'. *Policy and Internet* 7(1): 103–119.

Dowding, Keith. 2013. 'The Prime Ministerialisation of the British Prime Minister'. *Parliamentary Affairs* 66(3): 617–635.

Downs, Anthony. 1957. *An Economic Theory of Democracy*. New York: Harper and Row.

Druckman, James, Martin Kifer, and Michael Parkin. 2009. 'The Technological Development of Candidate Websites.' In *Politicking Online: The Transformation of Election Campaign Communications,* edited by Costas Panagopoulos, 21–47. New Jersey: Rutgers University Press.

Duverger, Maurice. 1954 [1967*]. Political Parties*. Science Editions, New York: John Wiley and Sons.

———. 1969. 'Personalization of Power'. In *Comparative Government: A Reader*, edited by Jean Blondel, 112–116. London: Macmillan.

Eder, Nikolaus, Marcelo Jenny, and Wolfgang C. Müller. 2015. 'Winning over voters or fighting party comrades? Personalized constituency campaigning in Austria'. *Electoral Studies* 39: 316–328.

Egle, Christoph, and Reimut Zohlnhöfer, eds. 2007. 'Ende des rot-grünen Projekts. Eine Bilanz der Regierung Schröder 2002–2005'. Wiesbaden, VS Verlag für Sozialwissenschaften.

Eldersveld, Samuel J. 1964. *Political Parties: A Behavioral Analysis*. Chicago IL: Rand McNally.

Elections Canada. 2016. 'Final Election Expenses by Registered Political Party'. *Elections Canada*. http://www.elections.ca/content.aspx?section=fin&document=index&dir=ot h/pol/finalexp&lang=e

Elgie, Robert. 2011. 'Core Executive Studies Two Decades On'. *Public Administration* 89(1): 64–77.

Enli, Gunn Sara, and Eli Skogerbø. 2013. 'Personalized Campaigns in Party-Centered Politics: Twitter and Facebook as Arenas for Political Communication'. *Information, Communication & Society* 16(5): 757–774.

Enyedi, Zsolt. 2010. *The 2010 Hungarian Candidate Study*. Machine readable data files.

———. 2011. 'Politikai képviselet és intézményi alternatívák. Felfogások a polgárok és a politikusok körében'. In *Részvétel, képviselet, politikai változás*, edited by Tardos, Robert, Enyedi Zsolt, and Andrea Szabó, 243-265. Budapest: DKMKA.

Errington, Wayne, and PeterVan Onselen. 2007. *John Winston Howard: The Biography*. Melbourne: University of Melbourne Press.

ESRC Party Members Project. 2016. 'Explaining the Pro-Corbyn Surge in Labour Membership'. http:/esrcpartymembersproject.org/2016/11/21/explaining-the-pro-corbyn-surge-in-labours-membership/

Evans, Jocelyn. 2014. 'We Know Where You Live: The Importance of Local Candidates'. In *Sex, Lies and the Ballot Box: 50 Things You Need to Know About British Elections*, edited by Philip Cowley and Robert Ford, chapter 26. Biteback Publishing.

Farrell, Brian. 1971. *Chairman or Chief? The Role of Taoiseach in Irish Government*. Dublin: Gill & Macmillan.

Farrell, David M., and Michael Gallagher. 1998. 'Submission to the Independent Commission on the Voting System'. *Representation* 35(1): 53–62.

Farrell, David M., and Ian McAllister. 2006. *The Australian Electoral System: Origins, Variations and Consequences*. Sydney: University of New South Wales Press.

Faucher, Florence. 2015a. 'New Forms of Political Participation. Changing Demands or Changing Opportunities to Participate in Political Parties?' *Comparative European Politics* 13(4): 409–59.

———. 2015b. 'Leadership Elections: What Is at Stake for Parties? A Comparison of the British Labour Party and the Parti Socialiste'. *Parliamentary Affairs* 68(4): 794–820.

Fenno, Richard F. 1978. *Homestyle*. New York: Harper Collins.

Fieschi, Catherine. 2007. 'Laws, Sausages and Leadership Transitions'. *Parliamentary Affairs* 60(3): 482–491.

Finer Samuel E. 1975. *Adversary Politics and Electoral Reform*. London: Anthony Wigram.

Fiorina, Morris. 1987. 'Party Government in the United States – Diagnosis and Prognosis'. In *Party Governments: European and American Experiences,* edited by Richard S. Katz, 270–300. Berlin: de Gruyter.

Flanagan, Tom. 2010. 'Campaign Strategy: Triage and the Concentration of Resources'. In *Election*, edited by Heather McIvor, 155-173. Peterborough: Emond Montgomery Press.

Foley, Michael. 2000. *The British Presidency: Tony Blair and the Politics of Public Leadership*. Manchester: Manchester University Press.

Forum. 2015. 'Liberals Maintain Strong Lead'. *Forum Research Inc.* http://poll.forumresearch.com/data/ebd925a1-af27-4fd48122ae256d165044Federal%20Horserace%20New s%20Release%20%282015%2010%2014%29%20Forum%20Research.pdf

Fournier, Patrick, Henk van der Kolk, R. Kenneth Carty, André Blais, and Jonathan Rose. 2011. *When Citizens Decide: Lessons from Citizen Assemblies on Electoral Reform.* New York: Oxford University Press.

Fowler, Erika, and Travis Ridout. 2013. 'Negative, Angry, and Ubiquitous: Political Advertising in 2012'. *The Forum* 10: 51–61.

Franceschet, Susan, Karen Beckwith, and Claire Annesley. 2015. 'Why Are We Still Debating Diversity Versus Merit in 2015?' *Federation for the Humanities and Social Science*, November 20. http://www.ideas-idees.ca/blog/why-are-we-still-debating-diversity-versus-merit-2015

Franceschet, Susan, Mona Lena Krook, and Jennifer M. Piscopo, eds. 2012. *The Impact of Gender Quotas*. Oxford: Oxford University Press.

Franklin, Mark. 1992. 'The Decline of Cleavage Politics'. In *Electoral Change. Responses to Evolving Social and Attitudinal Structures in Western Countries*, edited by Mark Franklin, Thomas Mackie, and Henry Valen. Cambridge, 383–405. Cambridge University Press.

Freedland, Jonathan. 2016. 'Welcome to the age of Trump'. *The Guardian*, May 19. http://www.theguardian.com/us-news/2016/may/19/welcome-to-the-age-of trump?utm_content=buffer99672&utm_medium=social&utm_source=twitter.com&utm_campaign=buffer

Freeman, Patricia K., and Lilliard E. Richardson Jr. 1996. 'Explaining Variation in Casework among State Legislators'. *Legislative Studies Quarterly* 21(1): 41–56.

Fulton, Sarah A. 2012. 'Running Backwards and in High Heels: The Gendered Quality Gap and Incumbent Electoral Success'. *Political Research Quarterly* 65(2): 303–314.

Gallagher, Michael. 2005. 'Conclusions'. In *The Politics of Electoral Systems*, edited by Michael Gallagher, and Paul Mitchell, Michael Gallagher, and Paul Mitchell, 535–578. Oxford: Oxford University Press.

Garzia, Diego. 2011. 'The Personalization of Politics in Western Democracies: Causes and Consequences on Leader-Follower Relationships'. *The Leadership Quarterly* 22(4): 697–709.

———. 2014. *Personalization of Politics and Electoral Change*. Basingstoke: Palgrave Macmillan.

Gauja, Anika. 2012. 'The 'Push' for Primaries: What Drives Party Organisational Reform in Australia and the United Kingdom?' *Australian Journal of Political Science* 47(4): 641–58.

———. 2013. *The Politics of Party Policy: From Members to Legislators*. Basingstoke: Palgrave Macmillan.

———. 2015a. 'The Construction of Party Membership'. *European Journal of Political Research* 54(2): 232–48.

———. 2015b. 'The Individualisation of Party Politics: The Impact of Changing Internal Decision-Making Process on Policy Development and Citizen Engagement'. *British Journal of Politics and International Relations* 17(1): 89–105.

———. 2017. *Party Reform: The Causes, Challenges and Consequences of Organizational Change*. Oxford: Oxford University Press.

Geddes, Barbara. 2003. *Paradigms and Sand Castles: Theory Building and Research Design in Comparative Politics*. Ann Arbor: University of Michigan Press.

Geer John. 2006. *In Defense of Negativity: Attack Ads in Presidential Campaigns*. Chicago: University of Chicago Press.

Gerl, Katharina, Stefan Marschall and Nadja Wilker. 2017. 'Does the Internet Encourage Political Participation? Use of an Online Platform by Members of a German Political Party'. *Policy & Internet*. Early View Online.

Gibson, Rachel, Fabienne Greffert, and Marta Cantijoch. 2017. 'Friend or Foe? Digital Technologies and the Changing Nature of Party Membership'. *Political Communication* 34(1): 89–111.

Gibson, Rachel, and Ian McAllister. 2015. 'Normalising or Equalizing Party Competition? Assessing the impact of the Web on Election Campaigning'. *Political Studies* 63(3): 529–547.

Gibson, Rachel, Andrea Rommele. 2005. 'Truth and Consequence in Web Campaigning: Is there an Academic Digital Divide?' *European Political Science* 4(3): 273–287.

Gibson, Rachel, and Stephen Ward. 2009. 'Parties in the Digital Age – A Review Article'. *Representation* 45(1): 87–100.

Gibson, Rachel, Stehpen Ward, and Wainer Lusoli. 2002. 'The Internet and Political Campaigning: The New Medium Comes of Age?' *Representation* 39(3): 166-180.

Gibson, Rachel, and Stephen Ward. 2000. 'A Proposed Methodology for Studying the Function and Effectiveness of Party and Candidate Web Sites'. *Social Science Computer Review* 18(3): 301–319.

Gidengil, Elisabeth, André Blais, Richard Nadeau and Neil Nevitte. 2000. Are Party Leaders Becoming More Important to Vote Choice in Canada? Paper presented at the annual APSA conference, Washington, DC.

Gidengil, Elisabeth, André Blais, Neil Nevitte, and Richard Nadeau. 2004. *Citizens*. Vancouver: University of British Columbia Press.

Gidengil, Elisabeth, and Joanna Everitt. 2003a. "Conventional Coverage/Unconventional Politicians: Gender and Media Coverage of Canadian Leaders' Debates, 1993, 1997, 2000." *Canadian Journal of Political Science* 36(3): 559–557.

———. 2003b. "Talking Tough: Gender and Reported Speech in Campaign News Coverage." *Political Communication* 20(3): 209–232.

Gidengil, Elisabeth, Neil Nevitte, André Blais, Joanna Everitt, and Patrick Fournier. 2012. *Dominance and Decline: Making Sense of Recent Canadian Elections*. Toronto: University of Toronto Press.

Giugal, Aurelian, Ron Johnston, Mihail Chiru, Ciobanu Ionut, and Alexandru Gavris. 2017. 'Gerrymandering and Malapportionment, Romanian Style – the 2008 Electoral System'. *East European Politics and Societies* 31(4): 683–703.

Goldfarb, Martin, and Thomas Axworthy. 1988. *Marching to a Different Drummer: An Essay on the Liberals and Conservatives in Convention.* Toronto: Stoddart.

Gomez, Chelsea, and Chantal Da Silva. 2015. 'MAP: Tracking the Leaders'. *CBC News*, May 21. http://www.cbc.ca/news/multimedia/map-tracking-the-leaders-1.3081740

Goodyear-Grant, Elizabeth. 2013. *Gendered News: Media Coverage and Electoral Politics*. Vancouver: UBC Press.

Haleva-Amir, Sharon. 2011. 'Online Israeli Politics'. *Israel Affairs* 17(3): 467–485.

Hart, Roderick P. 1994. *Seducing America: How Television Charms the Modern Voter*. New York: Oxford University Press.

Hartley, Jean, and John Benington. 2011. 'Political Leadership'. In *The Sage Handbook of Leadership*, edited by Allan Bryman, David Collinson, Keith Grint, Brad Jackson and Mary Uhl-Bien, 203–215. New York: Sage.

Hayes, Danny. 2009. 'Has Television Personalized Voting Behavior?' *Political Behavior* 31(2): 231–260.

Hayward, Margaret. 2010. 'Leadership and the Prime Minister'. In *New Zealand Government and Politics*, edited by Raymond Miller, 226–242. Melbourne: Oxford University Press.

Hazan, Rueven, and Gideon Rahat. 2010. *Democracy within Parties: Candidate Selection Methods and Their Political Consequences*. Oxford: Oxford University Press.

Heffernan, Richard. 2005. 'Exploring (and Explaining) the British Prime Minister'. *British Journal of Politics and International Relations* 7(4): 605–20.

Heitshusen, Valerie, Garry Young, and David M. Wood. 2005. 'Electoral Context and MP Constituency Focus in Australia, Canada, Ireland, New Zealand, and the United Kingdom'. *American Journal of Political Science* 49(1): 32–45.

Heldman, Caroline, Susan J. Carroll, and Stephanie Olson. 2005. 'She Brought Only a Skirt: Print Media Coverage of Elizabeth Dole's Bid for the Republican Presidential Nomination'. *Political Communication* 22(3): 315–335.

Hennessy, John. 2001. 'Churchill and the Premiership'. *Transactions of the Royal Historical Society* 11(6): 295–306.

Hennl, Annika, and Simon Franzmann. 2017. 'The Effects of Manifesto Politics on Programmatic Change'. *In Organizing Political Parties: Representation, Participation, and Power*, edited by Susan E. Scarrow, Paul D. Webb and Thomas Poguntke, 259–289. Oxford, Oxford University Press.

Hennl, Annika, and Thomas Zittel. 2011. 'Personalized Election Campaigns and Representation in Mixed Member Systems. Strategies for Electoral Gain or Pandora's Box?' Paper presented at the ECPR General Conference, Reykjavik, Iceland.

Heppell, Timothy. 2010. *Choosing the Labour Leader: Labour Party Leadership Elections from Wilson to Brown*. London: I. B. Tauris.

Hermans, Liesbeth, and Maurice Vergeer. 2012. 'Personalization in e-Campaigning: A Cross-National Comparison of Personalization Strategies Used on Candidate Websites of 17 Countries in EP Elections 2009'. *New Media and Society* 15(1) 72–92.

Hix, Simon and Klaus H. Goetz. 2000. 'Introduction: European Integration and National Political Systems'. In *Europeanised Politics? European Integration and National Political Systems,* edited by Simon Hix and Klaus H. Goetz, 1–26. Orchester: Frank Cass Publishers.

Holmberg, Sören. 2009. 'Candidate Recognition in Different Electoral Systems'. In *The Comparative Study of Electoral Systems*, edited by Hans-Dieter Klingemann, 158-170. Oxford: Oxford University Press.

Holmberg, Sören, and Henrik Oscarsson. 2011. 'Party Leader Effects on the Vote'. In *Political Leaders and Democratic Elections*, edited by Kees Aarts, Andre Blais and Herman Schmitt, 35-51. Oxford: Oxford University Press.

Holtz-Bacha, Christina, Ana Ines Langer and Susanne Merkle. 2014. 'The Personalization of Politics in Comparative Perspective: Campaign Coverage in Germany and the United Kingdom'. *European Journal of Communication* 29(2): 153–170.

Huddy, Leonie, and Nayda Terkildsen. 1993. 'Gender Stereotypes and the Perception of Male and Female Candidates'. *American Journal of Political Science* 37(1): 119–47.

Hutchins, Aaron. 2015. 'The Numbers are in – and Millions Watched the Maclean's Debate'. *Maclean's*, August 12. https://www.macleans.ca/politics/the-numbers-are-in-and-millions-watched-the-macleans-debate/

Ibbitson, John. 2015. *Stephen Harper*. Toronto: Signal/McClelland and Stewart.

Ilonszki, Gabriella. 2007. 'From Minimal to Subordinate: A Final Verdict? The Hungarian Parliament, 1990-2002'. *The Journal of Legislative Studies* 13(1): 38–58.

Indridason, Indridi H. and Gunnar H. Kristinsson. 2015a. 'Primary Consequences: The Effects of Candidate Selection through Party Primaries in Iceland'. *Party Politics* 21(4): 565–76.

———. 2015b. 'Democratising Candidate Selection in Iceland'. In *Party Primaries in Comparative Perspective*, edited by Giulia Sandri, Antonella Seddone, and Fulvio Venturino, 161-80. Farnham: Ashgate.

Inglehart, Ronald. 1990. *Culture Shift in Advanced Industrial Society*. Princeton: Princeton University Press.

Irish Times. 2016. 'Brendan Howlin Chosen to be New Labour Leader'. *Irish Times*, May 21. http://www.irishtimes.com/news/politics/brendan-howlin-chosen-to-be-new-labour-leader-1.2655555 accessed May 21, 2016/

Jackson, Nigel, and Daren Lilleker. 2009. 'MPs and E-representation: Me, MySpace and I'. *British Politics* 4(2): 236–64.

Jeffrey, Brooke. 2010. *Divided Loyalties: The Liberal Party of Canada, 1984–2008*. Toronto: University of Toronto Press.

Jenson, Jane. 'Party Loyalty in Canada: The Question of Party Identification'. *Canadian Journal of Political Science* 8(4): 543–53.

Jewish Women's Archive. 2016. 'Women Members of Knesset'. http://jwa.org/encyclopedia/article/women-members-of-knesset

Johansson, Jon. 2013. 'Prime Ministers and Their Parties in New Zealand'. In *Understanding Prime Ministerial Performance,* edited by Paul Strangio, Paul t'Hart and James Walter, 193-200. London: Oxford University Press.

———. 2015. 'Leadership in a Vacuum: Campaign '14 and the Limits of Followership'. In *Moments of Truth: The New Zealand General Election of 2014*, edited by Jon Johansson and Stephen Levine, 88-103. Wellington: Victoria University of Wellington Press.

Johnston, Richard. 1988. 'The Final Choice: Its Social, Organizational, and Ideological Bases'. In *Party Democracy in Canada: The Politics of National Party Conventions*, edited by George Perlin, 204–243. Scarborough: Prentice-Hall.

———. 1992. 'Party Identification Measures in The Anglo-American Democracies: A National Survey Experiment'. *American Journal of Political Science* 36(2): 542–59.

———. 2002. 'Prime Ministerial Contenders in Canada'. In *Leaders' Personalities and the Outcomes of Democratic Elections*, edited by Anthony King, 159–84. Oxford: Oxford University Press.

———. 2006. 'Party Identification: Unmoved Mover or Sum of Preferences?' *Annual Review of Political Science* 9(3): 329–51.

Johnston, Richard, André Blais, Henry E. Brady and Jean Crete. 1992. *Letting the People Decide: Dynamics of a Canadian Election*. Stanford: Stanford University Press.

Jones, G. W. 1964. 'The Prime Minister's Power'. *Parliamentary Affairs* 18: 167–85.

Judge, David, and Gabriella Ilonszki. 1995. 'Member-Constituency Linkages in the Hungarian Parliament'. *Legislative Studies Quarterly* 20(2): 161–176.

Kaid, Lynda, and Anne Johnston. 1991. 'Negative Versus Positive Television Advertising in U.S. Presidential Campaigns, 1960-1988'. *Journal of Communication* 41(3): 53–64.

Kanter, Rosabeth Moss. 1977. *Men and Women of the Corporation*. New York: Basic Books.

Karlsen, Rune. 2009. 'Campaign Communication and the Internet: Party Strategy in the 2005 Norwegian Election Campaign'. *Journal of Elections, Public Opinion and Parties* 19(2): 183–202.

———. 2011. 'A Platform for Individualized Campaigning? Social Media and Parliamentary Candidates in the 2009 Norwegian Election Campaign'. *Policy and Internet* 3(4): 1–25.

Karlsen, Rune and Eli Skogerbø. 2015. 'Candidate Campaigning in Parliamentary Systems: Individualized vs. Localized Campaigning'. *Party Politics* 21(3): 428–439.

Karvonen, Lauri. 2004. 'Preferential Voting: Incidence and Effects'. *International Political Science Review* 25(2): 203–26.

———. 2010. *The Personalisation of Politics: A Study of Parliamentary Democracies*. Colchester: ECPR Press.

Katz, Richard S. 1980. *A Theory of Parties and Electoral Systems*. Baltimore, MD: Johns Hopkins University Press.

———. 1986. 'Party Government: A Rationalistic Conception.' In *The Future of Party Government – Visions and Realities of Party Governmen*t, edited by Rudolf Wildenmann and Francis G. Castles, 31-71. Berlin/New York, Walter de Gruyter.

———. 1987. 'Party Government and Its Alternatives'. In *Party Governments: European and American Experiences,* edited by Richard S. Katz, 1–26. Berlin: de Gruyter.

———. 2005. 'Why Are There So Many (or So Few) Electoral Reforms?' In *The Politics of Electoral Systems*, edited by Michael Gallagher and Paul Mitchell, 57–76. Oxford: Oxford University Press.

———. 2013. 'Should We Believe that Improved Intra-Party Democracy Would Arrest Party Decline?' In *The Challenges of Intra-Party Democracy*, edited by William P. Cross and Richard S. Katz, 49–64. Oxford: Oxford University Press.

———. 2014. 'No Man Can Serve Two Masters: Party Politicians, Party Members, Citizens, and Principal-Agent Moels of Democracy'. *Party Politics* 20(2):183–93.

———. 2017. 'Political Parties'. In *Comparative Politics*, edited by Daniele Caramani, 207-223. Oxford: Oxford University Press.

Katz, Richard S., and Robin Kolodny. 1994. 'Party Organization as an Empty Vessel: Parties in American Politics'. In *How Parties Organize: Change and Adaptation in*

Party Organziations in Western Democracies, edited by Richard S. Katz and Peter Mair, 24–29. London: Sage.

Katz, Richard S., and Peter Mair. 1993. 'The Evolution of Party Organization in Europe: The Three Faces of Party Organization'. *The American Review of Politics* 14(Winter): 593–617.

———. 1995. 'Changing Models of Party Organization and Party Democracy: The Emergence of the Cartel Party'. *Party Politics* 1(1): 5–28.

———. 2009. 'The Cartel Party Thesis: A Restatement'. *Perspectives on Politics* 7(4): 753–66.

Keen, Richard. 2015. 'Women in Parliament and Government'. *House of Commons Library*. Briefing Paper Number SN01250. http://researchbriefings.parliament.uk / ResearchBriefing/Summary/SN01250#fullreport

Keing, Ofer. 2009. 'Classifying Party Leaders' Selection Methods in Parliamentary Democracies'. *Journal of Elections, Public Opinion and Parties* 19(4):433–447

Kenig, Ofer, William P. Cross, Scott Pruysers, and Gideon Rahat. 2015. 'Party Primaries: Towards a Definition and Typology'. *Representation* 51(2): 147–60.

Kernell, Samuel. 2006. *Going public: New Strategies of Presidential Leadership*. Washington DC, CQ Press.

Kinder, Donald R., Mark D. Peters, Robert P. Abelson and Susan T. Fiske. 1980. 'Presidential Prototypes'. *Political Behavior* 2(4): 315–337.

King, Anthony. 1969. 'Political Parties in Western Democracies: Some Skeptical Reflections'. *Polity* 2 (2): 111–41.

King, Gary, Michael Tomz, and Jason Wittenberg. 2000. 'Making the most of Statistical Analyses: Improving Interpretation and Presentation'. *American Journal of Political Science* 44(2): 347–361.

Kirchheimer, Otto. 1966. 'The Transformation of the Western European Party Systems'. In *Political Parties and Political Development*, edited by Joseph LaPalombara and Myron Weiner, 177–200. Princeton: Princeton University Press.

Koop, Royce. 2011. *Grass Roots Liberals: Organizing for Local and National Politics*. Vancouver: University of British Columbia Press.

Kreiss, Daniel. 2012. *Taking Our Country Back: The Crafting of Networked Politics from Howard Dean to Barack Obama*. Oxford: Oxford University Press.

———. 2016. *Prototype Politics: Technology-Intensive Campaigning and the Data of Democracy*. New York: Oxford University Press.

Kriesi, Hanspeter. 2012. 'Personalization of National Election Campaigns'. *Party Politics* 18(6): 825-844.

Kruikemeier, Sanne. 2014. 'How Political Candidates use Twitter and the Impact on Votes'. *Computers in Human Behavior* 34: 131–139.

Kruikemeier, Sanne, Adrian Aparaschvei, Hajo Boomgaarden, Guda Van Noort, and Rens Vliegenhart. 2015. 'Party and Candidate Websites: A Comparative Explanatory Analysis'. *Mass Communication and Society* 18(6): 821–850.

Kruikemeier, Sanne, Guda van Noort, Rens Vliegenthart and Claes H de Vreese. 2013. 'Getting Closer, the Effects of Personalized and Interactive Online Political Communication'. *European Journal of Communication* 28(1): 53–66.

Krupnikov, Yanna. 2011. 'When Does Negativity Demobilize? Tracing the Conditional Effect of Negative Campaigning on Voter Turnout'. *American Journal of Political Science* 55(4): 796–812.

Laing, Matthew, and Brendan McCaffrie. 2013. 'The Politics Prime Ministers Make: Political Time and Executive Leadership in Westminster Systems'. In *Understanding Prime Ministerial Performance*, edited by Paul Strangio, Paul t'Hart, and James Walter, 79–101. London: Oxford University Press.

Langer, Ana. 2007. 'An Historical Exploration of The Personalisation of Politics in the Print Media: The British Prime Ministers 1945–1999'. *Parliamentary Affairs* 60(3): 371–387.

———. 2010. 'The Politicization of Private Persona: Exceptional Leaders or the New Rule? The Case of the United Kingdom and the Blair Effect'. *The International Journal of Press/Politics* 15(1): 60–76.

———. 2011. *The Personalisation of Politics in the UK: Mediated Leadership from Attlee to Cameron.* Manchester University Press: Manchester.

LaPalombara, Joseph. 1964. *Interest Groups in Italian Politics.* Princeton, NJ: Princeton University Press.

Larsson, Anders. 2016. 'Online, all the Time? A Quantitative Assessment of the Permanent Campaign on Facebook'. *New Media and Society* 18(2): 274–292.

Larsson, Anders, and Bente Kalsnes. 2014. 'Of Course we are on Facebook: Use and Non-Use of Social Media Among Swedish and Norwegian Politicians'. *European Journal of Communication* 29(6): 653–667.

Lau, Richard, Gerald Pomper. 2004. *Negative Campaigning: An Analysis of U.S. Senate Elections.* New York: Rowman & Littlefield.

Lawless, Jennifer. 2009. 'Sexism and Gender Bias in Election 2008: A More Complex Path for Women in Politics'. *Politics & Gender* 5(1): 70–80.

Laycock, David, and Lynda Erickson. 2015. *Reviving Social Democracy. The Near Death and Surprising Rise of the Federal NDP.* Vancouver: University of British Columbia Press.

LeDuc, Lawrence. 2001. 'Democratizing Party Leadership Election'. *Party Politics* 7(3): 323–341.

LeDuc, Lawerence, Harold Clarke, Jane Jenson, and Jon Pammett. 1984. 'Partisan Instability in Canada: Evidence from a new Panel Study'. *American Political Science Review* 78(2): 470–484.

LeDuc, Lawrence, Richard G. Niemi, and Pippa Norris. 1996. 'Introduction: The Present and Future of Democratic Elections'. In *Comparing Democracies. Elections and Voting in Global Perspective*, edited by Lawrence LeDuc, Richard G. Niemi and Pippa Norris, 1-48. Thousand Oaks: Sage.

Lehmbruch, Gerhard. 1976. *Proporzdemokratie. Politisches System und politische Kultur in der Schweiz und in Österreich.* Tübingen: Mohr.

Lehner, Franz, and Benno Homann. 1987. 'Consociational Decision-Making and Party Government in Switzerland'. In *Party Governments: European and American Experiences,* edited by Richard S. Katz, 243–269. Berlin: de Gruyter.

Lev-On, Azi. and Sharon Haleva-Amir. 2018. 'Normalizing or Equalizing? Characterizing Facebook Campaigning'. *New Media and Society* 20(2): 720–739.

Levi, Margaret, Audrey Sacks, and Tom Tyler. 2009. 'Conceptualizing Legitimacy, Measuring Legitimating Beliefs'. *American Behavioral Scientist* 53(3): 354–75.

Li, Yaojun and David Marsh. 2008. 'New Forms of Political Participation: Searching for Expert Citizens and Everyday Makers'. *British Journal of Political Science* 38(2): 247–72.

Liberal Party, Canada. 2009. 'Advancing Change Together: A Time to Act'. Report of the Change Commission of the Liberal Party of Canada.

Lijphart, Arend. 1968. 'Typologies of Democratic Systems'. *Comparative Political Studies* 1(1): 3–44.

Lilleker, Darren, and Karolina Koc-Michalska. 2013. 'Online Political Communication Strategies: MEPs, E-Representation, and Self-Representation'. *Journal of Information Technology and Politics* 10(2): 190–207.

Lipset, Seymour Martin, and Stein Rokkan. 1967. *Party systems and Voter Alignments: Cross-National Perspectives* (Vol. 7). Free press.

Livak, Lior, Azi Lev-On, and Gideon Doron. 2014. 'MK Websites and the Personalization of Israeli Politics'. *Israel Affairs* 17(3): 445–66.

Lobo, Marina Costa. 2014. 'Party and Electoral Leadership'. In *The Oxford Handbook of Political Leadership*, edited by R. A. W. Rhodes and Paul t'Hart, 362–376. Oxford, Oxford University Press.

———. 2015. 'Party Dealignment and Leader Effects'. In *Personality Politics? The Role of Leader Evaluations in Democratic Elections?*, edited by Marina Costa Lobo and John Curtice, 148-166. Oxford, Oxford University Press.

———. 2017. 'Personality Goes a Long Way'. Government and Opposition 53(1): 159–79.

Lobo, Marina Costa, and John Curtice, eds. 2015. *Personality Politics? The Role of Leader Evaluations in Democratic Elections?* Oxford, Oxford University Press.

Lundberg, Thomas Carl. 2006. 'Second-Class Representatives? Mixed-Member Proportional Representation in Britain'. *Parliamentary Affairs* 59(1): 60–77.

Mair, Peter. 1994. 'Party Organizations: From Civil Society to State'. In *How Parties Organize: Change and Adaptation in Party Organizations in Western Democracies*, edited by Richard S. Katz and Peter Mair, 1–22. London: Sage.

Mair, Peter. 2013. *Ruling the Void: The Hollowing of Western Democracy*. London, Verso Press.

———. 2008. 'The Challenge to Party Government'. *West European Politics* 31(1–2): 211–34.

———. 2011. 'At CEU, Political Party Expert Peter Mair Talks Governance and Party Politics'. *Youtube.* https://www.youtube.com/watch?v=mgyjdzfcbps

Malloy, Jonathan. 2013. 'The Relationship between the Conservative Party of Canada and Evangelicals and Social Conservatives'. In *Conservatism in Canada*, edited by Jim Farney and David Rayside, 184-206. Toronto: University of Toronto Press.

Manning, Jennifer, and Ida A. Brudnick. 2015. 'Women in Congress, 1917–2015: Biographical and Committee Assignment Information Listings by State and Congress'. *Congressional Research Service.* https://www.senate.gov/CRSReports/crs-publish.cfm?pid=%270E %2C*PLS%3D%22%40%20%20%0A

Mansbridge, Jane. 2003. 'Rethinking Representation'. *American Political Science Review* 97(4): 515–528.

Marichal, José. 2012. *Facebook Democracy: The Architecture of Disclosure and the Threat to Public Life.* Farnham: Ashgate.

Marien, Sofie, Bram Wauters, and Anke Schouteden. 2017. 'Voting for Women in Belgium's Flexible List System'. *Politics & Gender* 13(2): 305–335.

Marsh, Michael. 2007. 'Candidates or Parties? Objects of Electoral Choice in Ireland'. *Party Politics* 13(4): 500–27.

Martin, Shane. 2011a. 'Parliamentary Questions, the Behaviour of Legislators, and the Function of Legislatures: An Introduction'. *The Journal of Legislative Studies* 17(3): 259–270.

———. 2011b. 'Using Parliamentary Questions to Measure Constituency Focus: An Application to the Irish Case'. *Political Studies* 59(2): 472–488.

Mayhew, David. 1974. *Congress: The Electoral Connection.* New Haven: Yale University Press.

Mazeruuw, Peter. 2017. 'Why the Conservative Membership Total Blew Away Insider Projections'. *The Hill Times*, May 3. https://www.hilltimes.com/2017/05/03/conservative-membership-total-blew-away-insider-projections/105287

McAllister, Ian. 2007. 'The Personalization of Politics'. In *The Oxford Handbook of Political Behavior*, edited by Russell Dalton and Hans Klingemann, 571–588. New York: Oxford University Press.

———. 2015. 'The Personalization of Politics in Australia'. *Party Politics* 21(3): 337–345.

McKelvey, Fenwick, and Jill Piebiak. 2016. 'Porting the Political Campaign: The Nation Builder Platform and the Global Flows of Political Technology'. *New Media and Society*. Online First.

McLeay, Elizabeth. 2006. 'Leadership in Cabinet Under MMP'. In *Political Leadership in New Zealand*, edited by Raymond Miller and Michael Mintrom, 93–112. Auckland: Auckland University Press.

Meeks, Lindsey. 2012. 'Is She "Man Enough"? Women Candidates, Executive Political Offices, and News Coverage'. *Journal of Communication* 62(1): 175–193.

Mendelsohn, Matthew. 1993. 'Television's Frames in the 1988 Canadian Election'. *Canadian Journal of Communication* 18(2):149–171.

———. 1996. 'Television News Frames in the 1993 Canadian Election'. In *Seeing Ourselves: Media Power and Policy in Canada*, edited by Helen Holmes and David Taras, 8–22. Toronto: Harcourt Brace.

Micheletti, Michele. 2003. *Political Virtue and Shopping: Individuals, Consumerism and Collective Action.* Basingstoke: Palgrave.

Micheletti, Michele and Dietlind Stolle. 2008. 'Fashioning Social Justice Through Political Consumerism, Capitalism, and the Internet'. *Cultural Studies* 22(5): 749–769.

Michels, Robert. 1915 [1959]. *Political Parties.* New York: Dover Publications.

Miller, Melissa K. 2017. 'Mothers and the Campaign Trail'. In *Mothers & Others: The Role of Parenthood in Politics*, edited by Melanee Thomas and Amanda Bittner, 155–178. Vancouver: University of British Columbia Press.

Miller, Melissa K., Jeffrey S. Peake., and Brittany Anne Boulton. 2010. 'Testing the Saturday Night Live Hypothesis: Fairness and Bias in Newspaper Coverage of Hillary Clinton's Presidential Campaign'. *Politics & Gender* 6(2): 169–98.

Miller, Warren, and Merrill Shanks. 1996. *The New American Voter*. Cambridge, MA: Harvard University Press.

Mo, Cecilia Hyunjung. 2014. 'The Consequences of Explicit and Implicit Gender Attitudes and Candidate Quality in the Calculations of Voters'. *Political Behavior* 37(2): 357–95.

Montgomery, Kathleen, A. 1999. 'Electoral Effects on Party Behavior and Development: Evidence from the Hungarian National Assembly'. *Party Politics* 5(4): 507–523.

Morley, Terry. 1992. 'Leadership Change in the CCF/NDP'. In *Leaders and Parties in Canadian Politics: Experiences of the Provinces*, edited by R. Kenneth Carty, Lynda Erickson, and Donald Blake. Toronto: Harcourt, Brace, Jovanovich.

Morton, Ted. 2013. 'Leadership Selection in Alberta, 1992–2011: A Personal Perspective'. *Canadian Parliamentary Review* 26(2): 31–38.

Mughan, Anthony. 2000. *Media and the Presidentialization of Parliamentary Elections*. Basingstoke: Palgrave.

———. 2015. 'Parties, Conditionality and Leader Effects in Parliamentary Elections'. *Party Politics* 21(1): 28–39.

Murray, Rainbow. 2010. 'Second Among Unequals? A Study of Whether France's 'Quota Women' are Up to the Job'. *Politics & Gender* 6(1): 93–118.

Nordlinger, Eric A. 1967. *The Working-Class Tories: Authority, Deference and Stable Democracy*. London: MacGibbon & Kee.

Norris, Pippa. 1995. 'Introduction: The Politics of Electoral Reforms'. *International Political Science Review* 16 (1): 3–8.

———. 2000. *A Virtuous Circle: Political Communications in Post-industrial Societies*. Cambridge: Cambridge University Press.

———. 2004. *Electoral Engineering. Voting Rules and Political Behaviour*. Cambridge: Cambridge University Press.

———. 2011. 'Cultural Explanations of Electoral Reform: A Policy Cycle Model'. *West European Politics* 34 (3): 531–50.

Nugent, Mary K. and Mona Lena Krook. 2016. 'All-Women Shortlists: Myths and Realities'. *Parliamentary Affairs* 69(1): 115-135.

Nye, Joseph S. 1990. 'Soft Power'. *Foreign Policy* (Autumn): 153–71.

O'Leary, Eimear. 2011. 'The Constituency Orientation of Modern TDs'. *Irish Political Studies* 26(3): 329–43.

O'Neil, Clare, and Tim Watts. 2015. *Two Futures: Australia at a Critical Moment*. Melbourne: Text Publishing.

O'Neill, Brenda, and David K. Stewart. 2009. 'Gender and Political Party Leadership in Canada'. *Party Politics* 15(6): 737–57.

Ohmura, Tamaki. 2014. 'Voting without the Party: Voting Behaviour on Issues of Conscience in the German Bundestag (1949–2013)'. Paper presented at the ECPR General Conference, Glasgow, Scotland.

Ohr, Dieter. 2011. 'Changing Patterns in Political Communication'. In *Political Leaders and Democratic Elections,* edited by Kees Aarts, Andre Blais and Hermann Schmitt, 10–34. Oxford: Oxford University Press.

Ontario Human Rights Commission. 2017. 'Gender Identity and Gender Expression (brochure)'. http://www.ohrc.on.ca/en/gender-identity-and-gender-expression-brochure

Panebianco, Angelo. 1988. *Political Parties: Organisation and Power.* Cambridge, Cambridge University Press.

Papp, Zsofia, and Burtejin Zorigt. 2017. 'Political Constraints and the Limited Effect of Electoral System Change on Personal Vote-seeking in Hungary'. *East European Politics and Societies.* Online First.

Parker, Brian T. 2012. 'Candidate Brand Equity Valuation: A Comparison of U.S. Presidential Candidates During the 2008 Primary Election Campaign'. *Journal of Political Marketing* 11(3): 208–230.

Parliament of Canada. 2016. 'Women Candidates in General Elections – 1921 to Date'. http://www.lop.parl.gc.ca/About/Parliament/FederalRidingsHistory/hfer.asp?Language=E&Search=WomenElection

Passarelli, Gianluca. 2015. 'Parties' Genetic Features: The Missing Link in the Presidentialization of Politics'. In *The Presidentialization of Political Parties: Organizations, Institutions and Leaders,* edited by Gianluca Passarelli, 1–24. Basingstoke: Palgrave.

Pilet, Jean-Benoit and William P. Cross, eds. 2014. *Leadership Selection in Contemporary Parliamentary Democracies: A Comparative Study.* London: Routledge.

Poguntke, Thomas. 2014. 'Towards a New Party System: The Vanishing Hold of the Catch-all Parties in Germany'. *Party Politics* 20(6): 950–963.

———. 2015. 'Die Präsidentialisierung des politischen Prozesses: Welche Rolle bleibt den politischen Parteien?' In *Parteienwissenschaften,* edited by Julian Krüper, Heike Merten and Thomas Poguntke, 261–282. Baden-Baden, Nomos.

Poguntke, Thomas, Susan E. Scarrow and Paul Webb, et al. 2016. 'Party Rules, Party Resources and the Politics of Parliamentary Democracies: How Parties Organize in the 21st Century'. *Party Politics* 22(6): 661–678.

Poguntke, Thomas, and Paul Webb. 2015. 'Presidentialization and the Politics of Coalition: Lessons from Germany and Britain'. *Italian Political Science Review/Rivista Italiana di Scienza Politica* 45(3): 249–275.

———, eds. 2005. *The Presidentialization of Politics — A Comparative Study of Modern Democracies.* London: Oxford University Press.

———. 2005. 'The Presidentialization of Politics in Democratic Societies: A Framework for Analysis'. In *The Presidentialization of Politics. A Comparative Study of Modern Democracies,* edited by Thomas Poguntke and Paul Webb, 1–25. Oxford, Oxford University Press.

Poletti, Monica. 2016. 'Why Labour Party Members Still Back Jeremy Corbyn as Their Leader'. *The Conversation,* September 24. http://theconversation.com/why-labour-party-members-still-back-jeremy-corbyn-as-their-leader-65974

Popescu, Marina, and Mihail Chiru 2013. *The 2012 Romanian Candidate Study.* Machine readable data files.

Pruysers, Scott. 2014. 'Reconsidering Vertical Integration: An Examination of National Political Parties and their Counterparts in Ontario'. *Canadian Journal of Political Science* 47(2): 237–58.

———. 2015. 'Two Political Worlds? Multi-level Campaign Integration in Canadian Constituencies'. *Regional & Federal Studies* 25(2): 165–82.

———. 2016. 'Vertical Party Integration: Informal and Human Linkages Between Elections in a Canadian Province'. *Commonwealth & Comparative Politics* 54(3): 312–30.

Pruysers, Scott, and Julie Blais. 2017. 'Why Won't Lola Run? An Experiment Examining Stereotype Threat and Political Ambition'. *Politics & Gender* 13(2): 232–252.

Pruysers, Scott, and William P. Cross. 2016a. 'Negative Personalization: Party Leaders and Party Strategy'. *Canadian Journal of Political Science* 49(3): 539–58.

———. 2016b. 'Candidate Selection in Canada: Local Autonomy, Centralization, and Competing Democratic Norms'. *American Behavioral Scientist* 60(7): 781–98.

Putnam, Robert. 2000. *Bowling Alone: The Collapse and Revival of American Community*. New York: Simon & Schuster.

Quintal, David P. 1970. 'The Theory of Electoral Systems'. *Western Political Quarterly* 23(4): 752–61.

Rahat, Gideon. 2008. *The Politics of Regime Structure Reform in Democracies: Israel in Comparative and Theoretical Perspective*. Albany, NY: SUNY Press.

———. 2011. 'The Politics of Electoral Reforms: The State of Research'. *Journal of Elections, Public Opinion and Parties* 21(4): 523–43.

Rahat Gideon, and Ofer Kenig. Forthcoming. *From Party Politics to Personalized Politics? Party Change and Political Personalization in Democracies*. Oxford: Oxford University Press.

Rahat, Gideon, and Tamir Sheafer. 2007. 'The Personalization(s) of Politics: Israel, 1949-2003'. *Political Communication* 24(1): 65–80.

Rahn, Wendy M., John H. Aldrich, Eugene Borgida, and John L. Sullivan. 1990. 'A Social- Cognitive Model of Candidate Appraisal'. In *Information and Democratic Processes*, edited by John A. Ferejohn and James H. Kuklinski, 136-159. Urbana: University of Illinois Press.

Ranney, Austin. *Pathways to Parliament: Candidate Selection in Britain*. University of Wisconsin Press.

Reed, Steven R., and Michael F. Thies. 2001. 'The Causes of Electoral Reform in Japan'. In *Mixed-Member Electoral Systems: The Best of Both Worlds*, edited by Matthew Soberg Shugart and Martin P. Wattenberg, 152–72. Oxford: Oxford University Press.

Reinnemann, Carsten, and Jurgen Wilke. 2007. 'It's the Debates, Stupid! How the Introduction of Televised Debates Changed the Portrayal of Chancellor Candidates in the German Press, 1949–2005'. *The Harvard International Journal of Press/Politics* 12(4): 92–111.

Rentoul, John. 2017. 'If Emmanuel Macron Wins the French Election Next Weekend, he Would Show that the Centre-left is not yet Dead'. *The Independent*, April 15. http://www.independent.co.uk/voices/emmanuel-macron-france-election-socialist-party-a7685176.html

Renwick, Alan. 2010. *The Politics of Electoral Reform: Changing the Rules of Democracy.* Cambridge: Cambridge University Press.

Renwick, Alan, and Jean-Benoit Pilet. 2016. *Faces on the Ballot. The Personalization of Electoral Systems in Europe*. Oxford: Oxford University Press.

Rhodes, R. A. W. 2006. 'Executives in Parliamentary Government'. In *The Oxford Handbook of Political Institutions,* edited by R. A. W. Rhodes, Sarah Binder, and Bert Rockman, 232–343. Oxford: Oxford University Press.

Rhodes, R. A. W., John Wanna, and Patrick Weller. 2009. *Comparing Westminster.* New York: Oxford University Press.

Rommele, Andrea. 2003. 'Political Parties, Party Communication and New Information and Communication Technologies'. *Party Politics* 9(1): 7–20.

Rosar, Ulrich, Markus Klein, and Tilo Beckers. 2008. 'The Frog Pond Beauty Contest: Physical Attractiveness and Electoral Success of the Constituency Candidates at the North Rhine-Westphalia State Election of 2005'. *European Journal of Political Research* 47 (1):64–79.

Roy, Jason. 2009. 'Voter Heterogeneity: Informational Differences in Voting'. *Canadian Journal of Political Science* 42(1): 117–37.

Roy, Jason, and Christopher Alcantara. 2015. 'The Candidate Effect: Does the Local Candidate Matter?' *Journal of Elections, Public Opinion and Parties* 25(2): 195–214.

Russo, Federico. 2011. 'The Constituency as a Focus of Representation: Studying the Italian Case through the Analysis of Parliamentary Questions'. *The Journal of Legislative Studies* 17(3): 290–301.

Ryan, Susan, and Troy Bramston. 2003. *The Hawke Government: A Critical Retrospective*. Melbourne: Pluto Press.

Samuel-Azran, Tal, Moran Yarchi, and Gadi Wolfsfeld. 2015. 'Equalization versus Normalization: Facebook and the 2013 Israeli Elections'. *Social Media and Society* 1(2):1–9.

Sanbonmatsu, Kira. 2006. 'Do Parties Know that 'Women Win'? Party Leader Beliefs about Women's Electoral Chances'. *Politics & Gender* 2(4): 431–50.

Sanbonmatsu, Kira, and Kathleen Dolan. 2009. 'Do Gender Stereotypes Transcend Party?' *Political Research Quarterly* 62(3): 485–94.

Sandri, Giulia, Antonella Seddone, and Fulvio Venturino. 2014. 'The Selection of Party Leaders in Italy, 1989–2012'. In *The Selection of Political Party Leaders in Contemporary Parliamentary Democracies: A Comparative Study*, edited by Jean-Benoit Pilet and William P. Cross, 93–107. London: Routledge.

———. eds. 2015. *Party Primaries in Comparative Perspective*. Farnham: Ashgate.

Sapiro, Virginia. 1983. *The Political Integration of Women: Roles, Socialization, and Politics.* Urbana: University of Illinois Press.

Savoie, Donald. 1999. *Governing from the Centre: The Concentration of Power in Canadian Politics*. Toronto: University of Toronto Press.

———. 2008. *Court Government and the Collapse of Accountability in Canada and the United Kingdom.* Toronto: University of Toronto Press.

Sayers, Anthony. 1999. *Parties, Candidates, and Constituency Campaigns in Canadian Elections.* Vancouver: University of British Columbia Press.

Scarrow, Susan E. 2015. *Beyond Party Members: Changing Approaches to Partisan Mobilization*. Oxford: Oxford University Press.

Scarrow, Susan E. and Bercu Gezgor. 2010. 'Declining Memberships, Changing Members? European Political Party Members in a New Era'. *Party Politics* 16(6):823–843

Schattschneider, E. E. 1942. *Party Government*. New York: Holt, Rinehart and Winston.

Schmitt-Beck, Rüdiger, Hans Rattinger, Sigrid Roßteutscher, Bernhard Weßels and Christof Wolf. 2014. 'Fazit und Ausblick: Langeweile und Extreme, Fragmentierung und Konzentration'. In *Zwischen Fragementierung und Konzentration: Die Bundestagswahl 2013*, edited by Rüdiger Schmitt-Beck, Hans Rattinger, Sigrid Roßteutscher, Bernhard Weßels, Christof Wolf, 355-357. Baden-Baden, Nomos.

Schulz, Winifred, and Reimar Zeh. 2005. 'The Changing Election Coverage of German Television. A Content Analysis: 1990-2002'. *Communications: The European Journal of Communication Research* 30(4): 385–407.

Schutz, Aaron, and Marie G. Sandy. 2011. *Collective Action for Social Change: An Introduction to Community Organizing*. New York: Palgrave Macmillan.

Schweitzer, Eva J. 2012. 'The Mediatization of E-Campaigning: Evidence from German Party Websites in State, National, and European Parliamentary Elections 2002-2009'. *Journal of Computer-Mediated Communication* 17(3): 283–302.

Seigfried, Andre. 1966 [1907]. *The Race Question in Canada*. Toronto: McClelland and Stewart.

Shepsle, Kenneth A., and Barry R. Weingast. 1994. 'Positive Theories of Congressional Institutions'. *Legislative Studies Quarterly* 19(2): 149–179.

Shugart, Matthew Soberg 2001. 'Extreme" Electoral Systems and the Appeal of the Mixed-Member Alternative'. In Mixed-Member Electoral Systems: The Best of Both Worlds?, edited by Matthew Soberg Shugart and Martin P. Wattenberg, 25–51. Oxford: Oxford University Press.

Shugart, Matthew Soberg, Melody Valdini, and Kati Suominen. 2005. 'Looking for Locals: Voter Information Demands and Personal Vote-Earning Attributes of Legislators under Proportional Representation'. *American Journal of Political Science* 49(2): 437–449.

Simpson, Jeffrey. 2001. *The Friendly Dictatorship*. Toronto: McClelland and Stewart.

Small, Tamara. 2010. 'Canadian Politics in 140 Characters: Party Politics in the Twitterverse'. *Canadian Parliamentary Review* 33(3): 39–45.

Smith, Graham. 2009. *Democratic Innovations: Designing Institutions for Citizen Participation*. Cambridge: Cambridge University Press.

Sniderman, Paul, Richard Brody, and Philip Tetlock. 1991. *Reasoning and Choice: Explorations in Political Psychology*. New York: Cambridge University Press.

Sourd, Cécile. 2005. "Femmes ou politiques? La représentation des candidates aux élections françaises de 2002 dans la presse hedomadaire." *Mots: Les langages du politique* 78: 65–78.

Stalsburg, Brittany L. 2012. *A Mom First and a Candidate Second: Gender Differences in Candidates' Self-Presentation of Family*. New York: Working Paper.

Stephenson, Laura, Andrea Lawlor, William P. Cross, Andre Blais and Elisabeth Gidengil. Forthcoming. *Provincial Battles, National Prize? Elections in a Federal State*. McGill-Queen's University Press.

Stewart, David. 1997. 'The Changing Leadership Electorate'. *Canadian Journal of Political Science* 30(1): 107–128.

Stewart, David, and Keith Archer. 2000. *Quasi-Democracy? Parties and Leadership Selection in Alberta*. Vancouver: University of British Columbia Press.

Strangio, Paul, Paul t'Hart, and James Walter. 2013. 'Prime Ministers and the Performance of Public Leadership'. In *Understanding Prime Ministerial Performance*, edited by Paul Strangio, Paul t'Hart; James Walter, 1–28. London: Oxford University Press.

Streb, Matthew J., Barbara Burrell, Brian Frederick, and Michael A. Genovese. 2008. 'Social Desirability Effects and Support for a Female American President'. *The Public Opinion Quarterly* 72(1): 76–89.

Sulkin, Tracy. 2005. *Issue politics in Congress*. New York: Cambridge University Press.

———. 2011. *The Legislative Legacy of Congressional Campaigns*. New York: Cambridge University Press.

Sulkin, Tracy, and Nathaniel Swigger. 2008. 'Is There Truth in Advertising? Campaign Ad Images as Signals About Legislative Behavior'. *The Journal of Politics* 70(1): 232–244.

Tallberg, Jonas and Karl M. Johansson. 2010. 'Explaining Chief Executive Empowerment: EU Summitry and Domestic Institutional Change'. *West European Politics* 33(2): 202–236.

Thayer, Nathaniel B. 1969. *How the Conservatives Rule Japan*. Princeton, NJ: Princeton University Press.

Theakston, Kevin. 2013. 'Evaluating Prime-Ministerial Performance: The British Experience'. In *Understanding Prime Ministerial Performance: Comparative Perspectives*, edited by Paul Strangio, Paul t'Hart, and James Walter, 221–241. London: Oxford University Press.

Thomas, Melanee. 2012. *Gender and Psychological Orientations to Politics*. PhD Dissertation, McGill University.

———. 2018. 'In Crisis or Decline? Selecting Women to Lead Provincial Parties in Government'. *Canadian Journal of Political Science* 51(2): 379–403.

Thomas, Melanee, and Amanda Bittner, eds. 2017. *Mothers & Others: The Role of Parenthood in Politics*. Vancouver: University of British Columbia Press.

Thomas, Melanee and Marc André Bodet. 2013. 'Sacrificial lambs, women candidates, and district competitiveness in Canada'. *Electoral Studies* 32(1): 153–166.

Thomas, Melanee, Philip Chen, Allison Harell, and Tania Gosselin. 2017. 'Gender Mediation, Character, and Competence: Comparing News Coverage of Heads of Government in the Canadian Provinces'. Paper presented at the Biannual Meeting of the European Conference on Politics and Gender, Lausanne, Switzerland.

Thomas, Melanee, Allison Harell, and Tania Gosselin. Forthcoming. 'Gender, Tone, and Content of Premiers' New Coverage: A Matched Comparison'. In *Political*

Elites in Canada, edited by Alex Marland, Thierry Giasson, and Andrea Lawlor. Vancouver: University of British Columbia Press.

Thomas, Melanee and Lisa Lambert. 2017. 'Private Mom vs. Political Dad? Communications of Parental Status in the 41st Canadian Parliament'. In *Mothers and Others: The Role of Parenthood in Politics*, edited by Melanee Thomas and Amanda Bittner, 135–55. Vancouver: University of British Columbia Press.

Tiffen, Rodney. 2015. 'Thinking of Dumping a Prime Minister? History isn't Encouraging'. *Inside Story*, February 8. http://insidestory.org.au/thinking-of-dumping-a-prime-minister-history-isnt-encouraging Accessed February 21, 2015.

Trimble, Linda. 2005. 'Who Framed Belinda Stronach? National Newspaper Coverage of the Conservative Party of Canada's 2004 Leadership Race'. Paper presented to the Annual Meeting of the Canadian Political Science Association, London, Canada.

———. 2007. 'Gender, Political Leadership and Media Visibility: Globe and Mail Coverage of Conservative Party of Canada Leadership Contests'. *Canadian Journal of Political Science* 40(4): 969–93.

Trimble, Linda and Angelia Wagner. 2012. 'Wildrose Wild Card: Alberta Newspaper Coverage of the 2009 Wildrose Alliance Leadership Contest'. *Canadian Political Science Review* 6(2-3): 197–207.

Tuchman, Gaye. 1978. *Making News: A Study in the Construction of Reality*. New York: Free Press.

Tudor, Sorin. 2008. *Politica 2.0.08: Politica Marketingului Politic*. Bucharest: Tritonic.

UK Labour Party. 2013. Labour Party Annual Conference, Conference Magazine, Brighton 22–25 September.

Vaccari, Cristian. 2013. *Digital Politics in Western Democracies: A Comparative Study*. Baltimore: Johns Hopkins University Press.

van Aelst, Peter, Tamir Sheafer, and James Stanyer. 2012. 'The Personalization of Mediated Political Communication: A Review of Concepts, Operationalizations, and Key Findings'. *Journalism* 13(2): 203–20.

van Holsteyn, Joop, and Rudi Andeweg. 2010. 'Demoted Leaders and Exiled Candidates: Disentangling Party and Person in the Voter's Mind'. *Electoral Studies* 29(4): 628–35.

van Santen, Rosa, Luzia Helfer, and Peter Van Aelst. 2015. 'When Politics Becomes News: An Analysis of Parliamentary Questions and Press Coverage in three West European Countries'. *Acta Politica* 50(1): 45–63.

van Zoonen, Liesbet. 1991. 'A Tyranny of Intimacy? Women, Femininity and Television News'. In *Communication and Citizenship: Journalism and the Public Sphere*, edited by Peter Dahlgren, Colin Sparks, 217–235. London: Routledge.

———. 2006. 'The Personal, the Political and the Popular: A Woman's Guide to Celebrity Politics'. *European Journal of Cultural Studies* 9(3): 287–301.

Vassallo, Salvatore and Gianluca Passarelli. 2016. 'Centre-Left Prime Ministerial Primaries in Italy: The Laboratory of the 'Open Party' Model'. *Contemporary Italian Politics*. Online First.

Verge, Tània and Raquel Pastor. 2017. 'Women's Political First and Symbolic Representation'. *Journal of Women, Politics & Policy*. Online First.

Vergeer, Maurice. 2012. 'Politics, Elections and Online Campaigning: Past, Present and a Peek into the Future'. *New Media and Society* 15(1): 9–17.

Vergeer, Maurice, Liesbeth Hermans and Steven Sams. 2011. 'Online Social Networks and Micro-Blogging in Political Campaigning: The Exploration of a New Campaign Tool and a New Campaign Style'. *Party Politics* 19(3): 477–501.

Vliegenthart, Rens, and Stefaan Walgrave. 2011. 'Content Matters. The Dynamic of Parliamentary Questioning in Belgium and Denmark'. *Comparative Political Studies* 44(8): 1031–1059.

Vowles, Jack, Hilde Coffé and Jennifer Curtin. 2017. *A Bark But No Bite: Inequality and the 2014 New Zealand General Election*. Canberra: ANU Press.

Vromen, Ariadne. 2017. *Digital Citizenship and Political Engagement: The Challenge from Online Campaigning and Advocacy Organizations*. London: Palgrave Macmillan.

Walker, James. 2016. 'All-Women Shortlists Have Starved Labour of Female Talent'. *The Huffington Post*, July 27. http://www.huffingtonpost.co.uk/james-walker/all-women-shortlists_b_11199646.html

Wattenberg, Martin. 1982. 'Party identification and party images: a comparison of Britain, Canada, Australia, and the United States'. *Comparative Politics* 15(2): 23–40.

———. 1991. *The Rise of Candidate-Centered Politics: Presidential Elections of the 1980s*. Cambridge: Harvard University Press.

Wauters Bram, Peter van Aelst, Peter Thijssen, and Jean-Benoit Pilet. 2016. 'Centralized Personalization at the Expense of Decentralized Personalization. The Decline of Preferential Voting in Belgium (2003–2014)'. *Party Politics*. Online first.

Wauters, Bram and Jean-Benoit Pilet. 2015. 'Electing Women as Party Leaders: Does the Selectorate Matter?' In *The Politics of Party Leadership: A Cross-National Perspective*, edited by William P. Cross and Jean-Benoit Pilet, 73-90. Oxford: Oxford University Press.

Webb, Paul. 2002. 'Conclusion: Political Parties and Democratic Control in Advanced Industrial Societies'. In *Political Parties in Advanced Industrial Democracies*, edited by Paul Webb, David Farrell, and Ian Holliday, 438-460. Oxford: Oxford University Press.

Webb, Paul, and Tim Bale. 2014. 'Why do Tories defect to UKIP?' *Political Studies* 62(4): 961–70.

Webb, Paul, and Thomas Poguntke. 2013. 'The Presidentialization of Politics Thesis Defended'. *Parliamentary Affairs* 66(3): 646–54.

Webb, Paul and Thomas Poguntke. 2005. 'The Presidentialization of Contemporary Democratic Politics: Evidence, Causes and Consequences'. In *The Presidentialization of Politics: A Comparative Study of Modern Democracies*, edited by Thomas Poguntke and Paul Webb, 336-56. Oxford: Oxford University Press.

Webb, Paul, Thomas Poguntke, and Robin Kolodny. 2012. 'The Presidentialization of Party Leadership? Evaluating Party Leadership and Party Government in the

Democratic World'. In *Comparative Political Leadership*, edited by Ludger Helms, 77–98. Basingstoke: Palgrave Macmillan.

Weber, Max. 1968. *Economy and Society: An Outline of Interpretive Sociology,* New York: Bedminster Press.

———. 1980. *Wirtschaft und Gesellschaft: Grundriß der verstehenden Soziologie.* Tübingen, Mohr.

Welch, Susan, John Gruhl, John Comer, and Susan Rigdon. 2010. *Understanding American Government.* Boston: Cenage Learning.

Weller, Patrick. 1985. *First Among Equals: Prime Ministers in Westminster Systems.* Sydney: George Allen & Unwin.

Whitaker, Reg. 2001. 'Virtual Political Parties and the Decline of Democracy'. *Policy Options*, June, 16–22.

Whiteley, Paul F. 2011. 'Is the Party Over? The Decline of Party Activism and Membership Across the Democratic World'. *Party Politics* 17(1): 21–44.

Williams, Andrew, and Kaye Trammell. 2005. 'Candidate Campaign E-mail Messages in the Presidential Election 2004'. *American Behavioural Scientist* 49(4): 560–574.

Williams, Philip. 1966. 'Two Notes on the British Electoral System'. *Parliamentary Affairs* 20(1): 13–30.

Winham, Gilbert R. and Robert B. Cunningham. 1970. 'Party Leader Images in the 1968 Federal Election'. *Canadian Journal of Political Science* 3(1): 37–55.

Wlezien, Christopher. 2009. 'Election Campaigns'. In *Comparing Democracies 3*, edited by Lawrence LeDuc, Richard G. Niemi, and Pippa Norris, 98–118. London: Sage.

World Bank. 2015. 'Internet users (per 100 people)'. http://data.worldbank.org/indicator/IT.NET.USER.P2

Wright, Katharine and Jack Holland. 2014. 'Leadership and The Media: Gendered Framings Of Julia Gillard's 'Sexism And Misogyny' Speech'. *Australian Journal of Political Science* 49(3): 455–68.

Young, Lisa and William P. Cross. 2002. 'Incentives to Membership in Canadian Political Parties'. *Political Research Quarterly* 55(3): 547–70.

Zamir, Sharaf, and Gideon Rahat. 2017. 'Political Personalization Online: Parties and Politicians in the 2015 Elections'. In *The Elections in Israel – 2015,* edited by Michal Shamir and Gideon Rahat, 167-192. New Brunswick: Transaction Press.

Zittel, Thomas. 2015. 'Constituency Candidates in Comparative Perspective – How Personalized Are Constituency Campaigns, Why, and Does It Matter?' *Electoral Studies* 39: 286–94.

Zittel, Thomas, and Thomas Gschwend. 2008. 'Individualised Constituency Campaigns in Mixed-Member Electoral Systems: Candidates in the 2005 German Elections'. *West European Politics* 31(5): 978–1003.

Index

Note: Page numbers in *italics* indicate illustrative material.

About the Contributors

Amanda Bittner is an Associate Professor of Political Science at Memorial University in Newfoundland. She specializes in elections and voting behavior and is the author of *Platform or Personality? The Role of Party Leaders in Elections* (2011).

Mihail Chiru is currently Research Director at the Median Research Centre Bucharest. He is mainly interested in legislative politics, and his work has been published in journals such as *Government and Opposition*, *European Union Politics*, *European Political Science Review*, *Journal of Legislative Studies*, and *East European Politics and Societies*.

William P. Cross is Professor and Bell Chair for the Study of Canadian Parliamentary Democracy at Carleton University. He is a student of comparative political institutions and his work emphasizes the internal organization of political parties. His recent (coauthored and coedited) books include: *The Promise and Challenge of Party Primary Elections* (2016), *The Politics of Party Leadership* (2016), *Fighting for Votes: Parties, the Media and Voters in an Ontario Election* (2015), *The Selection of Political Party Leaders in Contemporary Parliamentary Democracies* (2014), *The Challenges of Intra-Party Democracy* (2013) and *Politics at the Centre: the Selection and Removal of Party Leaders in Anglo Parliamentary Democracies* (2012).

Anika Gauja is an Associate Professor of Comparative Politics in the Department of Government and International Relations. She is the author of *Party Reform: The Causes, Challenges and Consequences of Organizational Change* (2017) and *The Politics of Party Policy* (2013) as well as the editor of several books on party organization and regulation.

Richard S. Katz is Professor of Political Science at Johns Hopkins University in Baltimore, Maryland. He was coeditor of the *European Journal of Political Research* (2006–2012). His books include *A Theory of Parties and Electoral Systems* (1980, 2006), *Democracy and Elections* (1997), *Handbook of Party Politics*, edited with William Crotty (2006), and *The Challenges of Intra-Party Democracy*, edited with William P. Cross (2013). He is vice-chair and treasurer on the Executive Committee of the European Consortium for Political Research.

Jonathan Malloy is Associate Professor and Chair of the Department of Political Science at Carleton University. His research focuses on parliamentary institutions, political leadership and Canadian national and provincial politics. Recent and forthcoming publications include *The Politics of Ontario* (2016), *Fighting for Votes: Parties, Voters and the Media in an Ontario Election* (2015) and "(Mis)managing Leadership Capital: Canadian Prime Ministers" in *The Politics of Leadership Capital: A Comparative Examination*, edited by Bennister, Worthy and t'Hart (forthcoming).

Jean-Benoit Pilet is Professor of Political Science at Université libre de Bruxelles (ULB-Belgium). He has recently coauthored with Alan Renwick *Faces on the Ballot. The Personalization of Electoral Systems in Europe* (2016), and with William Cross, *The Politics of Party Leadership. A Cross-National Perspective* (2016). He conducts research on electoral systems, political parties, Belgian politics and legislative studies and elections.

Thomas Poguntke is Professor of Comparative Politics and Director of the Düsseldorf Party Research Institute. He was series editor of the Routledge/ECPR Studies in European Political Science and has widely published in peer-reviewed journals including *West European Politics*, *Party Politics*, *European Political Science Review*, and *the European Journal of Political Research* and has written and coedited a number of books on comparative politics and political parties, including *The Presidentialization of Politics in Democratic Societies. A Comparative Study of Modern Democracies* (2005) with Paul Webb and *The Europeanization of National Political Parties* (2007) with Nicholas Aylott, Elisabeth Carter, Robert Ladrech and Kurt Richard Luther.

Scott Pruysers is a Social Sciences and Humanities Research Council of Canada postdoctoral fellow at the University of Calgary and a Bell Chair Visiting Scholar at Carleton University. His current research interests include party organization, intraparty democracy and political psychology. He has written on a variety of topics including multilevel party integration, party personnel selection, personality and politics and political ambition. His work has been published in a variety of national and international journals such as *Party Politics*, *Canadian Journal of Political Science, Representation, Regional and Federal Studies*, and *Politics & Gender* as well as chapters in a number of edited volumes. He is the coauthor of *The Promise and Challenge of Party Primary Elections: A Comparative Perspective* (2016).

Gideon Rahat is an Associate Professor in the Department of Political Science at the Hebrew University of Jerusalem. His research fields are comparative politics and Israeli politics. His interests include political parties, electoral reform, the personalization of politics and candidate-selection methods. He has published numerous academic articles and several books. He is currently working on a book (with Ofer Kenig) on party change and political personalisation.

Alan Renwick is Deputy Director of the Constitution Unit in the Department of Political Science at University College London. He was previously Associate Professor of Comparative Politics at the University of Reading. His publications include *The Politics of Electoral Reform: Changing the Rules of Democracy* (2010) and *A Citizen's Guide to Electoral Reform* (2011). His research focuses primarily on processes of electoral and broader political reform and how these are changing over time.

David K. Stewart is a Professor in the Department of Political Science at the University of Calgary. His research interests focus primarily on Canadian politics and relate to political parties, leadership-selection processes, provincial party systems, parliamentary government and political realignment. His work has appeared in journals such *as Party Politics*, *Canadian Journal of Political Science*, and *Canadian Political Science Review*.

Melanee Thomas is an associate professor in the Department of Political Science at the University of Calgary. Her research focuses on the causes and consequences of gender-based political inequality in Canada and other postindustrial democracies, with a particular focus on political attitudes and behaviour. She is the co-editor (with Amanda Bittner) of *Mothers & Others: The Role of Parental Status and Politics*. Her research appears in journals such as *Electoral Studies, Politics & Gender*, and the *Canadian Journal of Political Science*.

Paul D. Webb is Professor of Politics at the University of Sussex. He is an elected Fellow of the Academy of Social Sciences and a Fellow of the Royal Society of Arts. His research interests focus on representative democracy, particularly party and electoral politics. He is author or editor of numerous publications, including: *The Modern British Party System* (2000), 2nd edition forthcoming; *Political Parties in Advanced Industrial Societies* (2002) with David Farrell and Ian Holliday; *The Presidentialization of Politics: A Comparative Study of Modern Democracies* (2005, rev. ed. 2007) with Thomas Poguntke and *Gender and the Conservative Party: From Iron Ladies to Kitten Heels.*

Shahaf Zamir is a Ph.D. candidate in the Department of Political Science at the Hebrew University of Jerusalem. His research fields are political parties and web politics. His research compares online and offline political personalization. He also works as a research assistant at the Israel Democracy Institute. He has published a chapter in *The Elections in Israel 2015* with Gideon Rahat on online political personalization of Israeli parties.

www.ingramcontent.com/pod-product-compliance
Lightning Source LLC
Chambersburg PA
CBHW022349280326
41935CB00007B/136